Finding Palestine

Finding Palestine

One American's trek from the Midwest to the Middle East

Liza Elliott

Hope Publishing House
Pasadena, California

Maps reprinted by permission from *The Transformation of Palestine: Essays on the Development of the Arab-Israeli Conflict,* © 1971 by Ibrahim Abu-Lughod and published by Northwestern University Press, Evanston, IL 1971, pp. 22-23.

For information address:

Hope Publishing House
P.O. Box 60008
Pasadena, CA 91116 - U.S.A.
Tel: (626) 792-6123 / Fax: (626) 792-2121
E-mail: hopepub@loop.com
Web site: http://www.hope-pub.com

Cover design — Michael McClary/The Workshop

Printed in the U.S.A. on acid-free paper

Library of Congress Cataloging-in-Publication Data

Elliott, Liza, 1954-
    Finding Palestine / Liza Elliott.
        p. cm.
    Includes bibliographical references.
    ISBN 0-932727-97-2
    1. Arab-Israeli conflict--Health aspects. 2. Arab-Israeli conflict--Medical care. 3. Palestinian Arabs--Medical care. 4. Arab-Israeli conflict--Personal narratives, American. 5. Elliott, Liza, 1954- 6. Nurses--United States--Journeys--Arab countries. I. Title.

DS119.7 .E442 2002
956.04'092--dc21
                                                            2001051461
                                                            CIP

For

Ibrahim Abu Lughod

and

Peter W. Glaeser

Except for the extermination of the Tasmanians, modern history recognizes no cases in which the virtually complete supplanting of the indigenous population of a country by an alien stock has been achieved in as little as two generations. Yet this, in fact, is what has been attempted in Palestine since the beginning of the 20th century. Herein lies the nub of the crisis in the Middle East – at once its greatest tragedy and its most perplexing but inescapable problem. Our natural tendency to assume that what exists today has always been, may afford us psychic peace but only at the terrible cost of denying reality. And once historic reality has been denied, our capacity to understand and react meaningfully to the present is similarly destroyed.

–Janet Lippman Abu-Lughod, 1971
The Demographic Transformation of Palestine

Table of Contents

Acknowledgments

This story was assembled from the people, places and events that constituted my journey to Palestine. It recounts my private, interior awakening of self in a social and political context that came to demand more of me morally and spiritually than I ever imagined. Many more people and circumstances played a part in my life than appear in this recollection and their influence remains with me, even if unmentioned here. To you all, my thanks. Because Palestinians and their friends still suffer under Israeli military occupation, other than public figures, myself and my husband, all names have been changed due to requests and respect for concerns of privacy and security.

This book is better for the critical comments and advice generously provided by Professor Joseph Q. Reninger of Brescia University and the late Mr. Raymond F. Dunne. Ms. Faith Annette Sand, publisher, Hope Publishing House, courageously took up the manuscript and expertly directed its refinement and improvement. I am most grateful.

This book is dedicated to the late Professor Ibrahim Abu Lughod and Dr. Peter Glaeser. Ibrahim, Palestinian scholar and activist, was my teacher and friend. Pete, physician and professor, took up the challenge of Palestine and me.

Preface

Even though Palestine and the Palestinian people have existed in an unbroken bloodline that began before the time of Christ, for the past half century their new neighbors the Israelis – with the financial support of the U.S. and many Western nations – have been attempting to erase their connections to their homeland and push them off their native land.

It has been 25 years since I stumbled across Palestinians who were resisting with all their might the attempt to erase the lineage that holds them fast to their land. These were honorable people with a fervid desire to hold fast to their heritage – the heritage of the Holy Land. In "finding" Palestine I realized I had a new responsibility – a knowledge, a history that must be shared even at the discomfort of the teller or the listener.

My tale is a small fragment in this ongoing tragic saga. The only acceptable ending, yet to be written, is one that incorporates peace with justice, for until we establish peace with justice in the Middle East, none of us – in Israel, Palestine, Europe or the U.S. – will ever find true peace. Thus it is incumbent on us all to "find" Palestine.

PART 1 — CAIRO 1995

Chapter 1

Routinely, after sundown the security field lights of the Egyptian Military Hospital would crackle on, casting long shadows on my balcony. A dry greasy breeze rose from the open air *ta'mia* and *shawarma* stands which sold cheap fried food from steaming oil vats that smeared the air thick like Crisco. My 14th floor vista beyond the hospital across the Nile past fields to the Pyramids of Giza belonged to, as I did now, an Eastern world. Distant lights glittered up the horizon in victory for urban sprawl that shoved back the encroaching desert. The history of the city could be read by the altitude of lights, the ground-hugging lights, old dwellers and the high-rise lights, modern dwellers. Cairo at night.

My history could be assembled from the stories that glared from each copper table, brass vase or the cross-stitched cushions that rested in the *mashrabeya* furniture of polished wooden beads in my living room. This evening, standing alone on my balcony in the shadows, I found myself gazing on this scene and contemplating all the various roads not taken in my life, in contrast to those taken which led me here, to Cairo, my home.

Meeting Pete Glaeser, almost a fortnight before, had disrupted the rhythm of my satisfied existence. His impending departure from Cairo included a road wide enough for us to take together. This unsought possibility vexed me because it forced me once again to that risky brink where emotion, logic, pros and cons all converge, challenging me to decide whether to stay put or go for it. Be safe or take a chance. Content in my Cairo world, finding myself at this pesky spot again came as a total surprise.

Pete and his three colleagues had arrived on 6 October, a national holiday. Four emergency department physicians had come to teach a course in emergency medical care to Egyptian physicians sponsored by my development organization. For the eleven days of their stay, I was their boss and hostess in Egypt, *Um el Donya,* the Mother of the World.

Despite jet lag on the day they landed, the group had elected immediately to tour the Pyramids, so within an hour the five of us were balanced on camels, strung together with orange rope to form a caravan. We bobbed up and down with each gangly step of the camels, who followed the lead of a young tanned peasant boy winding us around the Pyramid grounds. I clucked in Arabic to my camel to stop spitting on Pete's camel, who insisted on walking next to us. Pete's camel spit back, the warm gastric slime slapped my arm and dripped off. "He likes you," Pete teased, laughing at my discomfort.

When next seen at the office, Pete's pink polo shirt and jeans were replaced with serious American khakis and a navy blazer. Despite the tidy professional look, his attitude and interactions remained unpretentious, easy as they had been the day before.

Shami, the driver for the office, patiently repeated and corrected Pete's attempts to master basic Arabic. "*Ezzayak*," said Shami slowly. "How are you. Same, same." Pete nodded to me he understood Shami's meaning that one meant the other. "*Ezzayak*, Shami." Pete tried again. His attempt to nail the accent brought an exasperated chuckle from Shami who commanded in accented English, "Again."

By the end of ten days Shami and Pete exchanged greetings and perhaps two sentences containing three or four Arabic words—the exact limit of Shami's English. Shami confided to me that he admired Dr. Pete very much. There was much to admire, I agreed, but I did not confide that to anyone.

My private playback of the last week was interrupted when I realized the wind had suddenly turned. Now it carried soft Nile air to my balcony making me sleepy. Reluctantly I abandoned the quieting Cairo night to curl up in bed. A few sleeping hours would keep my nagging dilemma at bay. But there was no escaping Pete's face— it appeared every time my eyes closed. His perfect lips tempted me, calling back old bourgeois notions of romance I long ago dismissed as phony. Yet it wasn't about kissing him. Being near him was dangerous, as the Arabs say.

He dared use me as the target of his irreverent jokes and instead of expressing outrage, my cheeks blushed as red and hot as a tomato on a shish-kebab stick. I'd rehash all the exchanges and wish I'd been cleverer when he had compared a local scene to a Monet painting. Besides everything else, he seemed to be an art connoisseur as well. This was not going to be someone easily brushed off.

I had slept fitfully until the five a.m. call to prayer got me out of bed. Today I would choose my future, *Inshallah*, God willing, but not until evening. First the whole day of touring *Misr Adeema*, the old Coptic Quarter, had to be lived through.

Only when the sun began sinking toward the horizon and Pete was sitting on my balcony nursing a fizzy tonic water, did I worry about what we would say to each other. We had never been alone. Each morning Shami and I picked up the group at the hotel. The day typically began with a personal message from Pete woven into the banter of daily greetings. "Good morning. That's a lovely outfit you're wearing, Dr. Liza." Then my reply, "Ah, Leave it to Beaver, now?" He'd slide onto the middle seat next to me and whisper, "Worked for Eddie Haskell." Without the group or the work, our need to communicate in awkward code vanished.

I didn't know where to begin, so finally I blurted, "I need to tell you a few things about my past and I'd prefer you to hear them from me firsthand." I glanced his way and was relieved to see a smile cross his face.

"Hey, I knew you had to have an exotic history; otherwise how could you have managed to end up here?" he swept his hand across my beloved view. "Besides, what could be so horrible?" asked Peter Glaeser of Milwaukee.

And so I set about my story. Cautiously, at first. "Regardless of how bad they are for you, I love potato chips. Long ago I quit hiding in the kitchen in order to snarf them down, to avoid lectures by sprouts and tofu *aficionados*."

"Is that it?" he replied with a skepticism that worried me.

"No, that's the tip. I don't do story problems, hate math, numbers and any game connected to them. No cards—ever." I stared out toward the Nile. "And there's more."

He nodded gravely, "Listen, this is my last night in Cairo. I wouldn't be here if I wasn't interested in hearing your story. Don't forget—it takes an awful lot to shock a pediatric ER doc from Wisconsin's biggest city. There's not much I haven't seen. Besides, no one can live 40 years and not have accumulated baggage."

His gentle words reassured. Besides, let's face it, he might have baggage of his own. I took a deep breath, looking at the first stars of the evening sky. The story I had to tell started in my first year of graduate school, but it made sense only in relation to what had happened early on.

My childhood died one sunny September morning in 1963. My father eased our car into the parking lot of St. Vincent's Hospital in Indianapolis to a spot where I could see the third-floor window of my mother's room. He left me with an old family friend while he went to fetch my newest sister—her delivery being my mother's seventh Caesarian section, six weeks premature, only ten-and-a-half months after delivering my sister Helen.

When my father returned, he was carrying a mound of blankets.

To my surprise, he opened my door, gently placed the tiny red-faced baby in my lap and said, "Here, Liza, you have to take care of your new sister now. Your mother is very sick and could die. You must help her by taking care of both your sisters." I was eight. I remember little of my life before this but I do know that I was expected to grow up abruptly that day. And I obliged.

Before we drove off, my father and I waved to the third floor window where I could see the blurry shape of my mother waving back. The thought she might never come home was intolerable, so I determined to do everything possible to bring her home. Riding home, Carol slept contentedly in my arms, oblivious to what was happening to our family.

A few weeks later my mother came home, sickly, but alive. Six months later she was at death's door again, this time from a pulmonary embolus, a blood clot to the lung. Again I jumped to help and protect her—anything to keep her alive. To relieve her fatigue I would bathe, feed and change the growing baby and almost-toddler before heading to school each day. At bedtime, I read them stories and sang them to sleep.

My brothers were spared the domestic chores and actually grew distant from me as I no longer was a playmate but a built-in maid. This pattern became permanent and even in high school they ignored me, never including me in their social life. They bought into the paternalism of our world and treated me like a donkey sister—good enough to wash their stinky football uniforms, but never deemed cool enough to include in their social set.

During my high school years my mother, a librarian, went to work when my father suddenly became unemployed. Her chores fell to me and my domestic skills were honed even more. Again my duty, my father reminded me, was to safeguard my mother's precarious health in this latest crisis.

With seven children, our fiercely tightened budget meant all extras were cut—at least for me. Ballet, which I adored, stopped.

Piano lessons ended, even though my older brother's lessons continued because he was to be the brilliant son and was not to be thwarted. I loved to sing and begged for lessons, but my mother's firm no was probably more driven by her need for my after-school chores than by not recognizing the love of music we had all inherited. Later I learned my grandmother had a lovely trained voice. In retrospect I felt even more the Cinderella when it dawned on me that during these so-called tough years, the rest of my brothers and sisters got to study violin, singing and piano whenever they expressed interest.

Normal socializing with kids my own age was even denied me, given my tight schedule. My mother ruled the activities of my life and tolerated no variation in her routine. Once I begged to sleep over at a girlfriend's house in the neighborhood. She grudgingly agreed but then humiliated me by calling the next morning at 7:30 with instructions to send me home to begin the Saturday chores. I never risked that one again.

In this world constructed and controlled by my mother, with my father in conspiratorial silence, the "Liza" belonging to my parents was all my brothers and sisters knew. Our mother fostered fierce competition among the siblings, and that separates us even today. She also tried to create dependency on her for each of us. She used to boast that she treated each of us as only children. The net result however was that we all competed for her limited time and as adults we are distant because we only relate to each other through the assigned role our parents established.

As long as I was home I carried the burden of preserving Mother's life. If I failed as a good daughter, it could ultimately kill her. So I made sure the household chores were done, kids picked up and even in high school when I got a part-time job, I would give my pay to Mother to help with buying groceries.

Fortunately my parents believed in a college education for all of us. Of course this was implemented along gender lines. My sisters and I went to public schools and state universities—adequate schools, but not choice enough for my brothers; they were sent to private prep schools and universities. Everyone in the family seemed to buy into the concept that the boys were more deserving than the girls.

My college years were spent in full-time class, three-quarters-time work plus the continuing house responsibilities. As a commuter student, I lived at home where the precious access to one of the two family cars came at the cost of picking up and dropping off brothers and sisters at their various activities. I was still expected to cook supper so it would be ready as usual for the six o'clock meal—all this with a ten o'clock curfew, even on weekends. When I started working the evening shift at the hospital, I was allowed 45 minutes to get home after my shift ended at eleven. Since my income went to pay tuition, I couldn't afford to buy my own car and so was tied to the rules.

I loved French and literature. Although my mother was a librarian, our family spent little effort on reading, exchanging ideas or discussing world affairs. Books, to my mother, were to be shelved in strict adherence to the Dewey Decimal System. The library was a well-oiled business, run smoothly for the patrons. Her love of the library was of its neat organization, its structure. When I tried to discuss my interest for college, she dissuaded me from the arts. "All you can do with those areas is teach. That's not a future. You should do something with science, something that will always be needed, like nursing."

This seemed to be the logical extension of all the care I'd given my family over the years, so dutifully I followed her advice. With only a semester away from graduating, I finally admitted to myself that I hated nursing. Luckily I discovered the emergency department—which I loved. Of course, my real fantasy was to leave it all behind and head to New York to take singing and dancing lessons and try my luck on Broadway, but-risk taking not being my forte, I stayed put. True to my Catholic roots, all I could do with profound unhappiness was to offer it up as a sacrifice to God.

I have often tried to understand why my parents held me hostage to a burden that over time no longer existed. Both are still alive and well today, but I suppose raising seven children under ten years of age overwhelmed them and the habits were set in place. Unfortunately it set a pattern for the life I would choose to live over the next few years. I was a dutiful daughter, out of touch with my own needs, always believing everyone was deserving of my care and protection, no matter what I got in return.

My first step towards freedom, which shocked my parents, was to announce I was going away to graduate school. So began the adventure that I would have to explain as best I could to my new friend Pete Glaeser if our friendship was to grow. I began the tale.

PART II - WASHINGTON, DC 1977-1979

Chapter 2

"What are you saying?" I asked the black haired, bearded man standing next to me on a steamy August afternoon in our nation's capital.

"My name is Soliman Munir," he said again, smiling a well-crafted smile.

"I don't understand what you are saying, speak English," I countered.

Another student came up and they slapped each other on the shoulders. This foreigner seemed to know everyone else in the groups and he also appeared to be going on the trip with us.

The bus driver motioned us on board and I chose a seat by myself in the second row because I knew none of the other new resident advisors going for a training weekend to learn what our responsibilities would be in the dorms this coming academic year. As a graduate student studying for my master's degree in nursing, I was grateful to have been chosen as a resident director. That spring I had searched desperately to find funding for the second year of my program.

Part-time night shifts at a local hospital's emergency department did not pay enough to cover living expenses. Awarded a traineeship for next year's tuition, I had searched for a way to cover living expenses. Suddenly a notice in the campus newspaper for dorm advisors appeared. Room, board and a small monthly stipend for a resident director seemed like the perfect answer to my needs. I applied and was accepted.

The others, all undergraduate juniors or seniors, saw me not as another student, but rather as a member of the professional housing staff. At 22, I was only a year older than many of the seniors, but to me this was strictly a job—being regarded as an outsider didn't matter.

The bus heaved out of the parking lot, lumbering past the swag-limbed oak trees that lined the curving campus road, past the stone, turret-framed social science hall to the street and then past the enormous National Shrine Cathedral. Once underway, those standing in the rear of the bus finally sat down. My worst fear came true. This man whom I could not understand sat next to me—and it was on purpose.

"Hi, I am Soliman Munir," he said again.

"I am sorry but I still can't understand what you're saying."

"You must be Liza. I am saying my name. It is not English."

"Oh. All right, say it again slowly so I can hear it."

He repeated his name and I pronounced it after him until I got it right. He was a graduate student in sociology with a university job—director of maintenance in the dorms. That was enough for me. I turned to look out the window not interested in talking to him or anyone else, even though I did notice the other students joked and laughed with him and he seemed genuinely kind to all of them.

We were headed for a lodge in the Pocono Mountains so the trip took several hours. Originally this now-tired lodge had been designed as a honeymoon haven. Vestiges remained: all the benches on the grounds were S-shaped so lovers could face each other, bathtubs in the cabins were heart-shaped in pink and black tile. Overgrown topiary heart-shaped arches framed the walking paths at various points. Honeymooners must be going elsewhere, so the lodge was being used for weekend retreats and training programs.

After dinner I went for a walk alone, feeling older and distant from the other students who had built bonds during their college life together. Suddenly I heard my name called. "Liza, wait, you should not walk alone." It was my bus companion, Soliman. Walking up the path toward me, his baseball jacket open, he seemed unwilling to consider I might resent his intrusion.

"Hi."

"Hi," he answered and then asked, "What did you think of today's program?"

"It was okay. Nursing school drowns in that stuff on active listening, open-ended questions and nonverbal communication," I answered, staring straight ahead at the path, not at him.

"Oh, so you are a nurse. Where did you go to nursing school?"

His question annoyed me because if he knew my name, he had more than likely seen my application. "Indiana University."

We walked on in silence a few yards. Not appreciating rudeness in others, I forced myself to be polite. "Where are you from?"

"Oh, far from here—as you might imagine," he replied with a wistful gaze over the treetops. "You've probably never heard of it."

"Try me." My father had been in the import-export business and traveled extensively. He would send me programs from the opera house in Paris, the symphony in London, operettas in Munich and post cards from everywhere. I loved anything international, the more exotic the better. Of course at that time, I was unaware how Euro-focused my knowledge was, mostly limited to Western classical music.

"Well, I come from what is called Israel, the north part, the Galilee," he stated with measured flatness.

"But you are not Jewish," I guessed from his name, "Isn't everyone who lives there Jewish?"

"Well, no. You are right. I am not Jewish. I am a Moslem, an Arab, but my family has lived in the Galilee for more than 800 years. We do not now live in our original village because we were forced to move after it was destroyed."

We kept walking in the pleasant cool mountain air. Finally I answered, "How awful. When was it destroyed?" I imagined it was hundreds of years before.

"In 1948."

He smiled at me, expecting some reaction but I was unaware of what had happened in 1948 to cause his village to be destroyed. There was no bluffing my way out of this one. "Would you refresh my memory of that time, I can't quite recall?"

"I am from the Holy Land. Palestine. I am Palestinian. Palestine has existed for centuries. In 1948 things changed for us." He kicked at a stone in the path like a belligerent child with unfocused, festering anger.

Scrolling through my memory searching for anything remotely related to Palestine, it came up blank. Prideful about knowing something about the outside world, I deplored my ignorance—so typical of the provincial Hoosiers from whom I was desperate to escape.

When I admitted my unfamiliarity with his history, Soliman rolled his eyes and sighed as if he expected my ignorance. With labored pleasantness, he began to recount words he had said many times before. "It is a very long story." He checked himself deciding not to tell it. "If you want to know more, I will give you some books to read and then answer any questions."

We walked on in silence but I wanted to know more. He had piqued my interest by not answering my question. His odd challenge to read on my own seemed rather rude. Why was he so reticent in talking about himself?

"Do you have brothers and sisters?" I segued into a harmless line of conversation.

"Yes, 13 brothers and sisters, all alive," he answered, "I am the oldest."

That evening we walked for an hour discussing our large fami-

Finding Palestine

lies, albeit mine was half his number. We found many topics of mutual interest—the university, resident advisors and directors, student activities in the coming year. When we reached the common area near the cabins, the undergraduate students began to whistle and tease us. We took it with good nature but their expressed immaturity offput me—had I known, at that point, I was to be assigned a fresh-person women's dorm to direct, I might have quit then.

But I still did not know the answer to what had happened to Soliman's village. Perhaps an earthquake or some other catastrophic event? Now curious, I decided his offer to read seemed friendly.

The next day I settled into the morning session in a large meeting room. Scanning the room, I noted an anorectic beauty queen and the shirtless, v-neck sweater cum gold chain adorning the housing office administrator. Then my eyes came to rest on Soliman's face. He led his small group discussion just like the other assistant administrators did in their small groups.

Detached and not engaged in the clucking chatter of small group talk, I was bored with the current project of planning new student activities. Here I was—an ER nurse accustomed to facing emergency after emergency. The last night I had worked there had been three codes—a cardiac arrest, a respiratory arrest and a diabetic coma, all arriving within 15 minutes of each other. I managed them all.

So my mind wandered. Who was this Soliman and what about his village? What did he want with a sociology degree? I admitted to myself he didn't really irritate me. His accent was pleasant, his English correct. He did not affect any foreign costumes—no over-sized suits with pants too long and too flared, no scarf, hat or turban. His clothes were casual, collegiate—at least what he wore that weekend. He fit in, but was still different—not enough to scare me away, only enough to intrigue me.

With skill, I pretended to listen to my small group, nodding at appropriate intervals. Instead, I wondered where I would see him again. Was he special? Perhaps my journey to new places, worlds, people had begun. After all that was why I came to do graduate school in Washington, DC—the capital of the United States, the capital of the world.

"I'm staying here this summer, with a job and a place to live," I repeated again to my mother. "Sublet a friend's room in a house in Georgetown. Yes, the other housemates are friends."

I hung up the phone—the break completed. I never went back to live in Indiana. Washington, DC became paradise that summer.

Busy with summer courses, full-time work in the emergency department, local DC activities, parades, theater, concerts and museums, I found each day delightful. I lingered on the terrace of the Kennedy Center after concerts mesmerized by lights on the Potomac River and I traipsed through the capital like a dutiful citizen. By far my favorite place was the National Library of Congress. The domed, wood-paneled reading room sheltered silent readers, hunched over the crescent reading tables—I intended to join their ranks.

One sunny summer afternoon after psychology class, my name sounded through the breeze. Soliman waved from his VW Sirocco.

"Liza. Hi, how are you?"

"Hi, what brings you over here?"

"Catch up on problems with the vents in the labs," he explained. "Didn't you go home for the summer?"

"No, I stayed to take a few courses and work full time. Makes my schedule a little lighter next school year."

"Well, see you soon." He shifted into gear and squealed up the steep path to the science hall. His button-down collar, yellow oxford cloth shirt with rolled up long sleeves gave him a continental air.

The few weeks before fall semester activities passed quickly. I stopped by the housing office to check my mailbox and found two books with no note or explanation: *The Evasive Peace* and Fouzi El Asmar's *To Be an Arab in Israel*.

"Hi. I'm Nancy, your RA," said a bubbly young woman with

straight brown hair who blinked her watery eyes a lot.

"Hi." I answered extending my hand. "When do you plan to move into the dorm?"

"This Saturday. My boyfriend is helping me. He's the RD on the extension campus dorm. How about you?"

"I'm moving in Saturday also. Perhaps we can have a meeting to set up our schedules and plans."

"That's fine. We aren't going out until later," she said, then squinted her eyes and hesitated.

"Look, Nancy, you don't know me at all but we will know each other very well soon enough. For now, you need to know that I am not interested at all in being anyone's boss, least of all yours. We are partners—work together, support each other. It's really quite simple. Now, ask me anything."

"See, I didn't know how you would be, being the RD. No one knew you," she said as if stating a decree.

"Well, alrighty then, see you Saturday."

"Oh, one more thing," she called after me. "Are you and Soliman a thing?"

"No, we are not a thing, nothing. Where did that come from? I just met the guy this past spring."

"Well, we saw you go walking with him and you were gone awhile." Her impish defensiveness was not lost on me. She glanced at the books in my hand.

"I don't know him any better than I know you or any of the other housing office staff," I retorted. "Don't you have anything better to do than speculate about my private life?"

"Well, like since we're friends now, I just thought I should tell you," she rambled.

"Tell me what?"

"He likes nurses," she announced with the caution of a fortune teller.

"Thanks for the tip." What did that mean? I dismissed the comment as typical from an immature coed trying to be cool. But such statements can haunt over time and this one surely did.

In mid-September I saw Soliman at the office. We chatted about the dorms and classes. It didn't take long for him to ask about the books. Not far into reading, I begged off talking about them for another week. We agreed to meet for coffee the next Friday.

"Two coffees, please," Soliman ordered. The coffee shop near campus was half empty—it being Friday evening.

"I read one book, *Evasive Peace,* but I don't understand what happened." His black onyx eyes examined me like miniature telescopes, always on the watch. They were not warm eyes, but rather cool like the glass lenses of a telescope. His unkempt hair gave the impression he had no vanity, but his look was well planned.

"What do you mean?" he asked.

"Before 1918 Palestine existed as a province of the Ottoman Empire, the empire of the Turks. After 1918 and the victory of the Allies in World War I, the Turk's Ottoman Empire collapsed. The winners, France and Great Britain, took control of the Arab world."

"Right so far."

"Palestine was assigned to Great Britain which had agreed in the Anglo-French Declaration of 1918 to give their Arab countries independence in exchange for their support of the Allies in World War I. Now let me see—that included Lebanon, Syria, Jordan, Iraq, Egypt and Palestine, according to my count."

"Keep going," he encouraged.

"But Great Britain reneged on Palestine. Instead it invoked the 1917 Balfour Declaration, a private letter recommending establishment of a Jewish homeland in Palestine. I don't get it." And looked up from my notes.

"What don't you get? What is your question?" he asked unimpressed with my recitation.

"Well, on the basis of a private letter, Britain gave Palestine away to European Jews? How can Britain give away a country full of people to anyone else?" I expected an explanation from him. "You are a Palestinian, how could that happen?"

Soliman winced. "How can that happen?" he stated with genuine weariness, as if he had asked that question himself many times over. "You tell me, America the great superpower. Tell me what right you and the Europeans have to take our homes away from us." His strident voice hinted at a contained rage within him.

What could I say? No one had ever asked me to explain the policies of the U.S. or personalized them with a direct question. I tried to deflect the attack, "Tell me what happened to your village?"

"My village was in the north part of the Galilee, the northern area of Palestine. My grandmother could tell us the family history lived out for at least 800 years on our hundreds of acres of olive trees. I was born in 1944." He took a sip of the coffee.

"Go on."

"I remember climbing our family's olive trees with Wa'el, my favorite cousin. While we were shouting to each other from different branches in the tree, a soldier with a strange accent appeared out of nowhere and began to beat us with a club. He told us our trees were Jewish and belonged to Jews only. Scared, we ran home to tell my father who ordered us to stay out of the trees for a few days."

"What year was this?" I interrupted.

"1948–the year the U.N. plan to divide Palestine was to take effect. I was four years old. One week after the soldier beat us in the trees, Zionist troops overran our village at four in the morning. As people staggered out of their beds, the soldiers machine-gunned down any teenage boys or young men they saw and threatened to rape some of the women."

"God, that is unbelievable, what did you do?"

"Families fled to villages north and west with just the pajamas on their backs. No one was allowed back to bury the dead. We camped under the olive trees because the still-untouched villages overflowed with refugees. Many families hiked to Lebanon for safety including some of my uncles, whose families still wait in temporary refugees camps for the day to go home. Since 1948."

"So you never went back to your village?" I hesitated to ask.

"Zionists routinely demolished villages and ours was no exception. Stone by stone, house by house, my village was blown apart, never to be inhabited again."

"Weren't you devastated by all this."

Soliman smiled a "you just don't get it" smile and shrugged. "My father refused to leave Palestine for fear he would never return. The families who fled to Lebanon thought they would be there for two weeks, waiting until order would be restored and they could return. My father could never imagine his Palestine divided and his family expelled because he lived in the U.N.'s newly designated Jewish part. He refused to give up his ancestral land and way of life, choosing the uncertainty of life under the brutal rule of Zionists rather than leave."

"Soliman, I hate to ask this question but I am just trying to understand, okay?"

"Sure, ask anything," he laughed. "Nurses are usually interested in people."

Nancy's cautionary warning came to mind at his comment, but I felt rather cool talking politics with a foreigner at a coffee house.

"Who were the Zionists?"

"You really don't know. Isn't it sad?" He shook his head with an air of righteous arrogance.

"No, I don't know and that is too bad. I am here to learn if you can get over your narcissistic self-pity."

"Oh, a hot temper, I must be careful," he laughed but his cool black onyx lenses studied me.

"I don't have a temper," I pressed, "but I am stubborn, so be warned."

"Back then, in 1948, Zionists meant the European Jewish settlers driven by the ideology of Zionism to establish a Jewish state. They're the ones that destroyed my village. In 1948, British colonial rule of Palestine was to end; however, instead of giving us our own independent state, the Zionists and their Jewish counterparts in America convinced the international community at that time of their right to our land."

"How can that happen?"

"The Zionist movement was founded in the 1890s by Theodor Herzl who envisioned an exclusively Jewish state as an answer to European Jewish national aspirations," he explained. "The Balfour Declaration bolstered Zionist efforts after World War I, despite years of protest to the British by my father's and grandfather's generation. The goal of a Jewish state picked up a lot of international support after World War II and the holocaust. The British betrayed us and let the U.N. divide Palestine."

"Well, the holocaust was a terrible tragedy, don't you think?" I interrupted, "You cannot dispute the horror that occurred."

"No one disputes the holocaust. After the war, the world wanted to show European Jews sympathy for what happened and deflect criticism of their own reluctance to intervene earlier when they should have."

"Well, don't you think sympathy was a reasonable response to the Jewish suffering ?"

"Sympathy at what price? The cheap, easy way. Console the conscience of the West by betraying their promise of independence to Palestine," he said.

"Why was it so easy to betray Palestine?"

"Why? Liza, it was very easy to betray a people who were 'not like us.' Palestinians were considered primitive compared to European Jews who looked like the British or Americans. Who cared what happened to us, far from the spotlight?"

"So Palestine was handed over to the Jews as an apology for the failure to stop the concentration camps on the part of the Allies?"

The idea astonished me. Soliman's eyewitness account transformed abstract history into a personal family story, but perhaps his embittered past made objectivity impossible. Concentration camp images from the newsreels came to mind—the faces, the suffering, the pain. If all he said were true, why was it a secret? Why was it not common knowledge? He couldn't have made this up just to get a date with me.

Still, the terrible wrong of the holocaust surely could not be righted by inflicting yet another global wrong on another people. "Never again" has to mean never again to anyone, not just "never again to Jews" otherwise the painful lesson of the holocaust is lost. Might would still be right at any cost, even one's morality. My startling reflection was cut short by Soliman's voice who signaled for the waitress to pour us some more coffee. "The net effect was that foreigners took our homes, our land, our country away from us by force."

"So that's what all the fighting is about over there." Over there. Fighting. No specifics. This inadequate vocabulary gave no identity, location or existence to the human beings of Palestine.

"What's wrong? Liza. You're upset?" asked Soliman.

"What do you expect? You've just told me an outrageous story that no one has ever heard of." Did my Midwest background make me an easy dupe for his version of *Tales of Arabian Nights*? "What about the Bible? The U.N.? What about terrorism, guerrillas?"

"Easy does it. This is a complicated story." He patted my hand which still gripped my empty mug. "Want some more coffee since you are working nights?"

"How did you know?" I demanded.

"Some of the nurses in your class told me you worked part-time at Provision Hospital in the ER."

"Whom do you know?"

"I know them all."

"So what? My nursing job doesn't interfere with my dorm

work."

"That's true."

"Thanks for the coffee and the talk. Work calls."

"You're welcome. We'll talk again. Just keep reading." A half smile escaped his cool face.

The farther my walk took me from Soliman, the more my skepticism grew. A conspiracy so large as to squelch the other side of a story so imbedded in our common collective memory seemed difficult to swallow. Yet in the day-to-day existence of Americans, did anyone really care which side of the story they heard, much less if it was the whole story? I wouldn't discount Soliman's story out of hand. What if it was true?

Discussing world politics exhilarated me, but the letdown afterward only reinforced the distance I felt from the powerful world of international politics. To do something meaningful and important required a cache of courage and conviction I didn't have. When I arrived at the hospital my musings were interrupted by a guard at the entrance, "Liza, I'll walk you to the ER," he announced with a no-nonsense air. "There's been one mugging here already tonight; no need for another."

"No, that's okay. Thanks." After the swish of the automatic doors closed behind me, I went to work.

Chapter 3

After a tedious three-hour lecture, the 20-minute walk alone to the dorm seemed like a victory prize. With luck I had avoided the nuns who usually walked with me. They made me feel phony because of a need to be cheerful around them when I wasn't. I had mostly attended public school, spending only a few early years in a Catholic school with the nuns—but the imprint was deep.

My Catholic heritage had less to do with theology and more to do with "The Fight Song of the Fighting Irish," the first song I ever learned by heart. All the men in my family were Notre Dame graduates. Shocked as a kid when I learned girls were not allowed there, I was slated to go to Indiana University, which was easier on the family pocketbook.

Catholic University served my graduate education interests but not because it was Catholic. If I wanted Catholic, it would have been Notre Dame. There was something else this university gave me. Escape. When I drew an eight-hour circle around Indianapolis on the map, Catholic University of America was outside the perimeter. That was farther than my parents would drive in a day. And it was in Washington, DC.

Despite the pretty campus and quality education I never got used to having nuns as classmates. Their lives reminded me of my

Finding Palestine

own life under my mother's unquestionable rigorous routine. Worse, I discovered, graduate nursing demanded we implement one of the competing nursing theories in our academic work. The faculty categorized us by the theory we chose and some were more fashionable than others. Prudent students did not criticize the theories, just as I never criticized my mother's regime. My informal journal club of three other classmates avoided any critical analysis of a nursing theory or any other theory. The only heated debates we had were about the best Irish bar in town and where to find flaky croissants.

One of our quartet gushed about Mother Teresa all the time, but wouldn't be caught dead at an international students' potluck dinner. She complained the Iranian graduate nursing students smelled and wore too much makeup. The other two aimed for the good life with their respective lawyer and physician husbands. A master's degree in nursing would fit their social status and guarantee a daytime job with an impressive title. On balance there was nothing wrong with those aspirations. I just didn't have them.

The boxy, red-brick dorm came into view around the hill. Students squatted outside the cafeteria with placards. Protesting for a better meal plan struck me as wimpy. The end of the 70s was a lot different from the start. Our college demonstrations tried to stop a war or improve civil rights. I had caught the bug of trying to keep justice on course and work for improved human rights for all. It still made sense to me. Emergency department nursing had meaning but I wanted a grander, global mission—a role in international health.

The phone in my room rang as I slid my key in the door. Tossing my backpack on the bed, I grabbed it mid-ring.

"Liza, how are you?" asked Soliman.

"Hi, fine."

"Are you free this evening? It is not Friday, you are not working?" he asked.

"What's up?"

"A friend of mine is cooking Palestinian cuisine."

"Sounds interesting. What time, where and all that?"

"I'll pick you up at five-thirty in front of the dorm. He lives in Silver Springs so it's a half hour drive. Is that okay?"

"That's fine. I'll be out front. See you."

"See you then."

Exactly on time the burnt-orange Sirocco squealed into the driveway of the dorm. "So, how have you been?" he asked as we headed away from the dorm. Pushing in a cassette he added, "You don't mind some Arabic music, do you?"

"No, let's hear some." I smiled at the memory of one of my father's albums—a scantily dressed, provocative woman with a vixen smile behind a sheer veil draped just below kohl-lined eyes on the cover—entitled "How to Make Your Husband a Sultan: Music for Belly Dancing." The record was never played as far as I knew, but as a child, I thought the woman beautiful.

"Who's singing?"

"Fairuz, a famous Lebanese singer." He hummed along with the strange sounds of strings and percussion mixed with almost no bass. Hers were the first Arabic words I had ever heard.

"What is she singing about?"

"The Mediterranean Sea, its beauty and how she loves her sweetheart. It is hard to translate word for word. Arabic music is very poetic," he explained. "Do you speak only English?"

"No, I can speak French."

"Good, if you ever go to Lebanon, you can use your French. It is practically a second language there. Many Arabs go to language schools as kids so they become fluent in several."

"Did you go to a language school?"

"Ha, never thought of it that way. I went to a school outside our new village, you know, the one we fled to during the raids. The school was run, as all the schools were, by the new Israeli government with Hebrew as the official language of instruction. Even though only Palestinian Arab students were in our school, the classes were taught in Hebrew which helped us communicate with our occu-piers. However, history class was the most amusing."

"What was so funny?"

"The teacher, a young zealot tried to tell us the official version of the new State of Israel. We kept asking questions about our dead and missing relatives in Lebanon. Every day we asked about going back to our original villages just to drive him crazy. Eventually he quit because he couldn't face us—the living truth about his new state." Soliman skillfully drove through the heavy traffic.

"Where did you learn your English?"

"We learned English all through primary and secondary school." He started to laugh. "I have a quick story to tell you."

"Okay."

"I came to America on a ship bound for New York, in the worst class of a cargo boat, but it was cheap. No one met me and it seemed every car honked and every bus growled in that city. I stood bewildered in my old suit jacket, stiff like a statue, with $200 U.S. dollars sewn into the lining of the sleeves. A yellow cab swerved toward me and stopped. The driver asked me where I wanted to go. "Washington," I yelled. He screamed, "Which one?" I didn't know there were two, so I yelled back, "The White House." He laughed at me, the foreigner, and drove off. Eventually I found the train and took it to Union Station."

"That sounds like a scene from a movie."

"I swear by Allah, I did not know at that time there was a state of Washington. For foreigners, there is only one Washington that matters—the White House Washington."

"No doubt your English improved once you settled here," I chuckled. "Which girl was the best teacher?"

"Liza, do you take me for that kind of man?"

"Absolutely. You are the guy who knows all the nurses."

"Ouch. Who told you that?" he demanded.

"All the nurses."

He drove down a tree-shaded lane in an old subdivision. Overgrown shrubbery and thick trees softened the sharp-cornered brick ranch homes in this cozy neighborhood. Pink big wheels abandoned on driveways and barking pets greeted us.

"Come on. They're all here," he said jumping out of the car.

Those already arrived sat in a glass sunroom—the type that doubled for a screened porch in the summertime. "*Marhaba, Marhaba, Ya habibi,*" Soliman greeted a tall bald man with a pot belly. They kissed three times; on the right cheek then left then right again. Another man and two women also kissed Soliman, but just twice.

"Liza," Soliman said while motioning me forward, "This is my good friend Fouzi El Asmar and his wife Maria."

I shook hands, guessing one doesn't kiss a stranger.

"Hello, how do you do." Formal, but safe for the author of the book I had recently finished. My curiosity grew in spite of my shyness.

"I am pleased to meet you." He turned to his wife. "Maria, see, she is also American, you will enjoy yourself."

"Liza, so nice to have you." She took my arm. "Let's go out to the kitchen and get you something to drink. I know what you want," she called to Soliman.

Her small kitchen percolated with color. The mustard yellow counter top contrasted with the jug of green olive oil, the cranberry glass canister of Turkish coffee and jars of colorful spices. Citrus and cinnamon steam escaped intermittently from the covered pots on the stove like white puffs from a steam engine.

"Please don't mind Fouzi's comment about being American. He knows I get tired of entertaining—actually serving is a better word for it—all sorts of people I will never see again," she apologized.

"I don't understand, what people?"

"You know, the politics. Fouzi is a journalist so all sorts of people come to see him to get his opinion on what's going on." She poured a diet cola over ice. "That's for Soliman, what would you

Finding Palestine

like?"

"Oh, the same is fine." Her weariness showed in her ruddy face and slightly smudged mascara. "May I ask 'what's going on,' that people come to see your husband about?"

Her turquoise-garnished small eyes widened. "You must be new to all this. Soliman has not talked to you about anything?"

"About what? He did give me a book written by your husband."

"Then you do know about Palestine," she commented. "Don't you realize the struggle that's going on? People come to see Fouzi for his reports and opinions about what is happening and what to do for resistance, for the struggle, the revolution."

Resistance, struggle, revolution? The words seemed incongruent with her suburban, dumpy housewife appearance.

"Me? I help Fouzi any way I can, typing, reading, welcoming. You don't know Arab culture, but everyone must have a coffee or tea and some sweets. Depending on who and the time of day, you have to offer them lunch or supper. Often, I don't hear a word of English. They all speak in Arabic. That's why Fouzi was glad you were American so at least I could talk to you and probably not about politics." She gave me a searching look, "How long have you known Soliman?"

"For a few months, since the start of the school year. I work in the housing office with him."

"He is a special friend of Fouzi's." She put Soliman's drink on a small silver tray. "But he has never brought anyone to our house so we were very curious about you. Come on, let's take this to him."

She presented the drink to him from the tray. He responded with a phrase in Arabic, but she answered in English. Then she picked up a tray of cucumbers and cheese and offered it to everyone who correctly took some and repeated the same Arabic phrase. Her performance was effortless. She took my arm and told them we would be in the kitchen arranging supper.

"Do you speak Arabic?" I asked.

"Not really. Fouzi tried to teach me, but it just doesn't work. I think you have to live in a place to learn its language." She shrugged.

"Arabic sounds are very different."

"That was simple, what you heard, all the proper phrases for just saying thank you. If you stick around this group, you'll find that there are all sorts of flowery phrases for what would be simple responses in English." She reached for some plates in one of the cupboards.

"So you know those lines?" I took the plates from her.

"Yeah, but I sound terrible so I stick with English. Fouzi wishes I would try more, but it's hopeless. I just let him speak Arabic to our daughter Latifa and I speak English. She knows them both now."

Maria flipped a pot of stuffed grape leaves onto a large tray and handed it to me. "In the center, please." She pulled a salad of parsley, lemon, tomatoes, cucumber and bulgur wheat from the refrigerator. "Fouzi insists I make the tabbouleh Palestinian style. He is a nationalist even down to his food."

"Is there that much variation in food?"

"Sure, there are regional differences, some use tomato sauces for stuffed grape leaves, some use plain lemon and salt, some make tabbouleh with more or less parsley and *burghul*. My mother-in-law taught me the El Asmar interpretation." She lifted out a casserole dish with eggplant and pine nut seeds from the oven.

"Did it take you a long time to learn all these things?"

"Only six years of marriage. That's when you really learn cooking because you start living two cultures together. The biggest problem is not cooking but eating humus and *baba ghannouj* with olive oil and bread for hours." She patted her round behind. "But it just goes to my hips. Come on, let's call them to eat. I'm hungry."

Maria went to get Latifa from the patio and called everyone to the table. Fouzi didn't look like the exotic person I had imagined from his book. This 18th-generation Christian Arab, a refugee from the town of Lydda, Palestine, appeared no different from any other middle-aged suburbanite in America. The other guests were a Palestinian couple on a short visit to Washington. Arabic dominated the conversation which Soliman did not translate. Maria and I chatted on the side clearly peripheral to Fouzi's comments which the couple had come to hear.

Soon after dessert, we all left. "Fouzi is an important man," Soliman remarked during the silent drive back to campus.

"So Maria said."

"Those other people were important with business to discuss and this was the only time they could see him," he explained.

"What was their business?"

"They were journalists based in Lebanon," he said flatly.

"Well, why didn't you say so?"

"There was no need." He glanced at me then added, "You found Maria nice, didn't you, with lots to talk about?"

"Yes, and she cares about Fouzi's work very much. Whom does Fouzi write for, a newspaper, a magazine? Does he write for the *Washington Post* or the *New York Times*?"

"He writes for Arabic newspapers and magazines."

"Why does he live here in the States? Wouldn't it be easier to live in the place you write about."

"He is not allowed to live in his hometown," Soliman sighed.

"Not allowed, by whom?"

"The Israeli government, which will arrest him if he tries to go back."

"Just because he is a journalist?"

"Because he is a Palestinian and a journalist who reports the real activities of the government and the occupation in West Bank and Gaza. The Israelis prevent him from living in his hometown because they are afraid his writings will provoke more resistance to the occupation. His articles threaten the prevailing myths of Israel."

"You are good friends, aren't you?"

He nodded as we swung into the driveway of my dorm. "You would like to meet some other friends too, yes?"

"Sure." I shrugged then ran up the steps to front door. What a strange evening—giving me a glimpse into Soliman's closely guarded world which was quite apart from his jovial façade of dorm maintenance director. The door to my room flung open with a push and I flicked on the light. Fouzi's book lay on the table, no longer inanimate, but alive with his kind face telling his sad story of betrayals, violence and the dismemberment of his home community.

Later, turning off the light, I recalled Maria's stuffed grape leaves. How did she keep them from unrolling while being cooked? Images from my busy day drifted in and out of my head. Sleep came late as usual.

Chapter 4

Generally I prefer to do academic assignments alone. So when the professor told us to choose a partner for our next one, my frown of frustration apparently amused the student sitting next to me. "My sentiments exactly," she leaned over to whisper. "My name is Rita."

We left the classroom together. Over the next few weeks Rita and I became friends. We shared the same opinion about graduate nursing's devotion to theory at the expense of attention to clinical issues. "I will listen politely to American theories and ideas, but then adapt everything to our Eastern Cape community. South Africa's needs are different from yours," Rita said. "Health education and community health measures empower the people against the oppression of apartheid."

She surprised me with a dinner invitation, which I readily accepted. Their neglected Black neighborhood in Northeast DC was sparsely dotted with gentrified three-story brick walk-ups, fortified with electronic security gates. Creaking up the stairs in the light of a single dangling light bulb to the third floor, I found Bo Rembutu waiting at the door. His intense bullet eyes winked a welcome to their tiny two room flat. Rita turned around from the stainless steel Pullman kitchen to wave with a long wooden spoon, "Welcome to our little home away from home, my sister."

Her apple red and black dress swished along the floor. Curls poked out around the edges of the tightly wound matching head scarf. To see South African fashion in the States was rare, this being pre-Alex Haley's *Roots*. African-American was a term yet to be coined. A picture of Nelson Mandela hung prominently in the room flanked by other political posters issued by the African National Congress. No one had ever called me "my sister" before. It had the sound of acceptance into a secret sect, the reward after proving oneself worthy in a rite of initiation.

"You notice our political expression. Does it bother you?" asked Bo. His words clipped by in an accent not quite British with an African rhythm.

"No, not at all."

"You know the phrase, the personal is political. Well, that sums it up for us." He motioned for me to sit down on the faded blue damask sofa. "Rita told me how much she has enjoyed working with you. Actually she said you were different from the others in your class." He leaned back in a frayed green plaid lazy-boy recliner, its stripped gears grinding before it popped into place.

"Oh, I don't know how different. Rita told me you are studying for a Ph.D. in political science. What is your dissertation about?"

"Colonialism. Actually, a comparative study of colonialism in South Africa and in Palestine. Are you familiar with either?" he answered.

"Not very, sad to say. What made you choose to compare South Africa with Palestine?"

"In part, both states conduct the most vicious variety of colonialism, that is, apartheid. But the Palestine case is especially unique so it works well for comparison purposes."

"Isn't colonialism a standard sort of thing?" Although desperately curious about world politics, knowing so little made me feel all the more inadequate. Bo and Rita's warm welcome allowed me to risk exposing my ignorance and allow them to teach me.

"No, there are variations. For instance, Britain and France are mother countries whose colonies in Asia and Africa enriched them with many resources that they took back home, thanks to the exploitation of the local non-white native populations. However, Zionism was a social movement, not a nation-state, which drew its members from many European nations and America. As a mixed bag of nationalities, but all Jews, Zionist colonialists hailed from no one shared country for whom the resources extracted from the new colony would be sent. Zionists colonized Palestine to set up a new country, Israel.

"Where do the British fit in then?" I continued

"At the time of World War I, Turkey ruled a vast empire including the Arab world. It allied with the Germans. So the British wanted the Arabs to revolt against the Turks and fight as allies of the British. After long negotiations, the Arabs agreed to do so in exchange for independence after the war. As allies and trade partners, Britain would get the coveted land route to India through friendly Arab countries."

"But it didn't happen?" The similarity to Soliman's account could not be an accident and intrigued me all the more.

"The British broke their promise."

"Was there no record of the deal with the Arabs?"

"Oh yes, the complete diplomatic correspondence between the British diplomat Sir Henry McMahon and the Arab leader, Sharif Husain, was known as the 'McMahon Correspondence.' The Arabic text of these papers widely circulated throughout the Arab world, even though the British people at that time knew nothing about it because an English translation was not released until 1938. British officials defended the cover-up with national security claims."

Rita joined me on the sofa. Bo continued to recount the modern history lesson. "Britain and France carved up the Arab world using the 'Sykes-Picot Agreement' in May 1916. They considered the Arabs too primitive and unsophisticated to rule themselves. The

Palestinian Arabs were neither passive nor primitive and proved difficult to control. Britain's solution lay with the Zionists—European colonials just like them. If Britain facilitated setting up a national home for the Jews in Palestine, then people like them would become the trading partners and allies they sought in the region."

While Bo spoke, Rita motioned us to the table where garlic lemon soup steamed from Pyrex bowls. We bowed our heads while Bo prayed the grace before meals.

The soup was good, but he quickly returned to his topic, "Basically the issue boiled down to land and labor."

"Land and labor?" I repeated quite aware that he was jousting with me. "What you are talking about."

"Getting control of the land is always essential to colonization. In the early days, the Zionists bought land in Palestine under cover of British banks and agencies and the Arabs did not catch on for quite a while. If you own the land and deny homes and jobs to the local population, they will move because they cannot survive. Britain facilitated the Zionists' encroachment on the Arab land and population."

Rita cleared the bowls away to make room for the vegetable casserole and chimed in, "Obviously the Jewish settlers knew they had to get rid of the Arabs in order to set up a pure Jewish state. It is like South Africa, no political rights unless you are white only and in the new Zionist state of Israel, no political rights unless you are Jewish. In both cases it doesn't matter that your family has lived there for hundreds of years and it is your land."

Bo added, "Because they all suffered from extreme arrogance, no one anticipated the level of resistance the Palestinians would muster. The PLO today is simply made up of the children and grandchildren of the native population who are still trying to resist, just like their fathers and grandfathers, this racist colonial movement called Zionism."

"Why do you suppose the Blacks of South Africa have managed

to make their case so well and the Palestinians have not?" I asked.

Rita chuckled. "Ten years ago no one listened to our plight. Finally the ANC managed to connect South Africa's national identity with racism. We internationalized our struggle as a fight against racism, which in America could be understood in the context of the civil rights movement. The resulting international isolation of the government of South Africa on the part of the world-wide intelligentsia and the corporations slowly worked to weaken the regime. Of course, as much as we need the support of intellectuals and politicians to fight apartheid, I am well aware of a certain level of hypocrisy."

"You might call it liberation fashion," Bo added.

"What do you mean?"

"The very people who boycott lectures in South Africa in support of Black liberation will trot off at a moment's notice to Tel Aviv and blindly give an anti-apartheid lecture in Israel, but refuse to acknowledge the squalor of refugee camps, the poverty in villages, the human rights violated daily by the Israeli government and its military occupation of Palestinians in their own homeland."

"Incredible," I said lamely, overwhelmed at the story which just kept getting worse. Rita's level of political knowledge daunted me and I hoped that as a nurse I could be as aware of my political surroundings.

Rita continued, "It cheapens Black suffering to be glamorized into a 'safe, chic cause,' when the violation of Palestinian human rights persists. And I will not be cheapened," she emphasized with a shake of her head.

"You see, Liza, Nelson Mandela taught us that human rights apply to everyone. No picking and choosing allowed. No convenient selectivity," added Bo.

"People won 't call for Palestinian rights or self-determination because they're afraid of being labeled anti-Semitic." Rita waved her hands in frustration, "That is absurd. Being for Palestinian rights and self-determination does not mean one is anti-Semitic or anti-Jewish. We must support the human rights of both Jews and Palestinians."

"While we welcome all support for our fight against white racism in South Africa, it is hollow if it is not genuinely meant for all people," explained Bo. "But, Liza, I meant to ask earlier: What makes you interested in Palestine, unlike most Americans?"

"Well, until I met this guy, Soliman ..."

"Ah, you know Soliman Munir? He is an acquaintance of ours. How did you meet him?" he interrupted.

"Through the housing office where I work as an RD. He gave me some books about Palestine."

"If he did, it is the exception. He usually doesn't talk about it," Rita added.

"We have commiserated with him about being second-class citizens in your own homeland with the restrictions on jobs and education, the like," said Bo.

"Yes, but despite all the problems, it is our home," Rita sighed, "and we must be there to continue the struggle against apartheid."

We finished the meal exchanging pleasantries about Washington, the university and Rita's media liaising work at a small nonprofit organization called the South African Human Rights Campaign.

Thinking about all this on my drive home, I was troubled to realize there were histories about which I knew nothing. I had stumbled on them, lately. But Fouzi's history I found in a book given me by an acquaintance—and I found out he just wants to go home to live near his ailing mother. How many Fouzis were there? In the open society of America, I couldn't even imagine where to look for a history of the Palestinian people. They simply didn't exist in our awareness, so how could their history exist?

Later that summer, Soliman and I both attended a going-away party for Rita and Bo. They had become dear friends—our relationship developed and was sustained on its own merits, separate from Soliman and definitely not the result of his introduction. Later it would always irritate me that strangers would automatically assume Soliman was my personal passport to the world.

In January of 1980 Soliman's lease ran out. He had been accepted to graduate school in Chicago but needed a place to stay for a few months. We were close friends and he suggested we get married. There was no rush of passion between us but the idea appealed to me because I liked the people he associated with. Slowly I began to affiliate with the men and women involved with liberation politics—Palestinian, South African, Nicaraguan. The reality of Western imperialism or colonialism in these peoples' lives demolished the pristine sanitized version of the America I had grown up with in Indiana.

The history of Palestine captivated me for its simplicity—colonial settler ambition based on lies, deception and violence. No one seemed to notice the current American role in perpetuating the misery of the Palestinian people.

Soliman was central to that life and an affiliation to him made access to various political groups and other interesting people easier. There was never talk of love between us. To this day I don't recall him ever saying "I love you," except under duress many years later. We fell into sex by proximity of sleeping—functional and fast. He didn't like to kiss, so we never did. Soon it didn't matter to me. Petty bourgeois notions of romantic love were anathema to me—the budding human rights activist. Falling in love would happen later, and then because mutual respect and care would have deepened.

With blind ease, I gave myself fully to the task of pleasing Soliman, earning his respect since he was so special, so deserving, reënacting my script learned so well growing up in my family. My escape from Indiana would be realized with marriage to Soliman.

After going through a perfunctory ceremony at the local city hall, Soliman told me we had an appointment at Immigration and Naturalization the next week. The Black immigration officer kept asking if I was sure Soliman was in love with me. Yes, I insisted. She only shook her head and told me, "Child, you can never be sure." With all the papers signed, Soliman could get a green card. It never occurred to me this was the reason for our marriage.

A few months later, the first of what would be the "rules" of our marriage evolved. Soliman had a night class downtown. Usually he arrived home by 10:30 p.m., but now it was long past midnight. By 3:30 in the morning I was scared enough to phone his friend Abbas who lived near the community college where the class had been. Abbas had not seen him. While at work the next day, I decided to call the police if he was not there when I got home at 4:30 that afternoon.

Finally home after work, I found the door ajar, Soliman on the sofa, with a frown on his face. "Don't you ever call anyone to look after me," he roared, shaking his finger at me.

"When you didn't come home," I protested meekly.

"What I do is not your business. My life is my own. If I am dead, I am dead. Nothing will change that, so what difference if you know now or ten days from now?"

"What do you mean, What you do is not my business?" I demanded. "As the one who pays the rent, buys the groceries, I am entitled to know at least whether to wait up for you or not."

"Who do you think you are, you think you own me?" he raged.

"Of course not, but didn't you think I would worry about you when you didn't come home?"

"For your own good, you should not know everything. And you will not, I assure you. So get used to it." He stood up and turned toward the window giving me his back.

There was nowhere else to go with the conversation. He protected me by not having me informed or involved with all his political activities. If he was so important as to have covert activities or need freedom of movement, then I must support him and the cause by living with a measure of mystery and uncertainty. Thus, the terms of our marriage were set. Soliman's work or activities were to be none of my business. I vowed never to worry about where he was, but in time this promise would almost drive me mad. We moved to Chicago in July so he could pursue doctoral study in sociology. Another rule for our marriage emerged: We were not to say we were married, only living together. This rule, I decided, must have something to do with culture or politics—the twin pillars on which I faithfully built the extreme denial I needed to sustain the relationship. I dared not see Soliman as he was, but only as I wanted him to be, inseparable from a mesh of politics and culture that I did not believe I deserved on my own.

Hell broke loose when my parents finally found out about my elopement six months earlier. As expected, my father disapproved my actions, but still loved me. According to my mother, she no longer had a daughter.

Soliman maintained we were not married. Yet there was never a question of not going with him for the adventure the future would hold. Committed to the Palestinian cause because it appealed to my nurse's heart that wanted to relieve human suffering, this was about human rights violations and I personalized the struggle through Soliman. My life in Indiana had prepared me to live obedient to whatever miserable arrangement I found myself in because I had no experience at all as an advocate for myself.

I was struggling for human rights for others perhaps out of a longing to find human rights for myself. I had been trained carefully to sacrifice for the greater good of those more important than I. At this juncture everyone else seemed more important. The disconcerting start of our legal relationship notwithstanding, pride kept me from admitting defeat to my parents and those in Indiana. This clumsy arrangement would work if it killed me.

PART III − CHICAGO 1980-1982

Chapter 5

We moved to a red brick three-flat, indistinguishable from all the other small flats of Chicago's working class neighborhoods. Hauling our furniture and books out of the U-Haul, we together hoisted it all up the four flights of squeaky stairs. Exhausted at the end of the day, we ate some gyros at a Greek diner five blocks away and then walked back to collapse.

The sun spilled through the sunroom windows the next morning. The tops of the trees shimmered close enough to touch. While I scrubbed the place down, Soliman went exploring the university campus five blocks away. He had insisted he wanted to live near the campus since he might have evening classes and long hours in the computer lab.

The next Monday morning my job began at a medical center and that evening Soliman informed me his scholarship would not start until the following academic year. His tuition was mine to pay for the first year. He was my husband even if no one knew it and we had moved here for him. The next day, every overtime sign-up slot bore my name.

The commute by "el," the elevated train, was pleasant enough if a bit long in the summer months. Up at five in the morning and out the door in thirty minutes, I could just make the train at 5:45

hoofing the five blocks briskly. The back windows and back doors of the flats and businesses along the route streamed by and I began noting who was up and who was still asleep. After Belmont station but before Fullerton station, I began noticing one window with the light on where a woman in a housecoat with a Peter Pan collar always sat at a round kitchen table smoking a cigarette, mug of coffee in hand. I identified with her and decided, like me, she was going to work somewhere and needed to be awake at this ungodly early hour. Soon I began intentionally to sit on the left of the train to watch for her, knowing that after her window, only ten more minutes remained before I had to change trains at the Washington station downtown.

The novelty of the commute quickly wore off as the weather changed. The colder it got and stronger the winds, the slower and less on schedule the trains seemed to me. No colder, lonelier spot on the face of this earth exists than the wind penetrating, rain pelting, snow blowing, unprotected canopies of the elevated platforms of the Chicago el in fall and winter. Especially at 5:45 in the morning.

My biggest disappointment occurred at work. I had been reassigned to an orthopedic/neurology unit. With no interest in this specialty, I protested to the nursing director only to get a take-it-or-leave-it response. The looming pressure of Soliman's tuition bill plus the excellent overtime pay with this ill-fitting job made my decision for me.

Of course none of this drudgery interested Soliman. He had been very restless those few weeks before his semester began, leaving early in the morning to return late at the end of the day. One day he left in the morning and did not return. Until midnight I waited in the sunroom, dark except for the blurry light from the street lamp. The next evening wore on with a repeat of waiting alone in the sunroom, torn between Soliman's directive not to inquire after him and my own fear that something awful had happened. Soliman was special and of course his harsh childhood and the pathetic plight of his country made him more sensitive so he needed more under-standing and acceptance of his behavior. My ability to rationalize what I did not like reached new heights, thanks to all my practice while growing up.

His callousness hurt me, his indifference to my concern for him baffled me. Yet this life's adventure, its meaning and exotic ambi-ance required his presence to legitimize my being there, since I did not yet believe in my own authenticity as an activist or advocate for a cause. Such maturation would take years for me to arrive at. So there was no going back, however distraught, to Indiana to listen to my family's endless "I told you so." Trained to be patient and defer to others, I was wrenched for four nights before he returned late one afternoon. He walked into the sunroom and stood in the archway.

"How are you?" My voice held evenly.

"Fine."

"Do you mind my asking where you have been." Staring out at the tree tops helped contain my anger.

"Yes, I do mind. You have no right to question me."

"Couldn't you have at least called once to let me know you were okay? Would that be too much to expect?"

"If I called you, then my friends would know about you. I did not want them to know anything. That's all." He turned, "What is for dinner tonight?"

"There's some spaghetti sauce already made. We can have that."

"Fine, I am going to take a shower now, then we can eat." He turned and walked down the hall to the bathroom.

What has happened? He was nothing like this in Washington. Then it occurred to me that maybe he was a sort of person that does not move easily. He had spent ten years in Washington before mov-ing to Chicago. The change might have disoriented him and not wanting to reveal his own fears and misgivings to me, he shut down and ran. For the first time I considered he might have basic flaws and be scared of the new direction he had taken. Perhaps because of culture, I rationalized eagerly, he could not express or confide those fears to me.

After a wordless dinner, Soliman got his pillow and a blanket and made up the couch for sleep. He flicked on the TV, then settled back to relax under the covers. Exhausted from the peculiarity of the silence, I got up to go to bed thinking how quickly five comes each morning.

"Are you coming to bed?"

"No." He turned the floor lamp off but the TV stayed on.

"Are you coming later?"

"No. Just leave me alone," he said, then cursed.

Sick to my stomach, I crawled into bed and set the alarm. When I left for work the next morning Soliman was still asleep on the couch. The morning ride on the el seemed to slip by. During morning report, the charge nurse droned on about the patients assigned to me that day. As the staff left the room to start the daily routine, isolation slowly wrapped around me tighter than ever.

My husband was my boyfriend, to these people an unexplainable deception. When I described him as a Palestinian, I would hear things like, "Oh, you mean Pakistani?" No one at work seemed to know or care about things international. To my surprise, Chicago, while much larger in population than Washington, seemed much more provincial.

Soliman kept to the couch until the second week after his classes began. He didn't touch me but it didn't matter. Relieved to see a change, I was glad when in time this pernicious phase passed. And so the semester ended without incident. We lived quietly and peacefully together. He revealed little to me—or perhaps he revealed a lot. At that time I was not yet an analytic reader of men. Besides, my attraction to him was in his context—politics and culture—not the man himself. How else could I ignore the ache of dysfunction that churned in my gut. It was too soon to recognize denial as pain.

My own work life remained dismal but dutiful. I showed up

every shift to work and refrained from any social life—which relieved me from expending psychic energy I didn't have or spending money which was resolutely saved for next semester's tuition. When January came at last, I was glad to note the sun was again trekking its way back on its northern route, reaching a little higher in the sky and setting later in the evening. The sharp shadows from the yellow winter sun brightened the colorless lawns, trees and buildings. My commute on the el no longer passed in total darkness. The renewal of each year, a prelude to spring, brought renewed sustenance for my soul.

Soliman's classes began but he also went downtown on a fairly regular basis. He told me he met with other Palestinian students.

"Liza," he began, after pouring a cup of coffee.

"Yes."

"I am going downtown tonight to a lecture by a lawyer about a case. If you want to go, you are welcome."

"Well, that would be interesting, but you're the judge."

"Not sure if it will be in English much, but you can observe," he commented.

"No problem, maybe I will learn a word or two."

"Well, there is no need to learn Arabic really," he replied. "We should leave by 6:30."

"Okay."

That night the lights from Lake Shore Drive high-rises glittered with extra shine. We whisked downtown in no time, then turned west out the Eisenhower Expressway. Although the event was scheduled to begin at 7:30, only a few foreign students milled around the university student center. Soliman told me to sit at a table and wait for him. He and some students walked off toward the area behind the lectern. By eight perhaps 20 other students had arrived, some women but mostly men. Judging by their dark hair and pensive faces they must be Palestinian. Arabic words filled the air.

At 8:30 a man dressed in a tie and a houndstooth check sport coat strutted in with the self important bustling gait of someone late but for whom it didn't matter. He knew the listeners would wait for him. Soliman and a few others came out and greeted him with great ceremony and respect. Homage paid, he ambled toward the lectern.

Just as they turned on the microphone a noise from the doorway had everyone jumping up to rush to the door shouting in Arabic—falling over each other to get there first. Some pulled the door back to reveal a plump woman in a white head scarf, red faced and huffing words of command, as she balanced a pot and a wide aluminum baking sheet on her head. She was upset because her small son had let the door smack into her. Um Samir, the mother of one of the students, had prepared sweets to be served after the lecture. The students took the tray and pot off her head putting them on a long table. She sat down noisily and then two other women, one young and slim, one older and plump, arrived, also armed with trays of sweets along with paper napkins.

Keenly aware of being an outsider, I knew this scene belonged to them, their culture, their language. It also reinforced my dependence on Soliman who provided me with access. Palestinian culture and its secrets lured me, but the amount to learn overwhelmed me. Then the lecture began.

Soliman introduced the speaker whose Arabic delivery was dramatic and palpable but incomprehensible to me. The audience clapped with gusto and charged the lectern afterward to ask questions or be near him. Some people grabbed for the sweets—similar to baklava—and little meat pies. Finally Soliman came over and said simply, "Let's go."

"Did the man say anything useful?" Indirect or peripheral comments, I had discovered, seemed less fraught with power and were more likely to be rewarded with an answer.

"He talked about a guy being held in the federal prison," he said looking at me. "The Metropolitan Correctional Facility to be exact."

"Who is this guy?"

"Ziad Abu Eain. He is from El Bireh, a city near to Ramallah."

"Why is he in the federal prison? Who was the speaker?" I waited nervously for an answer, mistakenly asking two questions in a row. The reprimand for doing so was usually the thunderous retort of "Do not interrogate me!" This time, he relaxed the standard and overlooked the error.

"He is there because the Israelis want him for a bombing incident in Tiberias. The lawyer, Omar Khatib, gave us an update on the case."

"Sorry, why he is being held?" Questions tagged with an apology were usually safe too.

"That is the point. He has not been charged with any crime. He is being held by your government only because Israel wants him sent back because they suspect he was involved," he sneered.

"Well, my government probably has an extradition agreement with Israel so they had to arrest him."

"They do, but that is the point," he shouted, "The U.S. has an extradition agreement that exempts people accused of political acts as part of resistance to state oppression. That protects political expression and human rights, but they won't apply it to Ziad because he is Palestinian."

"But isn't everything with the Palestinians political?"

"Sure, but Israel claims they want him for an ordinary criminal act, saying he is a common criminal, so it is okay to extradite him." He turned on the radio to a rock music station and said nothing the rest of the drive home.

Thrilled that he had taken me to a Palestinian gathering and further confided a current and local political controversy to me, I relaxed for the short ride home. A few days later he brought home the first of many bulletins about Ziad Abu Eain, a few in English, mostly in Arabic. There wasn't much to read, but that summer everything changed.

The spring semester passed uneventfully and we seemed to settle into a calm routine. My own triumph was getting a new job teaching nursing. Best of all, my commute to work shortened by half.

The summer arrived in Chicago, hot and humid. Soliman took summer courses and stayed busy with his political meetings. We decided to go to Evanston to a sidewalk sale. "See that man there with the wavy white hair, look there, in the pants section?" Soliman pulled me close to him and spoke into my hair. "Do you see him?"

"Yes, who is he?" I whispered.

"Now just pretend we're looking at these shirts," he said, examining a gaudy Hawaiian print.

I hissed, "How long are we supposed to look at the shirts?"

"Wait, he is walking the other way, relax." The man walked up the block toward the university campus. "That was Professor Mohamed Abu Jawad. A big shot."

"What makes him such a big shot?"

"He is a political science professor and also Palestinian. I have an appointment with him next week." He resumed admiring the shirts.

"An appointment?" Careful, don't ask too much.

"Remember the Ziad Abu Eain case? Well, he is putting together a defense committee. If he agrees, maybe I will be the director." He smiled as he clicked shirts one after another down the rack.

"That's exciting and very serious. You would be good for such a job."

"Of course, it is only volunteer," he added.

"Of course. No matter, the work is important." Disappointed that there was no money in it, my salary would remain stretched to the limit since it was already spent on his tuition. We lived simply so as not to accumulate abhorrent debt. I projected one more year of full-time class before he would do his dissertation. Then the same doctoral education journey would start for me.

"I will be very busy if I take this job, but you can help me too."

"You need help? Say when and where." We walked a few more

blocks, then got ice cream cones before returning home.

"Yeah, I can come down at around four." My new office window in a high-rise a few blocks east of Water Tower Place fogged up but the rain had stopped. At least the jaunt to Soliman's office in the south Loop would be dry. The second week of June and I was three weeks into the new job as an instructor of nursing. Best of all, Soliman had work for me to do at his office, the Ziad Abu Eain Defense Committee.

An hour later I knocked on the old heavy oak door in an ancient office building. A young Palestinian student named Assad unlocked and opened the door cautiously. Soliman said something to him in Arabic which made him open the door with a smile. I had discovered that although many Palestinian students could read and write English well enough to pass exams and write papers for their classes, they were notoriously weak in spoken English and shied away from us "foreigners" that they did not know.

"Come on in. Over here are letters to type," said Soliman looking up from his desk.

"Okay," I said, tossing my briefcase on a chair. "The same letter to many people or different letters to various people?"

"Let's see, this is one letter to these three people and these are four letters to whom they're addressed," he answered, arranging them in neat stacks near an old black IBM Selectric humming on the table. "What about one of those word processors—do you know anything about them?" asked Soliman.

"Not much other than they are a typewriter with some memory. They are not computers, you know. That is something altogether different," I replied pulling out the finished letter.

"What is in your office?" he persisted.

"We have IBM Selectrics like this. Although there is talk about computers, we don't have a budget for them for a few years. They are very expensive." I started another letter.

"It takes so much time to type each letter over and over again. If we could save the letter and just change the addressee it would speed up the work. We could also update bulletins and newsletters too." Soliman paced the office.

"Are you going to get a secretary?"

"Not if we don't have to. If you can come here each day for two to three hours, then we will be fine." He smiled at me with that "I know you will not refuse" look of his. "We also have weekends."

"Ah, ha." Soliman probably told that important professor he had a volunteer for secretarial work but did not manage to identify me by name or that we were married. For a moment I felt trivialized by my insignificance and yet mortified by my desire for recognition. Why was I such an embarrassment to Soliman that my existence had to be kept secret? Given my well-honed Catholic reflex to "offer it up," I tried to trust that Soliman had a reason as deserving as the sacrifice he kept asking me to make.

"What does 'ah, ha' mean?" Soliman quickly noted dissent.

"Nothing, just remember, I do have a job so don't save everything for one time. I'll need advance notice on big projects."

"Sure, sure of course. Assad can be here as much as we need him." He put his hand on the young man's shoulder.

"You speak English, don't you?" I asked him looking up from the typewriter.

"Yes, a little," Assad spoke softly, holding his baby face with big brown eyes at a bashful angle.

Soliman launched into a flurry of Arabic with gestures and smiles and reassuring slaps on Assad's shoulder. Assad nodded dutifully, glancing at me, then back to Soliman.

"I just told him that he was to do whatever you wanted and that you both report to me. He understands you are a volunteer but also my girlfriend." Soliman walked to his desk and sat down. He picked up the phone book. "What I said will help. He didn't know you and why he should take direction from you." Then he dialed a number on the phone.

He just didn't get it. The tiny nick to my heart cut each time my relationship to him was denied. Forget about it or be consumed—I decided to forget it and tried valiantly to abide by that position for quite awhile.

Soliman hung up the phone. "That was Ziad. He is happy his New York lawyer will be coming next week."

"You can call him anytime?"

"No, only at a set time," he replied, "It is not just any lawyer coming. Next week Ramsey Clark, you know, the former attorney general, and Abdullah Jamal who works with him are coming to meet with Professor Abu Jawad and me to plan some strategies."

"Will they speak to any of the students or groups around here?"

"Perhaps they will give an interview, then we can put that in our newsletter."

"That would be great, but don't you think the story needs to get into the mainstream press? Who reads our newsletters but people like us? Perhaps you could call a press conference or issue a press release?"

"We can try, but usually no one shows up. People are scared to identify with Palestinians. For one person who writes a story sympathetic to us there are hundreds who rush to write back to defend the Israelis. They confuse or ignore the facts. It is as if truth doesn't matter, only not saying a bad word about the Jewish community and Israel." Soliman stared at the ceiling and sighed. "I can tell you from growing up around them, the Israelis are not so fragile that they would break with a few words of criticism."

"Well, maybe some good press will come from this case," I suggested with dim hope.

We worked until seven that night and talked about Ziad whose family came originally from Lydda, the same town as Fouzi. They had been forced out in 1948 by the same massacre, expelled in the same death march. His family resettled in El Bireh in the West

Bank, later occupied by the Israeli army in 1967, so he grew up under the apartheid of Israeli occupation. Like many teenagers of his community, he resisted the oppression by spray painting anti-occupation slogans on walls and when caught spent a few weeks in jail.

"You know, Allah was with Ziad." Soliman commented.

"What do you mean?" I was surprised, for Soliman was not a devout Moslem and didn't pray five times a day nor go to the mosque. He disliked overt religious expression, which he associated with ultra-conservatism. His vision for Palestine was secular, not religious.

"On the day the bomb went off in Tiberias, Ziad was home. There are 13 sworn affidavits stating he was home that day. Why were the people, his neighbors and friends so sure?" He huffed, "Because his sister-in-law had a baby that day. Everyone was celebrating and congratulating him and the other family members. So the baby was a sign Allah protected him, giving everyone a reason to remember the day and prove Ziad was home and not in Tiberias."

"Then why are those people's statements not enough to prove his alibi? Holding him based on a forced confession from a tortured prisoner written in a foreign language violated everything our justice system stands for. How can an American judge even consider this as fair?"

"There was interference from the State Department. Wait and see, the ultimate decision will be made by Secretary of State Haig, and he is no friend to us, just like Reagan," he said. "This will be a long struggle."

A long struggle on many fronts I thought to myself.

"Oh, by the way, there is a meeting next week with the lawyers and I want you to take minutes. It will be mostly in English because of the legal discussion," he added. "I'll let you know the time. It will probably be an afternoon. That won't conflict with your schedule, will it?"

"No, afternoons are better for me. Just let me know soon," I replied, elated to meet these big shots and actually have a role in the meeting. It also pleased me to hear Soliman acknowledge I had a work schedule—these crumbs could appease me for now.

Dreary faux wood furniture and beige vinyl sofas rested on cheap Oriental carpets in the Lake Shore motel—just a few blocks from Chicago's Magnificent Mile, the chic north Michigan Avenue. It was perfect for our needs. Professor Abu Jawad arrived wearing his dark blue/black beret reminiscent of the World War II French resistance, a year-round accouterment. His blue eyes and light complexion contradicted the stereotype that all Arabs were dark-eyed and swarthy, and his sensual voice was pleasant to listen to.

The three lawyers arrived together. Ramsey Clark couldn't make this meeting. Instead, another local Chicago lawyer, Jim Fitzpatrick, came. With his dark wavy hair, piercing eyes and brick chin he had Jimmy Cagney's tough-guy look. Omar Khatib wore another houndstooth's check sport coat of colors so loud they barked. He strutted in grandly and studied the table carefully before choosing a place to sit. With showy flourishes, it took at least five tries before he was satisfied that his chair was set correctly beneath him.

Abdullah Jamal, Ramsey Clark's cohort, arrived in a boring suit and dull tie with his brow permanently knit in a pout of intense focus and parsimony. He wasted no words or time with chit-chat, the type Soliman was so expert at. He merely nodded once to those in the room.

"Liza, will you please just list the facts as I have related them?" instructed the professor.

"Yes sir. One, Ziad Abu Eain, a resident of El Bireh in the West Bank, visited his sister in Chicago because she was ill. Two, he left the West Bank through all normal channels and security checks and there was no objection by the Israeli officials at that time. Three, while a legally admitted tourist in this country, he came to the attention of the FBI. Four, the first time the FBI came to his

Finding Palestine

sister's apartment, he lied about his identity because he was scared of them, for anyone growing up under the occupation was scared of police. Five, the second time the FBI showed up, he gave himself up and was taken to the federal prison in downtown Chicago. Six, he has committed no crime in the U.S. and is being held without charge or bail, a violation of civil rights, because Israel asked the State Department to send him back. Seven, Israel wants to arrest him for a bombing in a town by using as the only evidence a forced confession from another suspect, in a language he does not read, write or speak—a confession that has since been recanted twice. Eight, there are many sworn statements made by citizens of El Bireh that give Ziad an alibi because they all remember the day as the same day his sister-in-law gave birth to a son and he was there to celebrate. That is all I have written."

"Good. Now that will form the basis of press releases, and a printed copy should be available to reporters who ask for back ground to the story," he ordered. "Let us pinpoint the key legal aspects of this case. They must be absolutely understandable to the lay public—not only the courts—who if mobilized can bring pressure on politicians and other officials. Now what are the key legal points?"

"There are really two points as we see it," replied Abdullah Jamal flipping through his notes. "The first has to do with probable cause. In other words, is a forced third-party confession alone with no other evidence enough to charge Ziad in the first place?"

"In light of the Israeli practice of torture and forced confessions of Palestinian prisoners, documented by the former U.S. vice-consul in East Jerusalem, in addition to various human rights watch organizations, we argue that a third party confession is by definition worthless and phony," added Jim Fitzpatrick.

"Right. The second legal point of the case is whether the bombing itself, regardless of who did it, including Ziad, is defined as a criminal act or a political act. If it is political, then Ziad cannot be extradited," concluded Abdullah Jamal glancing around the room.

"We know there was unprecedented interference by the State Department at the beginning of this case," Professor Abu Jawad said slowly, nodding at me so I could take his words down exactly. "Although there is supposed to be separation between the judiciary and the executive branch, officials at the State Department, as the executive branch, deliberately interfered with the courts by informing them of their view before the trial even began. They believed the forced third party confession was acceptable and labeled the bombing a criminal act so Ziad could be extradited and sent back. In effect the State Department preëmpted any honest attempt at defending Ziad's rights. Do you have all that down?"

"Yes."

"Typically, the State Department does not give its advice or opinion until asked at the end of a trial," he continued. "So the fact they did so in the beginning is evidence of official political interference."

"I think it is important to add," interrupted Jim Fitzpatrick, "that the defense lawyers tried to address these issues with the judge in many sound legal ways but were consistently overruled. We were never allowed to make the case that Palestinian violent acts are part of legitimate resistance to state terrorism conducted by the Israeli government as part of an illegal occupation. To label the actions criminal was to de-legitimize the Palestinian resistance."

"The political control of the case was obvious before the proceedings started, from the four-page letter sent by the head of the department of extradition to the chief U.S. attorney on the case. Then of all things, the Israeli Consul General and his advisor, a law school lecturer, sat in the front row where he was sure to be noticed throughout the whole hearing," fumed Abdullah Jamal. "And do you know what really galls me?"

"No, what?" asked the professor.

"We had the first hearing and lost. Then we appealed in the Second Circuit Court of Appeals in Chicago. We lost that and one

"Free Ziad now. Free Ziad now." The first of many chants reverberated off the high-rise office buildings of Clark Street where supporters noisily raised a loud ruckus on a march toward the Metropolitan Correctional Facility. August 21, 1981 marked Ziad's second anniversary of imprisonment. His case had been singled out to reorient the U.S. policy on extradition of persons who exercise activities of political opposition. The secondary effect reinforced the U.S. government's total support of Israel even at the expense of human rights.

The crowds on the street watched the demonstrators orderly progress carrying colorful Palestine flags which fluttered and snapped in the brisk wind of the Windy City. Children dressed in national colors of red, black, white and green skipped in front of parents, aunts and uncles as the Palestinian community came out to participate in a political and also a cultural event. The march provided a wonderful opportunity for them to show pride in their culture and heritage and feel proud of Palestine. It reminded the world that they wanted what ordinary people wanted—jobs, homes and self-determination in their own country.

Soliman walked at the head of the march with a few other community leaders, coördinating the affair with the Chicago Police assigned to parade duty. He was in his element, charming the police officers, who relaxed and helped. Clever and witty, Soliman had an unflappable charm which he turned on and off like water. With an ability to remember trivial details, he managed to project a false level of intimacy or camaraderie that somehow helped him get people to do anything—including me.

The stone courtyard of the prison facility filled up as the marchers assembled at their destination. The scratchy loudspeakers blared out the voices of those calling for justice and freedom for Ziad. Chanted responses acclaimed the words and sent a tower of sound to Ziad's window slit many stories above, where he could hear but not see the gathering. After all the effort, only one local TV station carried the event on the news.

This anniversary evening program drew a moderate crowd. I couldn't wait to write Rita and Bo about seeing Professor Dennis Brutus, the famous South African poet, himself in political exile and threatened the U.S. with extradition back to apartheid South Africa. His poetry recitation poignantly captured the cruelty of political manipulations. His defense committee urged us all to write the Immigration and Naturalization Service to grant him permanent residency in the U.S.. If Professor Brutus was extradited he would sit in prison like Ziad, one a distinguished scholar and poet, the other a youth, alike only in their desire to live in freedom, alike in the denial of their human rights by racist governments.

Other speakers discussed Ziad's case in the larger context of the national struggle of Palestinian people. Musicians played between speeches to encourage audience participation. Young and old sang together familiar songs with the zest of proud nationalism. The Jesuit activist Dan Berrigan as keynote speaker gave a fiery speech lambasting the complacency of Americans and the role of the U.S. in escalating world-wide militarism. His remarks were not considered newsworthy in this hawkish Reagan era. Not a word was mentioned in any media.

A decision was made by December 12, 1981, Ziad's last day in the U.S., but this was not made public. That morning Soliman talked to Ziad at 11:30 for half an hour as they routinely did each Saturday. Soliman, lazy that day, lounged around doing nothing in particular, so four hours later he was still home to catch a phone call from Mim Khatab, a dedicated Palestinian woman who volunteered with the Defense Committee.

His face chalky pale, he grabbed a pen and wrote a few words. "You're telling me you called just a few minutes ago and the guard told you Ziad was gone, his cell empty," he repeated. "And the guard told you he was moved but could not say where?" He paused, then added, "Just wait at home. I'll call you when I know something more. Thanks for letting me know."

Without a word he dialed a new number. "Mister Ramsey Clark please," he asked in a steady voice. "Please ask him to call Soliman Munir please. He has the number. It is urgent."

He put down the phone and grimaced, "They did it."

"Who did what?"

"Mim just called Ziad to chat as she has been doing regularly. The guard told her he has been moved. The only reason he would be moved is if he was going to be taken out of the facility. Who knows where he is right now." Soliman paced around the room.

"Now what can you do?"

"I've called Ramsey Clark. There is nothing else to do now. The guard told Mim that Ziad wasn't allowed to call his attorneys to inform them what was happening." He swore in Arabic.

"Shouldn't you call Professor Abu Jawad and the other attorneys?"

"Yes, but I don't want to miss Clark's call." In minutes he called them all. Then the phone rang. "Yes, Mister Clark, that's what happened." He explained the day's events as we knew them. "Yes sir, thank you sir, I'll be in touch."

He sat back on the couch and stared into the room. Which was worse: the fact Ziad had been furtively swept out of his cell, new location unknown, on a Saturday afternoon when key people would be hard to locate or that suddenly Soliman would be without a focus? Never moving from the sofa, he caught the phone about two in the morning. "Okay. Bye."

"Who was that?"

"Not Mister Clark, someone else. At 6:30 yesterday evening they took Ziad to a waiting plane and flew him to New York. At midnight he boarded an El AL jet, sat in first class to arrive at Ben Gurion Airport this morning." Soliman leaned back on the couch. "Very slick."

"What do you mean?"

"He's gone, just gone. The Supreme Court will never have to give a decision. The government didn't want to wait so they just sent Ziad back. Just like that to please Israel. So what human rights? Arrogant hypocrites in Washington. What do we have to do?"

"About what?"

"What do Palestinians have to do to prove we are human? No wonder no Palestinian believes in American justice."

Soliman ranted and raved the entire next day. Every conversation soaked in rage. His heart and soul thrived on political work and Ziad's Defense Committee had been the ideal venue for him. My personal concern was on what would he do now.

After the dull gnaw of defeat from Ziad's case ebbed somewhat, Soliman began to spend lots of time with the director of the Chicago office of the League of Arab States. He didn't say what he was doing, but kept busy with the United Fund, a humanitarian organization which supported preschools, kindergartens, clinics and hospitals in the West Bank, Gaza and the Palestinian Galilee area of northern Israel. The UF had chapters in many U.S. cities but Chicago was the headquarters.

My contribution to the Palestinian struggle continued as an invisible subsidy, a private donor supporting Soliman's education and political work. The greater measure of commitment was in the doing, so my role as breadwinner made me feel progressive and proud. My life split into two compartments, one for general nonspecific use, the other secret, guarded, only rarely exposed to those uninitiated into the rights and rhythms of opposition Palestinian politics.

Chapter 6

Ziad's defense committee disbanded almost immediately. Soliman filled his time with other political activities, confident of my support—moral and financial. My walks to the el station, my clinical work on hospital wards, my committee meetings with other faculty filled my time, but not my life. The noble cause for which I had worked so hard notwithstanding, I had nary a friend.

Without warning, things changed when Sally suggested we get a snack after work in the Water Tower. We had endured an excruciating meeting of dull wisdom provided by a senior professor during which Sally had twisted a lock of her blonde curls the entire hour while taking no notes. Her face scrunched from time to time when she disagreed with the speaker. Since my own boredom was so deep, watching her antics made the meeting tolerable for me.

She had joined the faculty that fall quarter but we did not teach in the same clinical area. Her invitation slightly unnerved me because we didn't know each other. After fighting the wind off the lake on the way to a Mexican restaurant, she hopped onto a swivel bar stool, slurped a gulp of limeade and asked about my boyfriend. Despite my chip addiction, the tortilla chips and salsa on the bar in front of us suddenly lost their appeal. Nothing killed my appetite faster than trying to explain Soliman.

Sally crunched on a purple chip with a quizzical look, "You have one, don't you?"

"Yeah, he's a political activist," my throat scratched out the words.

"Oh, what kind of politics—city, state?" She sipped her drink. Her blue eyes showed just above the horizon of the glass. A sympathetic face and feathery curls of long blonde hair—who wouldn't talk to her?

"Uh, Middle-East politics, Palestinian politics." I was normally hamstrung by Soliman's admonishments to keep a low profile lest it upset his ability to operate freely, but keeping my knowledge of Palestine private estranged me from average Americans. Sally persisted with questions that I felt obliged to answer lest she think I had some shameful secret to hide. It also helped that she did not cringe at Soliman's name or my explanation of his personal history and the Palestinian—Israeli conflict.

"There is enough of everything on this planet to share and it seems to me that is the solution. No one should dominate the other. You don't have to like your neighbors but you still respect each other and live side by side," was Sally's commentary.

"You are right in principle, but how do you get the Israelis to end the occupation of West Bank and Gaza?" My blunt words bubbled out, but it was too late to recoup. "Look, as long as an American Jew from Chicago can go to Israel or the West Bank and, on the basis of being Jewish, take the homes and land from the local Palestinian residents and be rewarded with protection under the Israeli law, the fight will go on."

"And on the American taxpayer's dollars," added Sally. "My husband never agrees with me on this."

"What do you mean?"

"Well, he is Jewish and very Zionist. We don't always share the same views on this which he attributes to my being just a Jewish convert after marriage. To me, the Jewish people got what they were after, a home of their own. This is where we differ. They must share with the Palestinians, but he says no. It would end quickly if the U.S. government just quit paying all the military expenses and other subsidies to the Israeli economy. There are plenty of other uses those billions could be going to, right here on Chicago's south side, west side, any side." She paused to motion for two more drinks toward the waitress at a nearby table. "The President should make a day's worth of home visits with me and see what we should be doing right here with all that taxpayer money."

Horrified to discover Sally was Jewish, my need to avoid conflict and not offend anyone since, of course, everyone was more important, roared to my foremost thoughts. She dismissed my apology as unnecessary and admitted she was probably an exception. Although proud of being Jewish, she did not support Zionism.

Noting the time, she realized her daughter Rachel was waiting at school for her. We stood up and shook out any remaining crumbs of tortilla chips and at the corner said good-bye. A rush-hour herd crossed at the light, pushing me toward the nearby el station.

Although it wasn't yet obvious to me riding home that night, an enduring friendship began that day. Sally set me on a task of self-examination, challenging me not to limit my own understanding of the Palestine story to narrow stereotypes and sub-standard analysis. Until Sally, non-Zionist Jews were unknown to me. My South African friend Bo Rembutu recommended I read Rabbi Elmer Berger's, *Memoirs of a Non-Zionist Jew.* Bo wrote that Berger's peace orientation irritated the militant political agenda espoused by ambitious Zionists. "Would colonialism never end?" Bo had asked in his letter. Meeting Sally motivated me to find the book as soon as possible.

Her practical approach to the resolution of the Palestinian struggle was a shock. She felt the problem was perfectly solvable—identifying money as the key component. Remove the U.S. budget that supported Israeli's occupation of the West Bank and Gaza and the conflict would resolve quickly. Her most powerful suggestion, from a political point of view, was that the Israelis share the land in dispute with the Palestinians. She articulated what later became known in political parlance as the Two State Solution.

Truly sophisticated Palestinian leaders had no fantasies about eradicating the existing State of Israel. Despite the need for a unified anti-Zionist rhetoric, particularly to their suffering constituencies, their readiness to live next door to their enemy was real and possible. But it was premature to advocate this position publicly. The intensity and brutality of Israel's recent attacks in Lebanon, West Bank and Gaza were too fresh to be answered except with stinging rhetoric and futile but dramatic small-scale military actions.

Walking home from the el that first day, I had a lighter step. The overwhelmingly ethnic atmosphere of my life was briefly replaced with the fresh air of normalcy thanks to Sally and some Mexican snacks. My controversial views had not put her off and over time I was delighted that she became one of my most treasured friends.

The tedious routine of work and silent support of Soliman's activism stretched out prairie flat—dry and wind swept. Although there is plenty of room to run, you never get anywhere for the prairie never ends. My Chicago world began to stifle me, reminding me of Indiana. International work was happening far from here, but no avenue of access had opened up for me. Soliman had not delivered on this promise of adventure, totally unaware it figured into my calculus of our relationship.

The man who would deliver, who would trust me with an important assignment, propelling me forever into the field of international health, became a life-long mentor and friend. Soliman had claimed to many that he was my promoter and friend, but a man unwilling to be identified as husband was neither. So the day we met Professor Mohamed Abu Jawad in his office to talk about Palestinian health care was a liberation day for me.

His office walls were bare but for a solitary map of Palestine scotch-taped above his desk. The signature beret lay tossed on top of a file cabinet and the early afternoon sun spiked silver highlights in his mostly white hair. One enormous boon was that he recognized me as distinct and apart from Soliman—a professional in my own right, with beliefs of my own. My confinement was over, the prairie had an end.

Moving two chairs closer to his desk, Professor Abu Jawad sat us down and then said. "Liza, you teach in the nursing school, so you have time off in the summer from classes, right?" he challenged me with a slight smile on his chiseled face

"Yes."

"Good, that's number one. Number two, we are looking for someone to go to Beirut, to South Lebanon specifically, to evaluate the feasibility of establishing an American clinic in a refugee camp." He paused, puffing on his pipe, "You see, there is already a fine Swedish-run clinic but we want to set one up in another camp."

"How is the Swedish clinic staffed?"

"Volunteers. The supporting humanitarian agencies in Sweden finance and arrange for their volunteers. There will be administrative tasks here as well as the clinical work in the camp. There are also some local nurses and physicians in the camps who would be employed in the clinics."

"That makes sense. It would be important to engage as many local experts as possible if for no other reason than the language."

"Quite right. So you must assess whether it is practical or not to do this. Report to me what it would take to set up a clinic and run it," he continued.

"My earliest time off comes in June. How long do you estimate this study will take?"

"Two weeks. You can stay as long as you like, however, if you find you need more time." He added, "This request is on behalf of the Palestine Red Crescent Society. Are you familiar with it?"

Throughout this conversation Soliman sat staring out the window, bored since he was not the center of the conversation.

I answered, "Since the Red Crescent Societies are the equivalents of Red Cross Societies in Islamic countries, I suspect the Palestine Red Crescent Society functions the same way?"

"Soliman, don't you discuss these things with her? She is your girl friend," the professor chided the sullen Soliman. "And this is the health care part of the struggle after all. Didn't you ever think of how much she could contribute?"

"She knows what is needed and it didn't come up before now," Soliman meekly protested.

Professor Abu Jawad proceeded to lecture me about the PRCS, as he called it. Designated by the Palestine National Council to oversee health care for all Palestinians, the PRCS performs the functions and duties of a ministry of health for the Palestinian people. Thus its scope is larger than the primary disaster and relief response of counterpart Red Crescent and Red Cross agencies throughout the world—all members of the International Federation of Red Cross and Red Crescent Societies headquartered in Geneva, Switzerland.

"But as a designate of the PLO, how could it work in West Bank or Gaza?" Soliman looked away with irritation because my question made him look worse in front of the esteemed professor.

"It cannot, obviously, so they support proxy institutions given the present circumstance," he explained. "The emphasis of PRCS's work is directed toward refugee populations in Lebanon, Jordan, Syria, Iraq, Egypt, even Gabon." He dug his ebony pipe into the small leather pouch for another scoop of fragrant tobacco.

"How do we proceed then?" My agreement set the two men in motion. In rapid fire Arabic they arranged everything. Minutes later, Professor Abu Jawad shook my hand and said he would be in touch.

The sun warmed our faces as we stepped outside of the political science building. The slight residue of the last snowfall glittered as it mutated into the gray slushy puddles along the curbs, typical of mid-March 1982. My patience had paid off. Last summer we spent frantically with the Ziad Abu Eain Defense Committee. This summer Lebanon would become the focus and my first Arab country to visit. There had been no mention of Soliman going with me, at least not in English, but his adroitness to scheme a way to accompany me could not be discounted.

Sally walked into my office as usual on Monday morning bringing along Lina, another colleague who had the toughest reputation on the faculty. Being a smooth psych-specialist, she analyzed you whether you asked for it or not. The students feared her, as we all did in certain degrees. Her self-confidence intimidated me and it made me hesitant to tell them of my summer news.

After filling their mugs with coffee, I began my nervous briefing. They reacted with silence. "If you want to work with Palestinians, why don't you go to Palestine?" asked Lina. Sally explained to her that for the moment, there wasn't a Palestine to go to. Lina flicked her fingers through her pixie hair and then asked why the Lebanese simply didn't absorb the refugees into the general society.

Her typical question could easily be answered and my own confidence increased. Lebanon refused to legitimize Israel's expulsion of the Palestinians, whom they recognized as a distinct nationality from their own. Their goal, as is any host country's goal, was repatriation of the refugees to their original homes. Further, national institutions such as the Palestine Red Crescent Society emerged amidst the chaos and the poverty of refugee camps to provide care for their people. The goal of returning to Palestine stayed alive.

"All well and good, their goals, but do they have any money?" asked Sally.

"Very little, that is why the clinic must be based on rotating volunteers from the States."

"It won't be easy," warned Lina.

"That's for sure!"

We trudged off together to a meeting with our mugs of coffee. The tiny box of my existence had stretched to accommodate no-nonsense Lina along with Sally. The additional space let me breathe easier and created a reprieve from the tense, guarded atmosphere of Soliman's regime.

PART IV - BEIRUT 1982

Chapter 7

The KLM 747 pushed up and away from the runway. Beirut–
looming ahead only a few hours away now–might be a new home.
The idea had originally come up at the Beirut Restaurant, a Middle
East restaurant at the corner of Foster and Clark on Chicago's north
side, during the going-away party for Professor Abu Jawad.

Professor Abu Jawad's wife, Jeanette, a quintessential scholar,
hosted their friends at the gathering, most of whom were professors
at other area universities. She admitted trepidation about her husband's new undertaking as president of the planned Palestine Open
University. His formidable task of building the structure, faculty and
operations for a university whose essence and execution relied on
the still untested notion of "distance learning" tantalized me. This
project would benefit those Palestinian youth denied access to higher
education by the Israelis while advancing the theory and method of
this new field of education.

Both Jeanette and Abu Jawad would take a year-long sabbatical
from their positions at the university to launch the project. Assuming
the best possible scenario, the Open University would come into
existence and need faculty about the time Soliman finished his
course work. He could write his dissertation while working at the
Open University and I could start my Ph.D. study at the American

University of Beirut. So, if no unforeseen obstacle developed, Beirut was going to be in our future—and the four of us would ultimately be working together helping to build Palestine.

Now we were flying toward this dream. Soliman, eyes closed, sat next to me. He had an irritating habit of resting his eyes while staying fully awake to listen and pounce on anything that caught his attention. He had convinced Professor Abu Jawad I needed a translator for my assignment and he of course volunteered. Unfortunately my experience of his translations were that they were usually severe abbreviations with purposeful omissions, but I chose not to share my reservation with the professor who seemed to regard Soliman highly.

Despite various efforts to learn at least conversational Arabic, Soliman always managed to thwart my attempts, which left him in the powerful position of being the communication filter. This also kept me an outsider and hindered my comfort level when participating in the ethnic community in which we moved. Beirut would at least solve this quandary since I could absorb the language by virtue of living there.

The rustling of passengers in preparation for landing wakened me from my revery. The sun dazzled the Mediterranean Sea creating a liquid mosaic of floating mirror shards. Beirut appeared flared out with congestion along the corniche, traffic packing the seaside boulevard. Cedar-covered hills and sharp mountains watched over the city as our jet circled around a massive oval of poured cement—obviously a football stadium now empty of any activity—and lumbered down to land at the nearby airport.

We whisked through customs and passport control—everything prearranged by Soliman's many connections. A short walk led us into a waiting area where a fence of thick black iron bars restricted friends and family. "Dr. Soliman, *marhaba, ahlan wa sahlan,* hello, welcome," greeted a well-dressed woman with almond eyes, bright-red lips and cascading mahogany hair held in place with a tortoise-shell clip. "I knew it was you from Professor Abu Jawad's description," she added with a light trace of Arabic accent.

"Madam Hala, *marhaba*," he replied smiling. "The director of public relations sent to meet us? We are honored."

"Please, follow me to the car. We will take you to the Hotel Beau Rivage to check in first. Then Dr. Fathi will pass by to discuss your program, *Inshallah*," she directed with the confidence of someone who knew she was in charge.

A stocky mustached man standing behind her took our bags and carried them to a waiting decrepit gray Mercedes that had rolled off the assembly line at least a decade before. Deftly he arranged our bags and settled us into the car and then burst away toward the city center along the corniche I had seen from the sky. The view of the sea reminded me of Lake Michigan from Lake Shore Drive, gray and green swells checked by an endless horizon.

On the land-side of the road the hilly city was terraced by layers of brown, pollution-stained cement buildings, balcony-trimmed at each story. These buildings ran up to the infamous green line that divided the Christian-East and Moslem-West Beirut and still were pockmarked with signs of the fierce fighting that had gone on here. The more protected high-rises on the corniche, European-style, with their sea views, swank restaurants and fringed awning canopies shading outdoor cafes had escaped the trajectory of artillery for now.

The farther you were from the sea the more modest were the high-rises. Here the ground-level shops tended to be small markets and service providers. Instead of genteel decorations, the alleys were littered with knotted plastic shopping bags bulging with garbage—waiting hopelessly for the city trash services, which had been discontinued long ago. The air hung heavy with an acrid sweet smell—from discarded and rotting fruits and vegetables in those sacks. Empty bottles and wads of newspaper littered the street.

Apparently city-wide trash pickup was no longer an option in areas where warring sectors were controlled by local militia who placed strict limits on who could or could not enter. The precarious water supply and sewage system impacted everyone's life adversely as did the sporadic supply of electricity—which precluded any traffic lights working to facilitate a drive through the city. My nurse's instinct clicked on and I began to wonder about the prevalence of infectious diseases and what provisions or contingencies were in place to respond to epidemics or emergencies that such conditions would foster.

After passing the UNESCO building and Beirut University's campus, we drove around the barbed-wire protected periphery of the Palestinian refugee camps. It looked like a tired war zone—scattered chunks of cement rubble lay about with twisted, rusting rebar protruding from construction projects long abandoned. Some buildings stood next to gaping holes left from demolished neighboring buildings. Potholed streets tormented the driver and I wondered how it would be to work in such a scene of destruction. I had no idea that first day how much worse it would eventually get. No one did.

A portrait of a community in collapse, Beirut in 1982 was a city which had relinquished its predictable routine to the morass of social disintegration, and signs of physical collapse were everywhere. What about psychic dissolution? What were the people like and how did they cope, living like this? My initial naïve enthusiasm began to wane, replaced with a tempered realism about the enormous crisis permeating this society. What could I possibly tell those back home?

Few pedestrians ventured on the streets. Yes, it was late afternoon so most of the town was napping off its usual three o'clock lunch, but I still felt a growing sense of alarm. Finally I spied ahead the pink and blue neon sign across the top of a high-rise—Hotel Beau Rivage—at last.

The driver squealed up the curved steep driveway and let us out at the front door. Madam Hala led the way. The desk clerk greeted her warmly like an old and dear customer and she and Soliman checked us in. Finished, he turned to me and handed back my passport and a room key. For a split second I was confused. Of course we would not be sharing a room, since no one here knew we were married. How could I have forgotten?

Madam Hala instructed us to gather in the lobby for lunch to meet Dr. Fathi. Soliman and I went to our separate rooms to freshen up. Locking my door, I felt relieved to be alone, yet wondered what kind of madness made me buy into this charade of his? Pacing the room, I tried to make sense of it all. Finally I resolved to confront the issue with Soliman once we were back in Chicago.

Soliman aside, I had become convinced the Palestinian issue was important. Here were a people whose rights had been violated and who suffered from the stigmas of racism all the violence one society could impose on a weaker one. I was committed to the cause, and now that a role for me, however minor, had emerged—thanks to Professor Abu Jawad—I would not allow Soliman to diminish my participation in this struggle, regardless of his fragile individual egocentricity, so help me.

Our marriage had never been about personal relationships anyway. Politics and culture, those twin pillars, still exerted their power to keep me in check now that I stood in Beirut. They deflected my eyes from the dysfunction of the marriage to the glamour of working with the PRCS. Human rights activism practiced at the grassroots level, just like Rita and Bo, beckoned me.

The adventure was enticing. From the knoll on which the hotel sat I watched the sun lowering towards the horizon. The city lay around me and I watched a woman in a shabby high-rise across the street gather in her laundry where it had been drying on her balcony, just above the Syrian tanks parked in the sand lot next to the hotel. Later I discovered the tanks had arrived under an Arab League Mandate as "peace keepers" in the Lebanese civil war. Many Lebanese opposed their presence fearing a long-term strategy by Syria to reacquire Lebanon into its own historic borders as it had once been during the time of the Ottoman empire.

But history never goes back, only forward. Even the Palestinians knew that. If only they could participate as a full member of planning that future with the Americans, the Israelis, the Egyptians, whoever was involved, instead of being ostracized and discounted as society's throwaways. This wretched policy of exclusion contradicted everything known about conflict resolution: the need for inclusion of all parties.

My hour was up so I headed down slowly in an empty lift to the ground floor. Soliman had not responded to my knock on his door, but that did not surprise me. Why would he have waited for me when truly important people were at hand? The lift's tinny doors creaked open near the front desk and I could see Soliman near the door silhouetted against the tanks and artillery only yards away and clearly visible from the glass lobby of the hotel.

Movement at the door caught my attention. Dr. Fathi Arafat had arrived and he and Madam Hala greeted Soliman and other hotel guests. As usual, it felt better to join the group quietly, so with little fanfare I slid next to Soliman, who remained oblivious to me for minutes. Finally Madam Hala took my arm and pulled me toward Dr. Fathi. "May I introduce Dr. Liza."

"Ah, dear Dr. Liza," he intoned, "at last."

His warm manner and obvious comfort with foreigners suggested years of experience with them. He certainly had a family resemblance to his brother, Chairman Yassir Arafat, but Dr. Fathi was bald unlike his brother, who always wore a military cap or *kouffiyah*, the black and white checkered scarf. But perhaps that was to cover his own baldness. Time would tell. Years later Dr. Fathi, always clean shaven, complained to me that he thought his big brother should have shaved that ugly beard.

"It is an honor to meet you, Dr. Fathi," I said knowing the custom in the Arab world is to use first names with the professional title, not the last or family name. "But please, I am not yet a doctor, just Liza is enough."

"Well, Miss Liza, welcome to Beirut," he obliged with a smile.

Soliman enjoyed being addressed as doctor although he had yet to finish his degree. The inaccuracy never seemed to bother him which struck me as slightly dishonest. We sat together in the turquoise lobby for about 15 minutes making plans. Agreeing that we must pay a courtesy call that evening to Professor Abu Jawad's home, Dr. Fathi wasted no time laying out the next day's schedule. "Miss Liza will tour some of the camps and see the rehabilitation center. Madam Hala, arrange a car to pick them up at eight in the morning. Start at Bourj el Barajneh Camp so they can see Dr. Jane, then Akka Hospital, then Fakhani Camp. That should be a good start."

"Yes, of course, Dr. Fathi, that sounds fine." Madam Hala smiled at me and continued, "Tomorrow night we have asked some of the responsibles, you know, the department directors within PRCS to have supper with us so they can meet you and of course you will have questions for them."

"*Ahlan wa sahlan*, welcome," Dr. Fathi concluded with the customary phrase of welcome. "Now, I must return. Madam Hala are you ready?"

We all stood at the same time.

"Yes, of course," she answered. "Soliman, you can take a taxi to the professor's home or shall I leave you the driver?"

"A taxi is fine, please do not worry," he reassured her.

"All right then, until tomorrow, all the best," said Dr. Fathi. His driver pealed away stirring up a wall of dust.

The front desk clerk called for a taxi. Within minutes we were headed across town toward the Al Hamra district, the exclusive neighborhood on a slight peninsula that gave most homes a view of the sea. Nightclubs, haute couture boutiques, jewelry stores, cinemas abounded here in the playground of upper class Lebanese who lived at the fulcrum of a social teeter-totter—the East on one end, the West on the other. Much of the glitter was now faded because those who could flee the war, had; worse, those who stayed had cut back on expenses. Hoarding and fiscal restraint by the leisure class is a fatal symptom of social collapse.

The American University of Beirut, the elite haven for ex-pat academics who loved the Arab world and for Lebanese academics who loved the West, spread along choice coastal property adjacent to the Al Hamra commercial avenues. Five-star hotels with empty discotheques dotted the district. Journalists and politicians favored the Mayflower Hotel. Just east and a little north, as it rounded Al Hamra district, stood the American Embassy.

Professor Abu Jawad's apartment a few streets back from the shore had a panoramic view of the Mediterranean Sea. His building had typical flourishes, decorative doorways and windows but it was essentially a modern building. The wrought iron filigree balconies completely ringed each of the five stories like a wrist adorned with perfectly spaced bangle bracelets. We knocked on the door of his second story flat.

"*Marhaba, marhaba,* come in, come in," greeted a smiling Professor Abu Jawad. He hugged Soliman and kissed me twice on each cheek then ushered us toward the balcony through the salon, a semi-round room with an extended dark blue crushed velvet sofa perfectly fashioned to spoon along the curve of the wall. Two matched chandeliers of ornate tarnished brass and crystal prisms hung at either end of the room.

Three men were already seated on the pink tiled balcony and they expanded their circle so we could join them. Everyone seemed a bit uncomfortable. The warm air clung to me, heavy with damp briny sea smells, but the steady rhythm of the surf stroking the shore soothed my ears. The men turned out to be journalists—two lived in Beirut and one, an American, was visiting from Memphis: Rick Chase was there to write about the current civil war. His Memphis-born Lebanese friends had put him in touch with Nader, a journalist for a Middle East newspaper, who had brought him to interview the professor. The third, Fouad, wrote for an Egyptian newspaper.

A plump short woman dressed in a pink *jalabiya*—a long-sleeved straight dress—with hair under a tightly knotted bandanna brought fresh drinks of lemonade to us. Placing the heavy copper tray on a table next to the professor, she beamed and nodded when he said something to her in Arabic. Soon she returned with three bowls of pistachio nuts and a tray of cheeses and sliced tomatoes.

The professor stood to ask Soliman something. The other men nodded assent so Nader went with him toward the salon returning with a tray of glasses and a bottle of scotch. Perhaps these men were Christian. I knew Christian Arabs generally drank alcohol, sometimes as a public sign so as not to be mistaken for being Moslem. Most Moslems followed their faith and did not drink, yet those who believed in secular politics generally would drink alcohol, typically scotch. This group on the balcony consisted of Arabs who strongly supported secular democratic governments, so being Christian or Moslem was in fact irrelevant. Scotch would be drunk all around.

Put it here," instructed Professor Abu Jawad, sitting back with ease in his chair. "Liza, do you need ice?"

"No, straight please."

"Good." He poured everyone a glass and pushed the bowls of nuts and the tray of cheese toward us all. "Now, where were we?"

"You were explaining some history to Rick to clarify why Lebanon erupted like it did," reminded Nader who spoke fluent English with a British accent.

"Oh yes, the main points: During most of the 19th century Lebanon was a stage for Western missionary action. The Jesuits had been here since 1625 but they greatly increased their presence in 1831 because of competition from American Presbyterians. Remember, Rome-oriented Christians had lived here since the time of Christ, but no indigenous Protestant community existed in the region so the Presbyterian missionaries were not converting Moslems but the Catholic Christians the Jesuits had already claimed."

He stopped to shell a handful of pistachios and then continued,

"In time, three competing groups operated—the French, the Americans and the Russians with their Orthodox faith. The missions operated schools because through education they could best proselytize and build Christian communities. The Moslem community feared proselytization and sent their children to the less glamorous state-run schools. There the language of instruction was Arabic, and indigenous values and traditions were emphasized."

"So the mission schools did not teach in Arabic?" asked Rick.

"They did, but the students also mastered the language of the foreign institution that financed the school. Take the French schools for example. Although their obvious goal was to provide the rising generations an education, they also wanted to shape their students' minds, outlook and allegiance toward France. Russia had the same ulterior aims as France, but they were clearly not as successful. The American and British missionaries were notoriously apolitical."

Completely absorbed with this private lesson, Rick sat very straight, leaning in with his hands clasped on his knees, his drink untouched. He asked, "Did it work, the allegiance to France?"

"Ask Nader, he grew up here. You are more comfortable in a bistro in Montparnasse than at the football stadium here, yes or no?" Professor Abu Jawad dug out a pipe from his pocket.

"That's not fair, I am a loyal citizen," protested Nader, "but who wouldn't like a bistro in Paris, even you, Professor?"

"See? You protest too much. You couldn't tolerate the rowdy crowd at a Beirut football game for one period. This is an example of the class cleavages that emerged. People here generally do not share a united national identity. Until now, you'd rather be a French-speaking Christian Lebanese than a Lebanese Arab. You only now recognize your Arab heritage at the price of a war."

"So the Christian Lebanese never supported an Arab national identity or pan-Arabism?" asked Nader.

"No, no, of course not," huffed the professor. "Don't you know your own history? The early enlightened Christians formed secret

Arab national societies aimed at overthrowing the Ottoman Turks who ruled Lebanon then, but the tyrannical rule by the Turkish leaders managed to stamp them out. Later Moslems formed secret societies to free Lebanon and the Arab world from Turkish rule."

"So with just an uncanny twist of fate the Moslems became the heirs to the original Arab National Movement formed by the early Christian Arabs," commented Fouad who until now had acted bored.

"No, it was not simple fate, there were reasons. Reasons!" Professor Abu Jawad scolded. "The Lebanese Moslems' own education had matured to a competitive level with the foreign schools, that's number one. Two, their organic connections through culture and language to Arabs of the gulf region, to Egypt and the Arab world beyond served to strengthen and legitimize their emerging leadership roles. During World War I both the British and Turks believed Sharif Husain, the Moslem Arab leader, could deliver the Arab world."

He paused, taking another sip. "It is absolutely essential to understand the history of this region if you want to analyze the current conflict. There are enduring historic clashes between the interests of the West and East, from the betrayal of the MacMahon Correspondence, to the Sykes-Picot Agreement. This civil war in Lebanon is the current exacerbation of the same unresolved conflict–the goal of the West to dominate this region."

The muggy, motionless air of the balcony made me shiver, but the others seemed oblivious to the weather and continued, "Who represents the West in Lebanon's civil war? Isn't that by definition an internal conflict?" asked Fouad with a slightly defensive air.

"As an Egyptian, you know the answer. Because Rick here probably would not be able to guess, I will tell you." Professor Abu Jawad glanced at Rick. "The West's enduring role is now played by Israel with its behind-the-scene patron, the US, providing its political and financial backing. The sad irony is that the U.S. taxpayer doesn't even know they are paying billions of their tax dollars for another country to wage war on other countries and peoples."

"You are right. I wouldn't have guessed it. How is Israel connected to Lebanese politics?" asked Rick. "Aren't they just after the PLO which happens to be here?" He leaned back in his chair, as if to better absorb the answer.

"Let me see," Professor Abu Jawad hummed. "I should be recording this so the next time one of you cocky young journalists decides to take a short course on history while drinking my scotch and eating pistachios on my balcony, I can just hand you a tape and say listen, then come later and be prepared to discuss."

"With all due respect, please finish your explanation about Israel's connection to Lebanon," I piped up. "Don't end at the very point which confused me.

"Liza. For you only I'll continue, since I got you into this mess here after all."

Rick stared at me but said nothing. Fouad shifted in his chair.

"Let's see, ah. As early as 1932 a Jewish Agency emissary visited Beirut to form an alliance with the Christian Maronites, regarded by the Zionist Jews as a natural ally against Moslem Arab nationalists. That's number one. Number two, Zionist Jewish aims for control of Lebanese resources, specifically the water from the Litani River predates the existence of their own state. Number three, the Zionist Jews and the Lebanese Christian Maronites represented a tremendous potential partnership."

"And they formed an alliance?" I asked.

"No, not then. The Christian Maronites opted instead for an alternative of peace with the Moslems recognizing that civil war was the only other alternative. They put off the Zionists for the time being. The Christian/Moslem peace spelled out in the 1943 National Pact secured Christian predominance in the Lebanese government, assuring them prosperity over the Moslem Lebanese. This pact held until the 1970s," Professor Abu Jawad explained.

"What destabilized it?" asked Rick.

"The pact broke down because in time the Christians controlled the wealth and the Moslems lived in poverty." He paused to call the plump woman for a glass of water. "Civil war broke out, exacerbated by the presence of Palestinians. The synergistic alliance of poor, disenfranchised Moslem Lebanese and the Palestinian refugees, mostly Moslem, complicated the civil war against the Christian-backed government."

"Then the Christian Maronites turned to Israel as an ally. That's when I discovered my Arab heritage. How could they do it?" interrupted Nader.

"You are referring to Saad Haddad?" asked Professor Abu Jawad.

"That," spat Nader.

"Easy does it, we have a lady in our presence." consoled the professor. "It happens. Soldiers being bought off by enemies has happened throughout history."

"I don't understand," I spoke up. "Who is this guy?"

"It's quite simple. During the 50s the highest circles of the Israeli government planned to carve up Lebanon to create a Christian state in the north with Israel taking the Litani River and the territory south of it. To do this, Moshe Dayan suggested they bribe an officer, a major, in the Lebanese army, getting him to announce he would save the Christian Maronites by establishing their own country. Then Israel would sweep in and take over his self-declared territory," recounted Professor Abu Jawad.

"And that's what happened?"

"In essence. In 1978 Israel invaded southern Lebanon. Through bribes they hooked their man, Major Saad Haddad, who deserted the Lebanese army. Israel equipped him with guns, tanks, anything he needed for his independent army to defend his independent state in southern Lebanon. In 1979 he declared his so-called state which Israel promptly confiscated in defiance of the United Nations which called for its return to sovereign Lebanon. For all intents and purposes, the plan of the 50s happened only a bit off schedule in deference to France. For some years Israel and France cavorted as allies. France believed it protected Lebanon so Israel wouldn't be so impolite as to invade an ally's protectorate." Professor Abu Jawad looked at us as if to make sure we followed.

"So the PLO presence in Lebanon is not the primary reason Israel keeps attacking Lebanon?" I asked. Soliman had yet to flash me a shut-up look, which bothered me. His wrath would appear later, it always did.

"No and yes. Israel attacks the PLO wherever it is. Lebanon is the current headquarters for its leadership. Clearly one goal is the destruction of the leadership, physically and psychologically, thereby eradicating once and for all any organized resistance to their colonization of complete Palestine. But the goal, as I explained before, to secure the water of the Litani River and all territory of south Lebanon was set 30 years ago. We are witnessing the implementation of that old expansionist, colonial plan. The PLO leadership being in Lebanon is accidental but provides highly convenient excuses for attacking Lebanon in order to get the Litani River and Lebanese territory. The PLO is a tragic decoy, but a decoy nevertheless."

Professor Abu Jawad gazed out to the sea as if staring at an old memory. I wondered about his own personal experience since he was one of the original Palestinian fighters in 1948. Maybe some day we would hear his story.

"It is very tense now," remarked Nader. "The PLO has maintained the cease-fire since last summer despite provocation bombing runs by the Israelis all year."

Professor Abu Jawad paused and asked his devoted audience, "Would anyone like some tea or Turkish coffee? And you are right, the PLO can maintain the cease-fire indefinitely but the question is, will the Israelis? I doubt it."

"So you really have to watch out for the Christians here," Rick commented. "Is that correct to say?"

"No, that is wrong. I caution you about stereotyping all Christian Arabs as Western sympathizers. They have historical organic links to Jerusalem and the early Christian movement in Palestine that are as real and valid as any Moslems' are to Jerusalem. Many Christian Arabs are historically Eastern-oriented such as the Copts in Egypt who claim to be the closest direct link to Christ's followers. The Copts have been loyal supporters of the Palestinian people's struggle against Zionism since day one. Their Pope refused to visit Jerusalem, the Copts most revered site, as long as it remains under Israeli control.

"Further, many Lebanese Christians support Arab national unity. Lebanon has many factions and militias whose alliances are based on political coalitions not religious beliefs. Religion is a useful tool for analysis but cannot explain everything," stressed Professor Abu Jawad. "Remember, this is a war about resources, control of resources, that is to say, political power and domination and securing Israel as the Western presence in the region. It is not a religious war."

"What about Palestinian Christians?" asked Rick impulsively.

"What about them? They too are indigenous people of the Holy Land. But their direct link to Christ's life in Jerusalem and Palestine is no protection against the Jewish aim to control the land. If the Jews did not accept Christ's message when he lived, they surely don't intend to now. The modern Palestinian Christians have been kicked out of their homes like all the Palestinians. They suffer under the military occupation like the rest of us," replied the professor.

He paused and said, "Rick, you might have the energy for another lecture but I don't. Anyway, you need to read more on the history of the region if you expect to write about it. No more Palestinian history tonight. If you can just get this Lebanon part accurately written that will be enough for now." He half grinned at me and said, "I am sure Liza has heard enough and I would like to hear about her mission."

I started an answer, "Well, Dr. Fathi has us touring around here tomorrow with a reception in the evening."

"Good. It is wise to begin in the city. You should see what resources are here in Beirut to backstop your clinic in the south. Soliman, you are with her all day?" he asked.

"Yes."

"I will take you to the south, then, the next day. I have some appointments and can make some introductions," he said.

"What clinic are you running?" asked Rick, for the first time showing awareness that he wasn't the only person listening to Professor Abu Jawad.

"A proposed clinic." I replied politely not sure what to think about him.

"Whom are you working for?" he persisted.

"No one, I am a volunteer for the PRCS."

"Well, best wishes. Perhaps we can do a story on it later," he suggested in a patronizing tone.

"Liza, we should go, you are tired and Professor Abu Jawad has other things to do," said Soliman.

"I almost forgot." I dug into my bag and pulled out the small stack of letters sent from his wife. "Here."

"Thanks. I will send a few back with you if you don't mind?" he said walking us toward the door. "Anyway, have a nice day tomorrow. I will see you in the evening. Soliman, we will talk more then. Take care of her, now."

"Thank you, good night," Soliman replied with a nod.

The ride home seemed quick. The door to the hotel appeared out of nowhere. Exhausted but content, I knew that playing on the global stage was exactly what I wanted to be doing. For a moment after the elevator door closed behind us, a fleeting notion to kiss Soliman lit on my heart, but flew away quickly as the common sense of experience warned me off of any change of routine. "See ya." was enough, alone in Beirut.

Chapter 8

Soliman and I bounced on the seats of the decrepit Mercedes as the driver skirted potholes and swerved by heaps of rubble. Finally on a small back street we pulled up to Bourj el Barajneh, refugee camp, our first stop.

The driver spoke to the guard, Kalashnikov slung over his shoulder, while the voice of Fairuz, the beloved Lebanese singer, blasted from some window in front of us. Suddenly we were off again, lurching as the driver swerved around crater-sized potholes in the dirt road. Rocking from side to side, the car progressed up a steep slope. The camp buildings were little more than poured cement shaped into large squares—and many of these were connected or adjacent or on top of each other, seemingly at random as if a block cubist painting had come alive in three dimensions. Staggered block steps, cemented on the outsides—no railings—served as staircases to upper levels. Half-built walls, half-bombed walls exposed threads of menacing rusted rebar rods protruding like malignant thorns threatening tetanus after any unlucky scratch.

Through the houses' small windows I could see thick walls painted turquoise or white. Two shutters served as doors that could be hooked in the middle. Most shutter doors had been latched open, some exposing hallways, the urban trails to other square rooms, tucked away, remote, deep in the maze of camp architecture. The aroma of freshly baked bread wafted from a 30-year-old temporary outdoor brick oven, its sides blackened from the wood-stoked fire at its base. What did this tanned old woman tending the oven think of her "temporary time-out" from her home village, most probably in the Galilee, which she had left some three decades before, expelled from Palestine?

Children stopped their play in the small patios or hung out window sills to see our newsworthy car pass. People were everywhere: preschoolers and toddlers played around their mothers' feet as they hung wet laundry on lines between the squares. Just as in Christ's time there were women getting water at a communal pump, filling jugs of all shapes and forms. Tiny children capered about trying also to balance water containers on their heads to general amusement. How many round trips a day would these women make to carry the water she needed to the square block where she lived? The density of people dwelling in these temporary squares made even the thought of privacy a luxury.

A wet trench dug in the center of the dirt road we traveled on was the open sewer. It snaked along all the pathways through the randomly built structures, with shallow connecting troughs that led to an occasional outhouse. At the top of the steep grade we parked by a cement brick building, more formal in mien, sporting a grand red crescent on the pediment above the main doors. "Palestine Red Crescent Society" gleamed in Arabic and English letters painted on the doors. We walked up the stairs to the hospital door.

"*Marhaba,* welcome," greeted Madam Hala with a big smile. "I hope you are feeling rested?" She was smartly dressed and her long tresses floated on the breeze from the open door.

"*Marhaba,*" replied Soliman, "We are fine. And you?"

We followed Madam Hala and the click of her chic black pumps up a flight of stairs to a small office. Dr. Jane greeted us with a thick Aussie accent and announced she would tour us around the hospital and answer any questions. The white zinc oxide cream protecting her nose from the adverse rays of the sun made her look like a swimmer.

Madam Hala left us, promising to meet us again later in Dr. Fathi's office and Dr. Jane wasted no time with chit chat, but led us to a room full of children and young women wearing blue smocks. Soliman grimaced as he watched one of the young women spoon feed a drooling child in a specialized chair, designed to help kids with cerebral palsy sit up in spite of their spastic uncoöperative muscles. All the kids in the room were CP.

"Haifa Hospital, named for the city of Haifa—you know all PRCS hospitals and facilities are named after Palestinian cities or villages," Dr. Jane explained, "is a specialized hospital for children with disabilities. We have a particular focus on CP, which occurs in higher-than-expected frequency for the population due to the stress of refugee life and lack of prenatal care. This is our combined day room, exercise room. Mothers come here and learn how to care for their children, how to feed them, exercise them and so on."

"So you have training here too, not just care?"

"We have a training program for young men and women who care for disabled children. It is important education for the young people who otherwise have no post-secondary education available to them. Here they learn and provide a service to their community. Besides, who else will do it if they don't themselves. Development of any society means developing the human capital, the people, don't you agree?" she challenged.

We followed her to a classroom where she interrupted the basic muscle anatomy class in order to introduce us, in fluent Arabic. Inquisitive shy smiles flashed from the young men and women. Anatomical charts, graphs and pictures with Arabic written under all the English words covered the walls. They are the future, Dr. Jane pointed out, as we climbed a short staircase to another floor.

A dark hallway led to a large sunlit room so bright that tears flooded my eyes as they squeezed to adjust. Mobiles of birds, stars and crescent moons hung from the ceiling, spinning slowly in the light breeze from the screenless open windows. At a long laminate table two women and a man sat motionless. Their stares made it obvious they were not seeing the pictures on the walls or the colorful mobiles; rather they had traveled to other places, to other eras, to other lives. Occasionally they gripped the clay mounds in front of them. A chipper young woman wearing a stained white artist's smock over black jeans bounced toward us.

"*Marhaba* Dr. Jane, who are your guests?" asked Muna. "Welcome to Haifa Hospital."

"This is Dr. Soliman and Miss Liza from America. They are touring the PRCS hospitals in Beirut. Miss Liza may work in the south," answered Dr. Jane. "Would you like to tell them about your department?"

"Yes, please. Excuse my English. My father who once taught English at a school in Haifa taught me and of course the BBC. It is not perfect," she apologized. Her coal black hair curled in long cork screws complemented her charcoal-gray eyes. She waved us toward a kiln used for ceramics. "This room is a craft room or art room. Here we try to encourage people who are depressed. Everyone in Bourj el Barajneh camp has had a relative killed in the Israeli bombings or the civil war. Some people lose hope. So when bombs come they are afraid. You never know if it will hit you or not. You cannot hide. Sometimes you see very bad things, smashed people or people without hands or faces. After some time, people cannot take it."

"What do they do?" asked Soliman.

"They stop eating or sleeping. They just stop. Or sometimes they become violent for no reason and when this happens their families bring them here. We try to talk to them, give them hope. Along with counseling we give them some activity therapy. Some make beautiful artwork. We always say that someday it will stop, this camp, the bombs. Then we will all return to Palestine and live in our own homes. It is more difficult than any other disease. When your spirit is killed, everything dies around you."

Her simple eloquence in a foreign language impressed me. Here under awful conditions, she articulated concisely the refugee life of homelessness, statelessness, poverty with the constant threat of unpredictable bombardment. How do the Palestinians endure this with no end in sight, I wondered.

"Muna is one of our best therapists. She has a talent for drawing out even the most isolative persons," praised Dr. Jane. "And she is an artist herself. See all the pottery on the shelves?" She pointed to the opposite wall full of jars, plates, bowls—painted in bright colors, perfectly glazed, ready to use. "Once in a while I insist she sell them, not just to make a little money, but because we run out of shelf space!"

"Thank you, Dr. Jane," blushed Muna. "Not all are mine, many belong to our brothers and sisters who made them as part of their treatment."

"The real cure for all of this is prevention," commented Dr. Jane running her hand through her hair again. "The real cure is peace and the return to their homes in Palestine. But as long as Israel tries to kill the refugees with bombing raids there will be no relief for any of us." Dr. Jane then thanked Muna and ushered us back to the hallway.

We turned another corner and stopped to notice a day-care room for disabled children, either from congenital defects or from wounds of war. Again Soliman appeared agitated when he had to look at the room full of struggling kids. Some children toppled over stuffed animals they tried to hold, their legs not sturdy enough to keep them upright. Others blandly struck at pictures of flowers with aimless attacks. A little boy rocked back and forth, his head protected with a padded helmet.

On the way to the orthopedic unit, Dr. Jane lectured us about the lack of burn care in the hospital. "There is no real treatment for extensive third-degree burns from standard bombs or phosphorus bombs," she said. "Dr. Fathi is trying to arrange a donation of Hubbard tanks and lifts—the equipment used in burn care and rehabilitation—but it hasn't happened yet. It would also be difficult to put them underground to protect them from the bombing. And the water is such a problem. You need lots of water." She added, "Of course most severely burned patients die from infection anyway. Since we can't cope with their initial acute care needs, there is little chance for rehabilitation."

My question about spinal cord injuries sparked a fierce response from the doctor. When she explained wheel chairs were almost impossible to maneuver around the camp where nothing is paved, ramps are unheard of and stairs the main access to anywhere, she concluded the plight of quadriplegics is basically a death sentence. "Assuming you can breathe on your own, there is not enough 24-hour care available by trained people. Most die within weeks of infection from bedsores, pneumonia or bladder infections."

Innocently Soliman asked if there weren't young people here that could be trained similar to those trained for CP. "Dr. Soliman, I don't know what sort of doctor you are, but it is not medicine or health care. In Australia or the U.S. you can get all the sterile and clean equipment, tubes, bags, medicines needed to keep a person alive. Here we know how, but we have no reliable way to get supplies. Remember, we are in a bloody refugee camp at the mercy of strangers to take pity on us and donate money or goods. Do you know when was the last time I had a complete stock of urinary catheters?"

"No," he said limply.

"Do you know I resterilize the ones I have even though they are disposable? I treasure glass syringes and my needle sharpener. My two functioning suction units are held together with electrical tape. I have to fight with Dr. Fathi constantly for the few things we have."

"Why?" Soliman had stepped back from her barrage of declarations, so she stepped closer, in his face.

"He says we must spend all resources in primary health care and prevention. I understand, but that does not answer the needs of people unlucky enough to be hit by bullets, shrapnel, bombs and falling debris. They have a right to treatment and rehabilitation too." Dr. Jane took a breath. "Our limited resources means those with severe injuries simply die."

Soliman nodded his head, chastised by her passion, but to his credit, in the future he worked hard to acquire the items she needed. He was grateful just then to see jolly Dr. Hassan, director of orthopedics, at the bottom of a long staircase outside the open door of a large woodworking shop. Saws, routers, drills, hammers, nails and foot forms were arranged neatly on pegboards or shelves. Along a wall stacks of wood leaned against supports and across sawhorses. Other shelves held molds of hands, hooks, wires and pulleys.

"*Marhaba,* Dr. Jane, what brings you down here?" welcomed Dr. Hassan, a large man with a robust smile and a neatly trimmed mustache. He slapped the man next to him, "I was just showing Iyad how to sand this wood which will be his new forearm." Iyad raised a below-the-elbow stump to show us.

"You look like a carpenter," joked Soliman to Dr. Hassan.

"Blame that on my father, a carpenter from Akka. I played in his workshop next to our house until I was five. Then in 1948, of course, we were expelled and have been here in this camp since. He set up another workshop in the camp. I apprenticed with him until I got a scholarship to go to medical school in Iraq. Carpentry is my first love so I decided to study orthopedics and prosthetics."

"Where did you get your workers?" Soliman asked hesitantly.

"I trained my own staff. All the men and women who work here are amputees and wear a prosthesis that they helped to build themselves. It's the best therapy. Not a better way to get over the shock and denial of losing a limb than by building your own replacement.

You get a new attitude and learn a skill." He waved around toward the room. "From shoe making, to wiring pulleys, to carving the limb or making plastic covers, there is a lot of work."

Dr. Hassan wanted us to have a Turkish coffee with him but Dr. Jane declined after realizing she was late for a meeting. She hurriedly bid us farewell and directed us to the front door where our driver waited, cigarette in hand.

The car wobbled back through the crowded noisy street. The whoops and hollers of children chasing each other up and down the precarious stairways competed with the cassettes blaring various songs and the late morning call to prayer from the camp mosque. Women cooked over small squatty kerosene tanks, notorious for exploding—usually fatally burning the cook. Men queued at water pumps to fill containers. Old people sat on door steps calling warnings to barefoot children playing with sticks and rocks on the open-sewer-lined street.

Teenagers hung out in boys-only and girls-only groups, safely kept apart by culture. Their separate doorway haunts, across the street from each other, kept them within eyesight. They listened to the same songs of love or patriotism as they eyed each other—still young enough to hope through love. Their fathers and uncles sat and chain smoked, emasculated by the absence of jobs. The mothers and aunts beat laundry on washboards, sympathetic to their men but helpless. Everyone endured the bleak void of wasted time that shrouded the endless future, smothering the faintest initiative.

I strained to see what was not there, like an artist focusing on the negative space of a composition—those structural shapes unnoticed but present without which there is no picture. There were no cinemas—nor libraries—nor gardens—nor swing sets. Nothing indicated simple pleasure, fun or entertainment, something to do, somewhere to go. I knew refugees of the camps were restricted in movement, not readily allowed to leave the camp boundaries. What on earth did these teenagers do?

Little corner shops operated below street level, tucked into a small squares of buildings where men sold sodas, cookies—called biscuits—simple toiletries and occasionally cheap lipstick. Vegetables ripened in the open air on flat-bed carts, cooled by the shade from buildings or by jerryrigged canopies.

When we reached the exit, two pensive soldiers approached the car and spoke to the driver and Soliman. One took a long drag on his cigarette, then pointed one way, then another. The driver nodded and gave the soldier a new pack of Cleopatra cigarettes. After the other soldier slapped the car onward, we sped away. Soliman then explained they had advised us to go a different route because of skirmishes on the main road. How odd, I thought, that he bothered to translate.

Some 15 minutes later we turned in to the entrance of Akka Hospital. A bland building next door, once white but now gray from war's pollution, contained the inconspicuous headquarters of the PRCS. The driver, pointing to a door, said something and I understood the name of Dr. Fathi. We went to his office first to make the customary courtesy call on the director before any other business proceeds. A receptionist stood up, adjusting her tight skirt, repositioning the scarf draped elegantly across her shoulders, "*Marhaba. Dr. Soliman and Miss Liza, we are expecting you. Welcome. Please follow me. I will take you to Dr. Fathi and the others,*" she greeted in perfect English. When she motioned for us to proceed, Soliman deferred and bowed to let her go first whereupon she flashed him a coquettish smile.

"*Marhaba, ahlan wa sahlan,* welcome, *ahlan wa sahlan.*" Dr. Fathi, who was in conference with another gentleman, sprang up excitedly from behind his immense mahogany carved desk. On the wall behind him hung a large framed picture of Yassir Arafat. In front of him was a panoramic poster of Jerusalem.

Later, he told me that the desk had been made in the PRCS carpentry shop which made all types of wooden furniture for the hospitals, schools, day-cares and offices. The PRCS encompassed not just hospitals and clinics but the complete social welfare institution for Palestinian refugees, providing employment for those of all the trades, crafts and skills necessary for maintaining the physical infrastructure and services of the hospitals. With electricians, laundry workers, housekeepers, orderlies, carpenters, doctors and nurses, the PRCS approached self-sufficiency. However, the demand for jobs by the refugees far outweighed the availability and PRCS could not employ everyone despite its ambitious mission.

"So what did you think of Haifa Hospital?" began Dr. Fathi, leaning forward on the crocodile-trimmed blotter on his desk.

"Your staff seems to do the impossible with very few resources and yet maintains professionalism and hope," I replied.

"Yes, yes," agreed Dr. Fathi. "Now, you did not yet meet Dr. Marwan, the director of the hospital. He is that red-haired tyrant over there," said Dr. Fathi pointing to the man sitting on a couch with whom he had been talking

"Pleased to know you are impressed with our humble efforts in a most difficult situation." Dr. Marwan spoke with a British accent. "We are all waiting for you to succeed with a new clinic in the south using American ingenuity."

"So you don't believe all Americans are the enemy of the Palestinians?" I ventured.

"None of us believe the American people are against us, just the American government. My years in the UK taught me to appreciate the gap between the government and the people even in so-called democratic societies. We are not so simple as to confuse the two. Anyway, welcome to Beirut and to the PRCS."

"We are not so simple … ," struck me as a profound statement of character. It turned out to be a phrase I heard repeatedly in the following years made by various Palestinians in all sorts of contexts. They understood that many Americans, regarding Palestinians as primitive, unconsciously assumed the mindset of the discarded colonialists in order to rationalize modern discriminatory policies towards Palestine.

These officials of the PRCS, fluent in several languages, many holding advanced medical degrees from British, French or American universities, married with children, did not live simple lives. The sophistication necessary to navigate the choppy waters of refugee life and/or military occupation required a resilience far beyond what life in America demanded. I toured the hospital with newfound respect plus an added frustration to my question why the Palestinians were still denied their basic human rights.

In the midst of our tour of the hospital a dainty woman approached me with great deference. "I would like to invite you to visit the PRCS Women's Association building. We teach handicrafts and embroidery to young women there. Would you like to see it?"

"Why yes, that would be lovely." I turned to Dr. Fathi, "Is there time today?"

"You can do it between the hospital and Fakhani camp as the building is located on the edge of the camp," he answered. "My sister Madam Khadijah wastes no time. She is in charge of the Women's Council. But I think you will like to see the embroidery?"

"Your sister?"

Madam Khadijah smiled. "We will be waiting for you." She left quickly after a wink to her brother.

As we resumed the tour of the main hospital with Dr. Imad, the medical director, escorting us, Soliman whispered to me that many of the people working here could be relatives of each other and to be careful about what was said to whom. A cute but rather plump nurse with a youthful face that did not fit her matronly figure had joined us. She was panting heavily by the time we climbed two sets of stairs to the inpatient ward which was lit solely by light from the outside streaming in through open, screenless windows—which kept nary any flies, mosquitoes or animals out, but did allow in the cooling sea breeze heavy with moisture which felt like thick ointment.

"This ward is a men's ward. There are 15 patients here," explained Miss Elham, the nursing director. "You can see the beds, made here in the workshop of iron piping, spray painted white. Once in a while we get bed donations from Europe."

There were no sinks in the room and the closest running water was in the small lavatory at the end of the hall. Simple pipes bolted together, attached to a tripod on wheels functioned as IV poles. Oxygen canisters without humidifiers leaned against the wall. One unused suction machine stood next to a chest tube using the old three-bottle system, but only one bottle rested on the triangular base.

The patients sagging against the pillows appeared listless and weak. On seeing us some pulled the rough gray wool blankets up around their chins despite the heat. Others sweated through their *jalabiya* pajamas, their covers lying shoved to the end of their beds. A few had visitors sitting idly nearby, all curiously watching us confer in English. According to Miss Elham, the women's ward had fewer patients but all beds were occupied. Having a relative stay with a patient in the hospital to help with the caregiving was a custom. If the beds were needed for a patient, the relatives slept in chairs or on the floor.

Dr. Imad defended the condition of the hospital. "As you can see, we are in a difficult situation. We know how you function, but we simply lack the facilities to do it here. My dream hospital is simple—just having central oxygen and central suction waiting in the wall behind the bed would be a wonderful luxury."

"There are many luxuries, Dr. Imad," countered Miss Elham. "My luxuries would be running water and toilets in all the wards, a few private rooms and clean and dirty utility rooms."

The building, donated to the PRCS, was never designed or intended for hospital use. The cost to retrofit it properly was prohibitive. Dependent on the intermittent and uncertain largesse of international aid agencies, this was the best they could do. Of course money was better spent on primary health care and prevention.

Finding Palestine

"Time is moving, we should go to the operating room," advised Dr. Imad. He and Soliman walked together in conversation along the way, no doubt discussing what he needed most in terms of equipment. Soliman was expert at procuring supplies and he could get people to donate. He charmed his way into their wallets or factories and was always ready to facilitate the delivery or customs involved. He knew all the tricks and became the great arranger.

Although we had climbed two flights of stairs up, we trudged down five into the underground. "All the operating rooms, emergency departments and ICUs are built underground to avoid repeated destruction by Israeli bombing," Dr. Imad explained at the door to the restricted area.

"Excuse me, Dr. Imad, perhaps this is naïve, but you built these departments underground for protection. Isn't bombing civilian areas, hospitals and schools forbidden under international law, the Geneva Conventions? Why are the Israelis bombing the camps and near hospitals?"

"Miss Liza, this question has many answers." Dr. Imad wrenched his face and took a deep breath. "The Israelis claim they are not bound by Geneva Conventions because we are not officially at war. They claim the PLO and the Palestinians are terrorists, criminals, so none of the protections apply to us. They can bomb freely, wherever they want. To them every Palestinian is a terrorist, my grandmother, my son, my sister, my wife, me, a doctor. No one in the international community recognizes our struggle as resistance to an occupation of our country based on broken promises to us. That, of course, gives the Israelis a green light to do what they want. Nobody dares stop them, nobody dares oppose them. Why?" He answered his own question, "The U.S. agrees with this line and the international community is weak. So we must build our operating rooms and emergency departments underground."

The impact of politics on Palestinian health care made me realize a bit more the challenge exacted by working with the PRCS. My clinic project grew in complexity as my understanding of the context in which it was to function matured. We found the underground OR had three connected rooms. Two men in green scrub clothes waved through the glass window as they wrapped surgical trays for various procedures to be autoclaved in an antique machine which we could see filled up the corner of one of the three rooms. I spied an anesthesia machine from the 50s next to a portable suction machine, some portable oxygen canisters, IV poles and Mayo stands. Everything looked kempt and sterile—but very basic and outmoded.

Soliman, who had never seen an American OR, was impressed by the bare-bones set up. Commendable under the circumstances, I agreed, but still this was 30-plus-year-old anesthetic and surgical equipment. There was no recovery room, Miss Elham explained, because there was neither space nor nurses for such. A set of double doors did keep dirt out and infection down. The hall opened onto a larger room with five cots divided by curtains between them. Sparsely supplied with IV solution, suture trays, one laryngoscope kit and one sink, this was the main trauma room.

There we found two men cutting sheets of gauze cloth while a woman rolled and packaged them to be sterilized in the autoclave. No nurse of my generation ever had to cut and roll gauze bandages. We were raised to believe gauze came in prepackaged sterile packs. Miss Elham then opened a door on a prehistoric X-ray machine caged in a small room which surely leaked radiation at a level prohibited back home. Still, no use pointing out the obvious. An X-ray machine was expensive. I made a note to urge Soliman, the great arranger, to locate a new one on his return to the US.

We climbed the ramp outside where hospital security guards were checking cars as they pulled into the driveway. Other men milled around, watching, talking, waiting. We continued on to a side building marked with a red sign in English and Arabic—"Lab." A chilly, squeaky clean white room hummed with spinning centrifuges and machines that slowly rocked tubes of blood back and forth. Two microscopes plus specimen containers with varying shades of yellow urine lined a corner counter. A refrigerator, the vintage of my mother's 1954-GE fridge that I vividly remember being commanded to defrost each week, stood in a far corner with an electrical cord connected to an enormous 220-to-110 converter.

"Ah, Dr. Refat. Come meet our guests," called Dr. Imad.

"*Marhaba, ahlan wa sahlan.* Well, this is the lab. Nice huh?" He stood up from behind a rack of test tubes."We like to put on a big show, you know, show how much we do with so little. But so what? Is anyone watching?" Dr. Refat shrugged. "I mean, is the queen watching, a president, a premier, any head of state? Or are we just the token poor people for this phase."

"Come now Refat, cheer up," cautioned Dr. Imad.

"Let's be realistic, we are nothing more than an irritant in the United Nations, a nasty cut in the fabric of nations that just won't heal. If we don't shut up they may amputate us all together," he groused in his crisp British accent.

"That guy is pretty full of himself," commented Soliman to me on the way back.

"Oh, he is just honest about the situation and probably tired of it. He is probably a tremendous asset precisely because he doesn't kowtow to everything." His blue eyes, dark wavy hair and rosy little boy cheeks were cute, but this observation I kept to myself.

We reached Dr. Fathi's office ten past the hour. "Welcome, welcome, how was your tour?" He tucked his faded blue short sleeve shirt into his baggy trousers. With his shirt unbuttoned at the collar, he could have been any worker at the PRCS.

"Dr. Fathi, I have a question." We sat down and soon someone brought sodas and placed them in opened bottles on the table in front of us.

"Please," he smiled. The ink of his fountain pen had leaked into the pocket of his shirt. He dabbed at the spot with a tissue.

"How does the PRCS work with UNRWA, the United Nations

Relief Works Agency, so there is no duplication of services?"

"Ah, this is an excellent question, Miss Liza." Satisfied that the shirt pocket was beyond rescue, Dr. Fathi gave up and leaned forward in his chair. "Well, as you know, UNRWA was set up by the United Nations to deal with the refugees coming to Lebanon and other Arab countries. People were suffering with no housing, no food, no facilities, so the UNRWA arrived with tents and shipments of flour and rice—the typical humanitarian relief supplies. But it was to be a temporary aid only a few months in duration because everyone thought the situation with the Israelis was temporary and the Palestinian refugees would return back to their villages. But of course, this has not yet happened."

"You see, Miss Liza," interrupted Madam Hala who had joined us, "This department of the U.N. operates until repatriation of the refugees. But it has limitations."

"Such as?"

"First, their great work—the schools, the small hospitals or clinics—are available only to those refugees of the original 1948 expulsion. The second wave of refugees coming in 1967 was not covered, so the PRCS, developed after 1967, meets the needs of the later refugees in addition to anyone from 1948. PRCS serves all Palestinians everywhere."

"We coördinate our services with the UNRWA services," added Dr. Fathi, "but you ask the people which they prefer? They will tell you PRCS, not because we are better, but because we are Palestinian. UNRWA is foreign-run, controlled by the United Nations which gave the green light for the Zionist Jewish state in the first place. The people prefer to go to their own national institutions."

"We, of course, welcome the UNRWA and are still waiting for it to assist us in returning to our homes," added Dr. Imad. "It showed that the international community knew exactly what it was doing in 1948 allowing the Zionists to expel us from Palestine. Later they were shocked at the magnitude of our misery, but not enough to stop the Zionists, of course. So we feel UNRWA, a whole powerless U.N. department devoted to Palestinian refugees, is nothing but guilt money."

"You're right. No one is fooled by the U.N.'s false charity," added Madam Hala.

"Well, enough politics. Is there anything else? If not, you and Dr. Soliman should leave for the next part. My sister, Madam Khadijah is already at her headquarters waiting for you. Dr. Soliman, the driver will park anywhere you want in the camp so you can take a walk, talk to some of the people. I am afraid I must keep Dr. Imad here for some work." directed Dr. Fathi.

"See you tonight at eight for our little reception," said Madam Hala. "Perhaps you should take some rest before. The jet lag must be catching up to you by now."

The edge of Fakhani Camp was visible from Akka Hospital but the route to the only entrance and exit was circuitous. Some ten minutes later we stopped in front of the Women's Association office where we were greeted enthusiastically by Madam Khadijah and three other women, who fussed over us as if we were high-ranking diplomats.

Their craft shop overflowed with embroidered pillows, eyeglass cases, purses and elegant black shawls with long black fringes embroidered with red gold, green and blue accents. They were beautiful and I wanted one. Soliman agreed and along with the shawl I bought some embroidered throw pillows. The refugee women's embroidery work was a source of income, a gender-specific way to support their families that did not compete with jobs the men otherwise might take.

Soliman was in his element here. He charmed the ladies, joked with them, flashed warm smiles and carried on in a rather flirtatious manner—never stopping to translate what he and these women who could not speak English were saying. To my surprise, one woman could speak French and started to communicate with me, but Soliman soon overrode the conversation in Arabic. Here he could be the wheeling, dealing arranger he loved to be and was discussing the possibility of importing their products to Chicago to find a better market for them. But even though I could have contributed to such arrangements, Soliman never included me in any of these projects.

After yet another cup of Turkish coffee and animated commentary, we said warm good-byes to the women and Madam Khadijah. I slipped my new shawl, carefully rolled in tissue paper, into my backpack with the similarly wrapped pillows and slung it over my shoulder. Soliman waved to the driver as we stepped out into the bright hot sun indicating we would walk for a bit. Five or six eight- or nine-year-olds surrounded us with curious grins showing their tetracycline-stained teeth. Their round tanned faces, girls with braids, boys with short tight curls, conveyed innocence and openness—no sign of the jaded skepticism and distrust of foreigners I'd seen on the older set. These probably still maintained a little naïve hope that their lives would actually improve. We smiled back and Soliman teased them with jokes.

On our stroll we passed a pretty woman knitting a blanket in the shade of a window shutter propped open. She proudly raised her knitting needles to display her work. I waved to her. She threw me a kiss from a smile so wide it would have been brilliant if only half of her teeth weren't gone. Nearby an old man sat hunched on a three-legged stool, both hands locked over the head of his carved cane. His eyes, opaque with cataracts, searched for recognition from Soliman who stopped and talked to the old man. I cringed inwardly knowing this man's eyesight was but a few thousand dollars away. Cataract surgery in the States had become almost like a drive-in laundry, in by ten almost blind, out by two with two good eyes. We'd recruit an ophthalmologist for the clinic to perform simple corrective surgeries.

The open sewer along the road stunk of ammonia and putrefying sludge, a rancid aroma steamed by the hot sun. Open doorways connected consecutive square blocks of all purpose rooms. Sleeping mats were piled against walls and the same room where a child napped, the mother cooked and the family prayed—some five times a day. Outhouses blended in with the scene. How could anyone do anything private where few discrete interior rooms existed? Where or when did couples find time for intimacy?

Soliman appeared at ease, confidently interacting with people. With his own people he was fine. Perhaps his inability to feel at ease outside a group of his own people might mean a move to Beirut would ease our problems. This became my new hope.

Fakhani camp had sustained severe damage from the Israelis' bombing raids the past July. I remembered reading about the casualties during our feverish work on the ill-fated Ziad Abu Eain case. The collapsed buildings and craters still were untouched. Energetic, apolitical weeds wove a green garnish over and between stones, rubble and exposed rebar rods. The camp once had boasted a six-story residential walk-up building which had relieved the congested population by expanding up, the only direction possible. Reduced by half during last summer's bombing raids, the standing half survived, sheared open to the wind which eerily tossed the shreds of curtains in ghostly billows and waves. The pink and green walls of the homes exposed looked eerily like the open side of a child's doll house. Pictures still stubbornly clung to the walls like social fossils documenting the fact that life had once been present.

BOOM. Jets streaked overhead, far past the point of their sound. Breaking the sound barrier reminded me of the pilots training from Grissom Air Force Base not too far from my home in Indiana. This was not Indiana. Suddenly our driver appeared screaming and waving his arms wildly, "Dr. Soliman, Miss Liza." He ran toward us screaming and pointing to the car. He talked hysterically in Arabic to Soliman, who stood motionless staring at the sky.

As usual, I understood nothing and waited until some other

visual cue offered itself up to provide meaning or direction. Finally I yelled at Soliman over the screams of people running after children and pulling them off the street, "What is it?" The cataract-ridden old man felt his way to the doorway of his square home. The blanket knitting, abandoned to the ground, spilled out of the yarn basket. The sun's scorching rays persisted.

I stumbled, although I hadn't taken a step. The earth beneath me resisted the walloping blow, shaking unnaturally, in a concentric wave wrung from ground zero. The earth did not split open under me, but it failed about 30 yards away. Splayed open as if gouged by a jagged router bit, the torn earth gulped the square houses of the refugees, as they caved into its violently exposed cavities.

Absolutely naïve, despite the crash of explosions, the fires, the burns, the screams and wails, the chaotic rush of people around me, all the objective evidence falling down around me, I stood with moronic calm to ask, Are these bombs? Are those American F-15s flown by Israelis bombing Fakhani Camp?

The bombs' tails of chalky white ribbons connected the jets to their targets of people and houses in the camp. Didn't the pilots know that I could see which jet dropped which bomb? Don't they feel shame at the unfairness of the fight? Jet dropped bombs on refugee camps? On children? On families? On civilians? Surely they were not absolved of their direct responsibility just because they could speed away from the destruction they rained so fast they could avoid watching and smelling the bloody hell wrought on the old man with cataracts, the knitting woman, or the kids with tetracycline-stained teeth?

"Miss Liza," implored the driver, who now pulled me along. "Dr. Soliman!"

Soliman began to run toward the car. Shells exploded all around us. Smoke, shrapnel and building debris clouded the air, blocking out the sun, substituting its heat with a suffocating film of hot sulfur and alkaline concrete dust. The overwhelming crescendo bit our ears and stubbornly lingered around us, amplified by the next explosion.

The building next to the car collapsed—a direct hit. The whoosh of implosion echoed surreally. The vacuum bomb pleated the building like a musician closing an accordion, all layers flattened and air tight, suffocating all life bigger than a microbe—luckless people smashed to death.

Soliman slammed my door and got in front with the driver. He shouted warnings to help the driver navigate out of the bombing target. Although only minutes had passed, the camp paths were empty. Most refugees hid in the protection of any underground structure, whether a garage or vegetable storage cellar. Reaching the main road outside the camp, the driver sped toward the protection of the sea.

The driver found the corniche and flew toward the Hotel Beau Rivage. We jumped out of the car at the front door. All hotel staff and guests filled the lobby standing in the center away from the plate glass walls surrounding them. Where else could they go?

More booms, more bombs landed. I thought of everyone I just met. Only hours ago we agreed to extract just a little more hope from the future with the clinic. The plate glass shuddered as the sound waves traversed through the city vibrating everything in its path. The Syrian regulars outside the hotel returned inadequate fire. Their artillery could not match the speed-of-sound getaways of the American F-15 and F-16 jets. Computer-generated, pinpoint bombing was the pride of American weaponry. For me, all the excuses for the civilian casualties vanished. If you can pinpoint bomb and civilians are killed, then you intended to bomb civilians.

Boom. Boom. The glass walls bowed but did not shatter. The bombs landed closer to the Hotel Beau Rivage than before. Soliman followed me outside to the patio. Neither of us wanted to die like a donkey with his head against the lobby wall.

The sun shone on the Mediterranean Sea but the sky was busy with traffic. The formation of American F-15s arched over and over again, playing with the Palestinians like a cat toys with a mouse, little slaps and nudges before the kill. When was the kill, later today, next week? When would Israel initiate its final solution?

The white threads of dispatched bombs told which jet had activated. They flew closer to us, swooping low, buzzing the high-rises of the Al Hamra district beyond. Turning around over the sea, two jets flew in fast and low, dropping several bombs at once at an area less than a mile away. The jolt from the impact knocked us to the ground. The sound crushed us. Dollops of oily black clouds billowed upward from the scarlet flames of the destroyed target.

Boom. More white threads trailed the jets and dissipated into the atmosphere, dispersed by the wind that transmits the screams of the dying and the grief of the living. These alarms of Palestinian human rights denied failed to impact the power elites, whose goal of world domination transcended the universal human rights of refugees or any people judged expendable. Freedom and the full restoration of Palestinian rights would not come in time for today's victims. Unfortunately they have yet to come at all.

Soliman stood apart from me, sadness contagious on his face, but there was no approaching him here in such a public place. How many people were killed in the last 45 five minutes? The putrid air stunk, soaked in a diffuse film of oily char, heavy with fear. What now?

The F-15s made a "so long for now" swoop, low across the rooftops of the high-rises on the hill of Al Hamra and aimed south to their bases where within the hour the pilots would probably meet at a local bar, drink and swap war stories, counting theirs hits, their kills, their goals, their scores, the ultimate "post-game wrap-up."

A messenger arrived from Dr. Fathi's office to verify our safety. He told us in addition to Fakhani Camp, Bourj el Barajneh Camp had damage, but Dr. Jane, her staff and patients hid in the basement and were safe. The casualties included ten dead and about 30 wounded. The big hit with the black clouds was the stadium. The

Israelis had reduced the sports stadium to rubble because they thought it held weapons.

Soliman swore at this news because the stadium functioned as a food and fuel storage area. Huge stores of Beirut's dry goods, vegetables and fuel blown up. He shook his head. "Do they really think the PLO is so stupid they would store guns and ammo in a totally open place that could not be guarded? But I don't think that was the intent anyway."

"What do you mean?"

"The Israelis wanted to destroy food and fuel. You know that any excuse to break the current cease-fire will be enough to start an invasion." Soliman stared south.

"What are you talking about?"

"You heard Professor Abu Jawad last night. The Israelis have big designs, they must occupy South Lebanon and colonize with military installations. They will yell security, their typical handy reason, for occupying a third of Lebanon. Wait and see if I am not right." Soliman nodded with the certainty of a prophet. "Something has happened. Something is going to happen. These raids are a cue, a signal of more to come. Bombing food and fuel is part of long range strategy, not just another run to scare people, to remind the Lebanese and refugees that big brother Israel is looking over their shoulder."

"What does this mean for us going to the south tomorrow?"

"We will find out tonight." He waved his head toward the door. "Come on, we should clean up and take a rest."

As the elevators opened on our floor, I stepped out and turned toward my room. To my surprise, Soliman followed me.

"What do you want?"

"You," he whispered. "Get your key out quick, open the door."

With the door closed and locked behind me, Soliman flopped on the bed, rolled on his back and beckoned me with his pat charming smile. What was this? We have just been bombed, some of our friends may be lying in pieces in the open sewers of the refugee camps. Does he think he is going to die and wants this to be his last act? This was not about drawing comfort or love from me by being close. I rationalized, for Soliman marriage was little more than a business, a system of exchanges, a perpetual continuity guaranteed with the security of a lifelong deal. For me I realized sex on demand was an exchange for the access to an adventurous life.

But whatever justifications I tried to muster, I was still revolted by the process. Unfortunately my malignant self-doubt paralyzed me and kept me from any corrective action. I also thought that perhaps Soliman would respect or at least appreciate me with a little bit more time. Besides, I couldn't bear the thought of returning to Indiana a failure. Ten minutes later, Soliman snored in spent satisfaction while my skin burned in the scalding soap and water of my Hotel Beau Rivage shower.

With my hair dryer switched to the 220 electric current mark, I fluffed my hair letting its noise drown out the remaining sporadic rat-a-tat-tat of the Syrian artillery, fired in stupid bravado at nothing. I woke Soliman from his snores and kicked him out to get cleaned up in his own room and then stood in my preppie skirt and blouse on the balcony vowing that some day I would have an apartment in a big city, with a beautiful view of water and a balcony to watch the sunsets.

Chapter 9

Soliman waited in the lobby for me that evening. A call from PRCS headquarters had let us know the reception was still on. In a sport shirt and khaki pants he looked like someone from the country club set and we set out in the only taxi waiting in the queue.

When we arrived several guards stopped us at a checkpoint outside the hospital driveway. Security tightened after a bombing. Crowds of wailing distraught relatives were milling around the entrance or sat with faces in their hands. A guard shouted to another at the entrance who cleared a path for us and then escorted us to the meeting room where Dr. Fathi and the others were assembled.

"Ah, Miss Liza," called Dr. Fathi as we walked into the room. "You are all right, *Al Ham du li'llah,* thanks be to God. Now you see for yourself what we live with, what we fight, daily. Dr. Soliman, *ahlan wa sahlan,* welcome. Please, let me get you a drink."

"Liza, I don't think this will last very long. Both of you can come to my place for awhile if you want." whispered Professor Abu Jawad in my ear as he kissed me on each cheek.

Madam Hala hugged me. She pulled my hand toward the chairs to sit together. "I was so worried about you in Fakhani camp with the first bombs. Only Allah could protect you. Do you see what we live with? We are grateful the casualties were so low but an invasion is sure now."

"Ten people dead is low? An invasion?"

"Yes, ten is not bad. It could have been much worse for the length of time and number of bombs dropped. As for an invasion, since your Philip Habib brokered the cease-fire from last summer's raids, we waited for the Israelis to find any pretext to break it. We have resisted all provocations, even today's, but they want to fight."

"What is so urgent just now?"

"The Israelis had to return the Sinai this past spring to Egypt, so they are aiming for new territory to grab to restore their wounded national ego. Egypt paid dearly to get it back, losing status and respect in the Arab world and the use of the land."

"How so?"

"Egypt will tolerate U.S. forces sitting in the Sinai for years, preventing its use to the Egyptians just to calm the nerves of the Israelis. As long as these soothing soldiers remain, the true sovereignty of Egypt over the Sinai is a façade, just to placate the Israelis who returned something they shouldn't have taken in the first place. It's Lebanon's turn now to feel Israel's expansionist ambition."

"So you think they will invade soon?"

"Did you see the papers?" Madam Hala replied, leaning over to reach for her briefcase.

"What do they say?"

"Just in case, I brought the *Herald Tribune* for you to see." She unfolded the front page. Under the main story were small headlines. The Israeli ambassador to the UK escaped an assassination attempt by the fringe group led by Abu Nidal. The date was June 3, 1982– yesterday.

"This will be the reason used to invade Lebanon. No matter that Abu Nidal is not part of the PLO. No matter that he has no base in Lebanon. No matter that his base in Iraq has to do with the Iraq/Iran conflict."

"No matter?"

"No matter. We will pay in Lebanon, young and old, with our blood because that is what the Israelis and Americans want." she lamented. "Tomorrow, the next day." She stared at me intently and continued, "You don't mind my remarks about the U.S.? From your presence here you are one of us."

"One of us," gave me the subtle feeling of being welcomed into some part of the inner circle. As Madame Hala patted my hand warmly, I somehow knew she was light-years ahead of me in worldliness and sophistication. Over the years this was confirmed as little by little I learned her story: Raised in an upper-class Moslem family from Jerusalem, she had attended a French school run by the Sisters of the Sacred Heart. A lawyer by training, she had become the personal secretary to the queen of Libya before the revolution of Colonel Qadafi. Madam Hala had managed to rescue the queen's personal jewelry from confiscation as "property of the state jewels" by arguing they were part of her wedding dowry so could not be touched. This brilliant argument, grounded in Arab culture and tradition, was honored by Qadafi who knew better than to anger the populace by daring to lay petty claim to a lady's wedding gifts from her husband. But this I was only to learn years later. This night I only knew this vibrant woman was committed to the national struggle for freedom of her people.

Professor Abu Jawad agreed with her prediction of the invasion. "Today or tomorrow. You saw the papers. That Abu Nidal story—even though it has nothing to do with the PLO or Lebanon. Make up any story, print it in the papers and let the wire services pick it up as if it is gospel." He lit his pipe. "That brings me to you, Liza. You are not going to the south tomorrow, until we know a little more. So you stay here in Beirut for one more day."

"Are you sure? I am not afraid."

"That's enough. You are under my direction. I will tell you when and if," he barked like a concerned father, "but I am happy you are still willing to go. This is just the beginning of a long association, if you want it. You must be patient and wise about how you work with us, no need to put yourself at risk. Bad enough our own people are killed. We don't want to lose you either."

"Okay."

"Liza, why don't you come to Akka Hospital tomorrow and spend the day with Miss Elham? There is a great deal she wants to tell you and she can be a big help to you for the clinic too," suggested Madame Hala and pointed to Dr. Fathi, who was about to make a public statement.

"Welcome, all of you here tonight," began Dr. Fathi, standing in the center of the room. The ink stain on his shirt was gone, but the fresh shirt was identical. "Today's example of Israeli aggression resulted in ten dead and about 40 wounded. Let us bow our heads in a moment of silence for our new martyrs—one a babe three weeks old—whose blood was shed because they were Palestinian."

Three weeks old? Was it the baby sitting on its grandmother's lap as we drove by? Was it the baby we didn't see, sleeping in one of the square homes?

"Thank you everyone today for your efforts to care for our brothers and sisters. I am proud to serve with you," Dr. Fathi nodded to everyone around the room. "We also want to welcome our guests, Dr. Soliman and Miss Liza from America. Perhaps, Miss Liza, you would like to say something to everyone here?" asked Dr. Fathi. He caught me off guard, but his smile and authoritative eyes told me this was a nonnegotiable request.

I learned to appreciate over the years his unique manner of sweetly commanding people to do, say and even eat something that ordinarily they would not. He would smile, lips closed, half wink one or both eyes and then give a quick nod. Only one. No more was needed. No one ever resisted. He embodied the honor and commitment to the cause of Palestinian human rights while inspiring trust. It was more than charisma. Dr. Fathi could connect, at some emotional level, to each newcomer to the cause that he met.

Standing in the middle of the room in front of people met only hours before, my heart felt anguish for their unrecognized bravery, their unrecognized lives, so casually dismissed as primitive by my own American society. What difference would a few words of thanks and compliments make to them? But I did feel grateful for their generous welcome and appreciated the belief they held that an American nurse might make a difference in their lives. My goal was to honor their trust and all this I told them.

Afterwards Dr. Fathi approached me, put his hands on my shoulders and kissed me on each cheek. Then he tousled my hair as if I was a young daughter. "You understand. You are one of us now." He said good-bye quickly because he still needed to visit the wounded in the Gaza Hospital. Little did I realize that evening that one day Dr. Fathi Arafat would rescue me from my own oppressive nightmare and become as dear as a favorite uncle.

The gathering broke up soon after. Madame Hala declined to join us at Professor Abu Jawad's flat because she had some telexes to send—the fax machine still being three or four years away. We left in Professor Abu Jawad's car and drove along the corniche to his flat in Al Hamra.

Once there, he turned to me solemnly and said, "Liza, I have had some news. You should go home tomorrow. The invasion has begun, for all intents and purposes. Most likely they will 'soften us up' with bombing raids. Then the full-scale assault will begin June 6, like Madame Hala said." He stared at me with authoritative eyes.

"Are you sure? Maybe nothing will happen."

"I am sure. Besides, the biggest problem is the airport. If they close the airport, you will both be stuck here. Even if you don't get killed, you don't know how long it will be before you can get out." He shook his head. "You have an American passport, but you, Soliman, what do you have? Are you a citizen?"

"No, a green card. I have an Israeli passport, of course, since I grew up there, but it is worthless outside the West. No Arab country will accept it, so I have a *laissez passez*," he answered lamely.

"That means you essentially have no passport," the professor affirmed. "No one cares about your application for a green card. You have nothing to prove you are an Arab, a Palestinian. Did you bring your Israeli passport? It will state you are an Arab at least."

"No."

"Great. Some ignorant or scared idiot could think you are a spy for Israel. *Laissez passez* is worthless here. You'll be arrested immediately at any checkpoint if you try to leave West Beirut. All the factions will suspect you. You are only safe here, protected by the PLO and the Lebanese National Movement where we can vouch for you," exclaimed Professor Abu Jawad. "So you must both leave tomorrow before the airport closes. There is no other choice. Go home and pack. I'll pick you up early. The first flight is always at eight. You will be on it, wherever it is going, just to get out."

We scuffed down the stairs in the darkness outside the door. The vague shadow of a taxi soon rolled to a stop on the corner of the street down the block. Soliman hailed it and within minutes we were back at the hotel.

The night passed but sleep never came. The sun rose just before a jet took off from the airport at six. A few minutes later Soliman knocked on my door. According to Professor Abu Jawad the airport had closed with that six o'clock flight. So many people were waiting to leave, the last jet was filled and took off. We were to relocate to the Weiner Haus, a hotel in the heart of Al Hamra a block from Professor Abu Jawad's flat.

The Weiner Haus blended in between other buildings; only its narrow tall marquee drew any attention. The lobby decor sparkled with chrome trimmed furniture in black and white—a modern style which already appeared dated. Checking in was easy since war created vacancies in tourist hotels. Professor Abu Jawad soon appeared at the front desk and ordered us to Akka Hospital for the day.

There we split up. It was still only seven-thirty. I went with

Miss Elham to the emergency room while Soliman went to Dr. Fathi's office. A nurse gave me a pile of cut gauze strips to roll. The other nurses, two men and one woman, smiled at me and talked between themselves. My lack of Arabic frustrated me. Unfortunately my French was no help. Miss Elham, away on an errand, had promised to return within 15 minutes but we didn't see her again until much later that day.

My small gauze bandage rolls, covered in brown paper, taped at the end and neatly stacked on a gurney, erupted into the air as a loud crushing explosion vibrated the hospital. Again the whistling whir of incoming shells (or was it the outgoing retaliatory response?) shattered the routine start of a typical hospital workday. The ground beneath us shook as bombs landed close by. Because we were already underground, the F-15s and F-16s breaking the sound barrier couldn't always be heard. Hospital staff ran in all directions to get to their wartime posts. A nurse patted my hand and smiled to reassure me. This was no game. The bombing continued unabated, one after another, like Fourth of July fireworks—but these fireworks were meant to kill lots of poor people with no place to go.

I watched my nurse colleagues. They had been through this before. They speedily connected IV tubing to the IV solution—D5W, 5% dextrose in water. The wrong solution for trauma, for hemorrhage, for lacerations, for fractures. A good choice only in head injuries at least that was the conventional wisdom then. Some 15 years later it was found D5W also had adverse effects in head injuries, so in retrospect it was the wrong solution for all cases, but it was all there was.

I searched the shelves for Lidocaine, an injectable local anesthetic. I saw one bottle, three-quarters empty. I found large curved needles and chromic. No nylon, no small gauge needles. There was only the very large chromic and cat gut. We did have rolls of gauze however. I picked them up off the floor and spread them out on the shelf. I thought about turning on oxygen and suction, routine, reflexive maneuvers in a modern American emergency department, inappropriate here. I would not squander what little oxygen was left in the tanks ahead of time, just to be ready. The suction machine would go to the one who needed it most.

The bombing remained steady, the crashing and shaking continuous. Bits and chunks of plaster broke loose from the ceiling and smashed into tiny sand storms of plaster talc on the floor, dusting the gray tiles with the slippery residue. Lights flickered as the current shorted out and on. The fan taped to a pole swayed with each frightening wave. I suspected Fakhani Camp across the highway was battered given the intense vibrations of the hospital.

Ten minutes from the start of the first wave of bombing, the injured began to arrive. I could smell them before I could see them. Burned flesh, sweat from fright and coagulating blood together created an odor of horror and repulsion. I braced myself. Odor was my weakness. I was okay until a person threw up. Then I would feel my own nausea surge, as a primordial response, forcing me away from the offensive smell. I had always overcome my own nausea as a professional duty to my patients. The odor I breathed before I saw these injured Palestinians smelled singed in the warm, stuffy air of the tunnel hallway. Underground, there were no windows. The meager spin of the fan in the main room mocked us with its false wind of fresh air.

I heard them before I could see them. The squeaking wheels of the flimsy pipe carts and stomping steps of orderlies grew louder. Shouts from men and women at the door punctuated the steady moans and wails of the injured people. I couldn't understand them, but I knew they shouted hurry, this way, don't worry we'll get help, hold on—the typical words spoken in situations of mass casualties that needed no translation.

Some people walked in bleeding, applying pressure from one hand against the bleeding hole in their other arm or shoulder. Heads were ringed in blood from slow dripping scalp lacerations—these worried me the most. Hair mashed into a clot of blood can mask an aggressive bleeding artery. Such can give way later, silently leaking unnoticed as the resting person sleeps into coma and dies quietly.

We met the first wave in the hall and triage began—sifting and sorting the injured according to their severity and needs. By nodding and pointing to the trauma room or an empty room where the injured could wait, we agreed on where to send the patient. The doctors began to treat immediately. Soon we were overcome by the volume and the increasing severity of injuries and then had to open a small room to be used as temporary morgue.

Nursing assistants or orderlies—people minimally trained to help during bombing raids—maintained order in the rapidly filling hallway and then tended to the less urgent injured. A doctor who had just arrived handed me a suture kit and told me to start suturing, so I did. Another doctor, examining a fairly deep scalp wound in a man about fifty, asked me to consult. "What do you think?"

"I think you can do a simple closure. It is deep and raggedy, but it is after all only the skin that is cut. Clean it well and close it." He didn't move, so finally I asked, "Do you want me to do it?" My suturing skills had been honed on many ER night shifts under the supervision of overworked physicians grateful for any help.

"Yes. If you don't mind, "the doctor replied, "I am a psychiatrist and haven't touched a needle in years."

"Gladly. This doesn't require any talk, but there are plenty of people out in the hall that need to talk. Why don't you go there and do what you are trained to do? If this isn't the time for crisis intervention, when it would be?"

"Thank you. Yell for me if you need translation or anything. And welcome to Palestine." He bowed and left.

He knelt to talk to a small child with burns on her arms and shoulders, shivering, lost in the throngs of shouting, crying, bloody people and then stepped back into the main room to grab a basin. Stuffing his lab coat pockets with gauze and two small bottles of sterile saline, he paused in the door way on his way out, catching my eye, "I can talk, but I can also treat these burns too. I'll send anyone needing stitches to you."

"Okay."

The 50-year-old man would have no anesthesia since we'd used the last drop a few patients before. His laceration was at least an inch and a half long and with cat gut about the size of upholstery thread and a big curved needle, suturing would hurt. I dabbed his wound with a piece of gauze and trimmed his hair close, then flushed it again, sparingly with the little bit of saline left. He winced but said nothing and blinked slowly to tell me to go ahead. I sutured quickly, leaving long thread tails so someone could find the stitches easily in a week or so to take them out. The psychiatrist came back and instructed my patient to return here or go to any PRCS clinic to have them removed.

"He will return here next week, *Inshallah*, for you to take them out." the psychiatrist related.

Suddenly, great shrieks of grief and wailing sobs swelled from up the hallway. The sound escalated with voices calling for Allah, calling for Jesus, calling for names of children. The psychiatrist rushed out to the hall to a man holding his head in his hand, rolling it back and forth.

"School buses. The Israelis bombed school buses filled with children on their way to school." He disappeared into the morass of stricken mothers and fathers.

Sweat from my chin dripped onto my watch: 8:15. The bombing had stopped in the last 15 minutes. It had been continuous between seven-thirty and eight, just when buses would be reaching schools. Were they bombing the highways? Pilots could see school buses from their F-15s and F-16s. Pinpoint bombing. Surely the Israelis would not claim that PLO soldiers rode school buses a half hour before school started to justify bombing them.

One after another, stretchers began to arrive with the children.

Burned, bleeding, missing limbs, some dead, some dying. The head nurse opened an empty locked room with a tiny window well and motioned for the least injured to be laid there while the temporary morgue began to fill up with dead school children.

The psychiatrist called to me, "Liza, this one is badly hurt. You must treat her." Two young men rushed into the room carrying a girl on a stretcher.

From her clothes and figure I could see she was a young teenager. Together we lifted her, limp body onto the cot. Her head lay askew, her gaze cast down toward her feet. Her eyes bulged out of their sockets, gray button mushrooms with dull black spots, unreactive. Her gray purple swollen lips fell apart, slack jawed. Watery pink fluid still dripped from her nose detailing the path of leaking cerebrospinal fluid mixed with blood. Her arms were broken above and below her elbows. I picked up each arm gently and repositioned them in anatomical correctness. Her silver rings had absorbed the heat from the bomb blast, burning ridges into her fingers, now swollen like boiled hot dogs. Her feet in white sandals were still connected to her legs, but her knees bent in the wrong direction. Her red plastic hair clips were melted on to only a few strands of a braid, most of which was singed off. Her small white patent leather shoulder purse hung around her, its buckle still locked securing a pen or a pencil or perhaps her favorite private possessions.

The head nurse looked at me and nodded. We lifted her back onto the stretcher with the help of her two waiting brothers and gently laid her on the tile floor of the temporary morgue, covering her with a torn strip of cloth from a wound-stained sheet. The brothers embraced each other, crying for their sister.

The dead children outnumbered the injured for a while. We made numerous trips between the treatment room and the temporary morgue working together for hours in silence. No words were needed. Nothing in my own emergency experience prepared me for this day. The results of murder, drug overdoses, hypoglycemia shock, stab wounds or car accidents in peace time do not compare to the breadth and depth of war trauma These poor refugees, disallowed by the world community, called up every last bit of decency and courage to care for themselves without whining, without pity.

By noon we had cleared out the last of the patients. Some were admitted upstairs, others went to the houses of relatives. The most serious casualties were sent directly to the OR which soon backed up with fractures, third-degree-burn debridement, amputations and various abdominal injuries.

A cleaning crew scoured the adjacent rooms and hallway. Orderlies transported bodies to a staging area on the main floor for identification, as burial had to be completed within the day according to Moslem tradition. The wails of mourning families filtered through the walls of the hospital to our ears in the underground emergency room. Their lament released a collective pain but no comfort answered them. We readied the room for the next onslaught of pointless casualties with depleted supplies and equipment.

Later, on my way to Dr. Fathi's office, I stood outside the door facing the crowded open area inside the gate. My eyes squinted at the brightness of the afternoon sun, yet the hot outside air felt cool and fresh on my face.

"Miss Liza, over here," called a British accent. Dr. Refat opened the lab door and waved.

"Hi."

"Hey, how are you? You were in the ER the whole day? This is terribly rough for a first day's outing." He put his arm around my shoulder.

"It's pretty awful, Refat. How do you manage day in day out?" I pulled away.

"We get used to it. There is no alternative. But you see why we are angry. This is senseless slaughter. It is state terrorism—genocide. But no one cares or cares to see it that way. You tell me. You live in the States. Tell us what we can do to get Israel to stop." He shrugged his shoulders. His crisp starched lab coat had wilted from his own sweat and the blood of many casualties sprinkled with the dirt of Beirut's refugee camps

"Where have you been all day? Surely not in the lab?"

"No, the ICU trying to keep alive those poor souls patched up by the surgeons. There is not much the lab does but type and cross-match potential blood donors from the relatives of the injured." He stopped to take a deep breath. "Where are you going?"

"To Dr. Fathi's office to meet Soliman at three. Can I ask you a favor?"

"Anything, my darling, anything," he sang.

"Could you take me there? I'm lost."

"Liza, you are not lost if you are with me. T'would be a pleasure to escort you." He offered me his arm with a slight bow.

"Dr. Refat, come quickly," called a nurse standing next to the hospital door. "It's Miss Amira."

A sobbing nurse had collapsed at the bottom of the stairs in a heap. Dr. Refat pulled her off the floor onto the steps and gently asked what was wrong. "My sister Muna is dead and her artist's hand is gone." Refat looked at me, shocked at the news, then ordered me to help him take her to Dr. Fathi's office. She limped along with our support. Muna, the artist with a chipper outlook and Amira, a nurse. Everyone was related in the PRCS so no one was insulated from tragedy.

When we stepped into the doorway of his office, Dr. Fathi jumped to his feet from behind his massive desk. "Ah, Miss Liza, you have been working so hard." His own shirt was stained with soot and sweat.

"Like everyone else, no more. How are you?"

Soliman, who was sitting in a corner engrossed in conversation with a woman, did not hear me come in with Dr. Refat.

"You know Haifa Hospital has been destroyed with casualties. Miss Muna, whom you met, was killed," he choked in a painful whisper. "You have seen Amira her sister?"

"Yes, she is with your secretary waiting for her father."

"There are many casualties at Sabra and Shatila." He shook his head at Dr. Refat. "Gaza Hospital was overwhelmed. Here at Akka we are over capacity now but we will make do. Would you like a coffee or a tea?" asked Dr. Fathi as he answered the red phone. I noticed the tissue to a red abrasion on the top of his bald head was weeping clear fluid, but not blood. He was dabbing it absentmind-edly as he spoke.

"A coffee please," I answered. Refat was trying to get Soliman's attention but I stopped him, "Just let him talk. It doesn't matter."

"Hm. Aren't you two a couple?" he queried.

"Yes, but so what if he talks to another person. It surely has something to do with his volunteer activities in Chicago."

"He is a professor or something," Dr. Refat said.

"Well, after he finishes his doctorate. Yes, he plans to teach sociology."

"Here is the coffee," he motioned for me to sit down. An old man brought several poured cups of coffee. Dr. Refat handed me one and took one for himself, sitting next to me.

"Liza, I didn't see you," called Soliman getting up from his corner chair. "This is Miss Daxon. She's with an international aid agency. This is Liza Elliott."

"How do you do?"

Tall, slim, she had thick brown hair swept up into a ballerina-style bun that accentuated her beguiling wide brown eyes and lush lips. "Hello, pleased to meet you. Are you working with the PRCS?" she asked flashing a broad smile.

"Yes. As a volunteer."

"Miss Daxon is going to show me her projects tomorrow. Her agency is involved in educational programs and child development programs," gushed Soliman, a little too enthusiastically for my taste. "What time tomorrow?" he asked turning to her.

"Let's meet here at eight. I'll have a driver tomorrow. We can spend the day out, unless you have any other commitments?" she suggested.

"No, the day is open. That sounds great," Soliman agreed.

"Well, I'll be off. Nice meeting you, Liza. Perhaps we will meet again in these next few weeks." She turned her enchanting smile to Soliman, "See you tomorrow. Ciao!"

"So, Liza, how did you manage this morning? It was bad in the ER?" said Soliman, chattering a bit too effusively, I thought. He looked at Refat who glanced away.

"Busy."

Miss Daxon's laugh in the distance yanked Soliman's eyes in the direction of the door. I could feel he was ready for tomorrow's appointment with her.

Dr. Fathi closed the phone gently and announced, "That was not good news." Patting the back of his head with quick rubs, he continued, "The situation in the south is very bad. We should expect a repeat of today, tomorrow. There are maneuvers in the south by the Israelis. Liza, you will not be going south. It's too dangerous. I don't know when it will be safe."

"This is it," stated Dr. Refat.

"Yes." Dr. Fathi wiped his eyes with his hand. "Dr. Refat, we must have an executive committee meeting tonight, here." He called his secretary on the blue phone.

"If you need us, we will be with Professor Abu Jawad tonight," Soliman said. He gave me a little shake of his head indicating it was time to go.

"Refat, thanks so much. I'll be in the ER tomorrow again. Goodbye, Dr. Fathi, see you tomorrow."

Soliman and I walked out together in predictable silence. We lived in separate worlds surrounded by the common context of Beirut, Israeli bombing and Palestine. A driver approached us to take us to the hotel.

Chapter 10

Before we left Professor Abu Jawad's place I had stood staring out to the Mediterranean Sea from his balcony while he and Soliman heatedly discussed something in the salon. It seemed liked a decade had passed since that morning, yet all I could think of was that 14-year old girl, dead on the emergency room cot. What was her name? Did she write poetry? Or did she draw? Play the flute? Was math her favorite subject? Perhaps she watched the moon and stars at night and dreamed of being a teacher. I would never know, but ever after her haunting image became a frequent visitor to my dreams for her picture somehow distills all the sorrowful, wasted tragedy of that day—her last day.

"Liza," said the professor, stepping onto the balcony. He sat down in front of me. "I will arrange for you to get out. As for Soliman, he cannot leave."

As he predicted, Soliman's *laissez passez* meant nothing. Even his own American passport meant nothing since he was too well known. The only way to get to a seaport required crossing the greenline into East Beirut which the Christian Phalangist militia and their allies controlled. "He'd be imprisoned or shot or both," the professor said, drawing a long breath on his pipe.

"But it is okay for me?"

"Two reasons: You are a woman and you are from America—

their patron after all. It would not be smart to kill an American citizen, a nurse, caught unexpectedly in the war." He studied me closely, scrutinizing me. "You will have to be smart. Don't speak of us. You must say you were helping at the American University hospital or something like that."

"I don't want to deny you."

"You are not denying anything. When you get back, you must write, speak, tell the world what you saw, what is going on here. You will have a lot to do that can help us if you choose to go on public record in support of Palestine." He paused and added, "And you must go and see Jeanette and tell her not to worry. She will be out of her mind. She always felt I minimized the risks of Beirut and she is right. But tell her I am okay and will be back. She will already know, if the invasion comes, the Open University project will be suspended for a while. I won't say it is doomed yet."

"Okay." My immediate future had been decided. We left soon after this discussion.

Morning came quickly. The rat-a-tat-tat of machine guns woke me by five o'clock. There were no jets as yet. Perhaps they were firing out to sea. Yes. That must be it. Suddenly I seized with the fear the building would collapse around me while I stood naked in the shower, my hair full of shampoo and nothing around me. The gunfire continued to terrify me. Frozen with the absurdity, I stripped and jumped in and out of the shower faster than possible and did not relax until my clothes were on.

"Ready to go?" called Soliman knocking on my door.

"Yeah."

We stopped first at Dr. Fathi's office. Miss Daxon was there, Dr. Refat, too, a crisp white lab coat on his arm which he handed to me, "This is for you. You might like to have one while you work here. Just exchange it at the ICU nurses' station for a fresh one before you go home." He laughed, "Now you are really part of the system."

"Why, thanks. That is so thoughtful. Do you think today will be like yesterday?"

"Be sure of it. Probably worse. It is early. They can bomb at any time. They vary it, just to intimidate, to antagonize, to make it worse. Maintaining full alert 24 hours a day is big drain," he explained. "Come on, I'll walk down with you."

Soliman already engaged in a conversation with Miss Daxon paused to say, "Meet here in the afternoon, around the same time if possible. Leave word here if there is any change," and turned back to Miss Daxon.

"Refat, what is she like?"

"Who, Miss Daxon? She's decent. She is very nice. She works hard and has been here about a year. Soliman likes her," he replied opening a door to the hallway.

"He is free to like whom he wants. He is not a medical person, so it is natural he would seek others who deal with education or general social services."

"You are pretty forgiving of his obvious interest in her. All of us can see it, by the way," he said. "I'd never do that to my wife."

"Your wife? Where is she? Does she work here?"

"No, she's in London where we live, but this bloody war will interfere with my return. Who knows when I will get back."

"So you are not permanently based here as the head of the lab?"

"As director of all laboratory divisions in the PRCS, I rotate a few weeks here every couple of months."

"What do you do in London?"

"Direct an organization that works to support the PRCS's activities."

"You mean like the fund that Soliman works for?"

"Well, yes, but his is for general social welfare, mine is specific for medical relief and the support of health care. Of course all these organizations are affiliates to the PRCS which is how it can build a world-wide network of support and people to work for it."

"Here's my assigned post."

"Good luck." He left me and headed to the ramp that led to the lab.

The nurses and doctors in the main room were already setting up supplies from the AUB hospital that had arrived only hours ago. I looked over the supplies and was pleased that today's casualties would be luckier than yesterday's—but still there was no local anesthesia for anyone today.

Boom. The sound barrier was broken overhead and soon the bombs began to land. The return fire from artillery represented an exercise in useless vanity, an utterly incapable defense against a superior military machine backed by a super power. Again, within minutes casualties flooded the emergency room.

"Liza! Good you are here. This man is burned," called the psychiatrist wheeling the cart into the room. His Buddy Holly glasses had slipped to the end of his nose.

"And it's a relief to have a translator around," I rejoindered.

"We'll be a good team," he replied running out the door to the hall. "Be back soon."

See you later, Buddy, I thought to myself.

The patient groaned. The second- and third-degree burns followed the edges of the pajamas he wore. Poor man, he probably was asleep when the bomb hit and woke up to this nightmare. Nahid the nurse said "operation room" in English to me. Nodding, I helped him wheel this man with flash burns around his face and respiratory involvement to the OR.

"Bring him this way," called Dr. Imad. "What's this? Burned in his bed?"

"Seems that way. He's yours now. Good luck."

"Thanks," Dr. Imad mouthed from inside the surgical suite.

We worked steadily, the air growing hotter, stuffier, smellier, even foul. The wounded and the dead began to blur for me and look the same after a few hours of relentless attack. I imagined the sky, textured like a basket, crisscrossed with the white thready trails of the bombs' paths to the ground from their F-16 dispensers. Perhaps you could no longer see the white threads obscured by the dark cloud of debris from the exploded buildings, trees, streets and people whose body parts vaporized, never to be identified or accounted for in the morgues of the hospital—only mourned by survivors.

There were no shifts, no fresh staff to relieve us. By late in the afternoon, some nurses and doctors left to find out about their own families. The bombing had stopped. The flow of casualties slowed down, but the severity of injuries remained high. After the early morning rush of burned patients, many more crush injuries of arms and legs, hands and feet arrived. Many more buildings had collapsed, exploding or imploding from blast bombs or vacuum bombs. Either way, they killed and maimed.

Two nurses, Mohamed and Mahmoud, with the help of the translating doctor, told me to leave for the day. They would sleep in the emergency room that night and promised to send for me if they needed help. Their families stayed with other relatives.

"Miss Liza. How are you?" bellowed Dr. Refat strolling into the main room. He spoke to the nurses and nodded. "They assure me you should leave. It is almost five o'clock in the evening. They say you haven't stopped since you came at seven this morning and are worried you will become sick."

Dr. Refat took me back to the hotel by way of the sea. His prescription for refreshing me was to walk along the corniche, a seaside stroll and glass of fresh lemonade. The bitter lemon cleansed the lingering chalky taste of the messy ER in my mouth and the sea breeze blew away the heaviness the scenes of suffering had layered on my mind. It was on this walk he confessed his attraction to me and I admitted my own for him, but he preempted the next step, a fiery affair, because he was an honorable married man and a gentleman. Soliman's treatment of me enraged him, but it was not for him to interfere. We agreed to be friends knowing our work would provide the lid of respectability, to cover a simmering heat which we promised never to let burn us.

It seemed impossible that something about me could move Refat to an emotional place so crucial he had to speak about it only days

Finding Palestine

after we met. It troubled me greatly that I had done something to evoke this, but nothing came to mind. With no confidence at all in my personal looks and a total void in relating to Soliman in any way other than use-values, it stunned me that a man would give me a second look. Our agreement avoided a catastrophe, yet provided me a lifelong friend whose advice and counsel throughout later complicated years only endeared him to me more.

Walking back to the hotel, we passed the destruction in the Fakhani camp. Its primitive skyline had been totally altered, reduced from neat flat roofs, supporting lines of flapping laundry to mounds of rubble, concrete and rebar with an occasional shirt still stubbornly snapping in the wind. Smoke rose in curls and waves from the freshly bombed neighborhoods outside the refugee camps. No one was safe, anywhere.

Back in my room only minutes, I head someone knocking on my door.

"Professor Abu Jawad, come in. Are you all right?" I pulled him into my room and sat him in the chair. Sweating, pale white, blue lips, a panic look on his face, my first thought was that he was having a heart attack. "Do you have chest pain?"

"No. It's not my heart. Just stay with me. Just stay with me. Let me sit with you," he gulped between breaths. I stroked his hand and wiped his forehead with a damp wash cloth. We sat for five minutes on the bed before he spoke.

"Next to my building. It's gone. They bombed it, a direct hit. It happened only a half hour ago. I was walking home," he panted. "It was so awful, just next door. The whole block is unstable now, my building's outside wall is cracked anyway." He put his head on my shoulder and took deep breaths. His white hair, tacky from panic made my shirt damp.

"You can stay here, there is plenty of space in the hotel."

"I called the house, but Jeanette was not there, just the cleaning lady. I miss her."

"Look, go and wash yourself off in the bathroom, you'll feel better. Take a shower if you want. Your color is back already. You'll be all right, you have just had a huge fright."

He steadied himself at the edge of the bed. "I have to go back to get my things, my papers anyway." He stood slowly and stepped gingerly to the bathroom to rinse off his face and chest. "Do you want to go with me?" he asked as he emerged, wiping his face with a towel.

"Sure."

We walked toward the war zone where his apartment stood, surrounded by smoking rubble. Every gust of wind lifted cement dust. The wounded had been evacuated to the AUB hospital nearby but the missing person count was still open. This was Al Hamra, where the elite lived, which the war was not supposed to touch. No refugees lived here in the city center of the mythic Beirut—the Paris of the Middle East.

It took only a few minutes for Professor Abu Jawad to pack a suitcase, gather his papers and his briefcase which we carried back to the hotel. Soliman had left a note on the door.

Professor Abu Jawad knocked on his door. "*Marhaba,* where have you been?" demanded Soliman. His dark eyes accused me.

"The ER until five. Dr. Refat brought me home. Then Professor Abu Jawad came and we had to get things from his place and we are back. Why? Where have you been?"

"We were stuck near Gaza Hospital. The roads were blocked. What happened to you?" he finally noticed Professor Abu Jawad's tired face.

"I'll explain. Just sit down," he commanded. He gently touched my shoulder and pointed to a chair. "You know, Soliman, there is no need to greet Liza the way you did. You are not the only one with important work here. In fact, weren't you to be her translator?" His gruff response to Soliman took me by surprise.

Soliman sulked at the rebuke. After hearing the story, Soliman stood and peered out the window. "Do you see those long shadows resting on top of the horizon?" he asked.

"Those are Israeli gunboats. They were responsible for the apartment building. The attack was launched from the sea, not the air. That building was exposed to the sea, the one with unobstructed views. They may hit tonight, again, if my sources are correct," commented Professor Abu Jawad. "I am worried."

"What can we do?"

"Nothing. Just hope they don't attack or if they do, that they miss us," Professor Abu Jawad said evenly.

The sound of artillery filled the air. The zoom, whir and hum began, both incoming and outgoing. We sat in the room quietly. Praying to God seemed pointless. Who was God? Where was God? Whose side was God on? I became resigned to God's abandonment of us and withdrew into my own private spiritual cave.

Soliman fell asleep, snoring deeply. Professor Abu Jawad and I listened for an hour more. Then it stopped. Eerie quiet followed. Professor Abu Jawad stood up from his chair and sat down on the other twin bed. He waved me good night and fell back in an exhausted slump. I went to my room and ached to sleep in the comfort of someone's arms, but ruefully recalled it doesn't matter.

Up early, I found the very strong black coffee in the lobby a welcome drink. It was only six, but since the bombing typically began by seven-thirty each day, no one dared sleep late. Who could know when their home would be destroyed or their relatives would die under rubble? The only constant for the refugees was a psychologically and physically destabilizing uncertainty—not unlike the uncertainty my psych-specialist friend Lina had described to me once that permeates the life of an abused child—living on the edge, watchful, waiting, tense, never knowing when the trigger of violence will be pulled, only that it will be pulled. Sometime, anytime.

"So you're off to the hospital?" Professor Abu Jawad joined me.

"Yes."

"And Soliman?"

"He may spend more time with Miss Daxon."

"Ah, here he is. Sit down. What are you doing today," quizzed

Professor Abu Jawad. "Translation for Liza perhaps?"

"Ah, no. Miss Daxon and I are going to formulate a plan for follow-up in Chicago," he said, waving for a coffee to be brought over. He put on his charming face for me. "You'll be at the hospital again?"

"Yes."

"Let's all meet here at six o'clock this evening, no exceptions," Professor Abu Jawad announced.

Soliman stopped to see someone at Dr. Fathi's office and then went on to his appointment with Miss Daxon. I proceeded to my post in the emergency department. Dr. Refat stopped by for a short chat, then raced off to the ICU when we heard the sound barrier break overhead. My watch read seven-thirty.

That evening we met at six o'clock, but there was no news about leaving. It would take time to find a way out. My days began to collapse into each other, undifferentiated from each other. It felt like having a job. The evenings would include Professor Abu Jawad's political analysis, assessment of damage and guessing the future. The bombing raids varied their time now. It was impossible to predict when the pilots would dump destruction onto the defenseless Lebanese citizens and Palestinian refugees living in underground urban caverns, tunnels, cellars or parking lots.

One afternoon Dr. Refat took me along to the Bourj el Barajneh Camp to find Dr. Jane. The camp had been reduced to mounds of rubble and debris. People doubled or tripled up in remaining buildings because they had nowhere else to go. The hospital lay pulverized in heaps of concrete chunks. Miss Muna's department of pink and blue pottery lay scattered about, broken shards gleaming in the sun. Her potter's wheel protruded from a grip of concrete wedges—a glob of clay dried to a wooden board, finger prints still visible in the once mushy stuff.

"Refat, look, a hand."

"Where?"

"There, behind that block of concrete. It's a right hand. It's

Muna's hand." The clay had dried between the fingers, on the ring and under the nails. The turquoise stone had cracked.

Dr. Refat covered the hand with a scrap of fiberglass ceiling panel lying nearby. My eyes bulged with tears that would not cry. He held me for a minute, but I just stood, unreactive to my sorrow for Muna and her pottery, never to be molded, colored and fired again, for Amira and the others. My suppressed, private reactions to everything I'd seen, heard or touched threatened to leak out now with, of all people—Dr. Refat.

"It is so hard, Refat. Your kindness to me only exposes petty needs I try to squelch."

"Are you saying kindness, thoughtfulness don't matter? All those things Soliman seems to have in short supply? You must believe there is more to life than causes or duties," he said.

"Oh, come on, Refat, romantic love is a Western bourgeois creation to support consumerism, the bridal industry, valentines, all that stuff."

"Now, see here, you are wrong. Dead wrong. Don't diminish other cultures or people because that's the only way you can maintain your unhappy relationship with Soliman. Don't insult the rest of us by using human rights and activism as a cover for your own disappointments. You are better than that. Do you think you need Soliman?" Refat lifted my chin with his hand.

"Please don't talk about this anymore." I lifted my chin out of his hand and began to walk to get a box for Miss Muna's artist hand. "Let's talk about something else, business, enough of sentiment."

"Such as?"

"Professor Abu Jawad is anxious for me to leave, to get some word out about the invasion. Who will listen? Who would believe what we saw just now? A hand. No body to be found. Do you really believe the average person riding the El to work in Chicago would care? Who would believe these atrocities were committed by the very people who chant 'never again'? Even I wouldn't have believed it without having seen it."

"Your worst hurdle is with the label anti-Semitic," he responded. Although you are not against the Jewish people, you are for the Palestinians. You must present Zionism as the ideological fuel for the destruction of Lebanon's and Palestine's people. Not every person follows an ideology that dismisses universal human rights."

"But to detach Zionism from being Jewish is considered provocative, even dangerous," I retorted. "That threatens to destroy the whole reason for creating a Jewish state in the first place. Who am I to raise such a profound critical ideological and political question? The whole Western world led by the super powers supports and enables the distortion of these two separate entities."

"Now, don't get angry. No one ever said this was going to be easy. This is a long struggle. Whose hand was it? We know it is Muna's hand. She is depending on you to explain where Palestine is located and why she isn't there now," said Refat.

We found Dr. Jane in the prosthetic room, her headquarters for the moment since it was underground. It was crammed with people so we didn't stay long. Dr. Refat conferred in private as artificial legs and arms were sculpted as if it was normal to make them in the quantity this shop produced. She gave him a box for the hand and we retrieved it for the family.

When Refat dropped me off at the hotel, I found Professor Abu Jawad sitting alone in the lobby, smoking his pipe. He motioned for me to sit down. "You are leaving tomorrow, early. It's all arranged. So pack your things and I will give you a few letters to take. Soliman is not back yet, by the way."

"Soliman is with Miss Daxon. There is a secret you must keep, promise? Take care of him while you are both here. Soliman is my husband."

"What? That jerk is married to you but carries on like he is not?" he gasped. "Why the secret?"

"That's the way he wants it—always alluding to some security thing. And don't ask me why I put up with it."

"Well, why do you? It is not right," he pushed.

"Oh, I keep thinking he will change. He is a Palestinian nationalist, a hard worker for the cause. He's just a bit off on the personal stuff."

"Well, okay, but two men asked me about you, if you are available, and I told them yes. Even Rick Chase asked me about you. Oh, well, you are leaving anyway. He is lucky, that Soliman, but he doesn't deserve you." He pulled me toward him patting me on the back. "Don't worry. It will all work out the way it is supposed to. Allah has His plan."

"Okay, now, but you know it will be hard to explain all these events, don't you?"

"Sure, but you should not attempt policy analysis. Let the policy experts do that. Your power lies in your eyewitness accounts. Only you can testify to the abuse, violence and destruction of our people. Simply tell the story, tell what you saw and what you did. You can humanize it and put a face on the Palestinian people. That's your power, and it is essential."

We gossiped about Rick Chase, who had left on the last plane, surely sorry he missed all the action. He expected to hear from me per Professor Abu Jawad's instructions to us both. The professor turned at the sound of the hotel door. Soliman strode in.

"*Marhaba,* how are you," he cheerily greeted us and flopped down next to me. The scent of roses confirmed my hunch. The slight pink smudge on his shoulder could only come from a cheek, perhaps laid there in fear or perhaps not, but still from a cheek not mine. No twinge of jealousy stirred me. He merely enacted his nature which according to his rules was none of my business. Rules understood, I left the men and went to bed. Soliman knocked on my door later but got no answer.

The next morning, Soliman tossed my suitcase into the trunk of a taxi. Professor Abu Jawad paid the driver a lot of money in U.S. dollars. We sped off toward the interior of the city, heading to the greenline where four heavily armed soldiers stopped us at the checkpoint. One pointed his machine gun and motioned me to get out. They shouted at each other arguing about me and my passport. A soldier harassed the driver who answered "tourist" with a French pronunciation. A third soldier asked the one with my passport in French if he believed I was a tourist.

I spoke up in French saying I was a tourist, but also a visiting professor at AUB in nursing and that the airport closing had stranded me. They reacted with shock at my French but believed me. Snarling words in Arabic, the senior soldier motioned me back to the car and the driver to go ahead. The driver, who spoke only Arabic, kept repeating "Merci, merci, merci, Madame" as we raced through artillery lined streets, still empty because of the early morning hour.

The urban density of Beirut proper disappeared within a half hour changing to the scenic steep foothills of the mountain range that ran the length of modern Lebanon toward our destination, Jounieh. Despite the war, this port city north of Beirut continued as the docking point for many ocean-faring ships from around the world. The word leaked out that these neutral ships would take any foreign nationals wishing to leave Lebanon to their scheduled next port of call for free. Professor Abu Jawad arranged for me to get there today, their departure date. I had to find the way to get on board one of them.

After many questions to many people, a Canadian man helped me. He had figured out the system and found the registration table. A Lebanese soldier told us to get on a bus to go to a staging area, but we worried the bus might be a trap. However, it arrived intact at a small stadium where we split up by nationality and sat in groups. Our names were taken and boarding proceeded by groups. The American group would go last, after eight hours of waiting and sweating in the blistering sun. The blame for the evacuation, the disruption of lives, the interruption of business and industry, the destruction of Beirut and Lebanon was laid on America so it seemed only just to the Lebanese in charge that we swelter the longest in the heat awaiting our turn.

The Americans corralled with me told stories of driving by refugee camps and ignorantly cursing them saying, "Why don't you just go home and leave Lebanon be?" I could hardly believe my ears—if Americans living in Beirut could be so uninformed, what about the Americans who had never left home? Go home? If only there was a home to go to.

With the sun now setting just under the horizon, the American group was finally called to board. Lebanese officers led us onto a landing craft. An Italian military ship was anchored out from the shore. The gray sea heaved and slapped the shore. With great dips and rises our small boat climbed the choppy waves toward the open sea. Standing against the side, someone called my name. "Liza, I have seen you before," a woman wearing jeans and a short jacket leaned past two other people to exclaim to me.

Who was she? I was sure I had never seen her before and turned away. I felt confident of my instincts and I decided this was no time to make a spy into a friend.

Our craft locked onto the staircase lowered from the side of the ship and one by one we climbed a narrow metal plank, slick from the splashing water. The main deck of the ship, a great open space, filled with people milling around. Some had set up camp complete with blankets, lanterns and cassette players. Sailing overnight, we would arrive the next morning in Cyprus.

With nothing to do, I explored the ship. A climb down a set of stairs took you to a large dormitory. The sailors had been ordered to give their swinging canvas hammocks to mothers with children which created a room full of crying, whining children and nursing mothers. In front of an interior room filled with tanks, artillery, guns and the tools for war were dingy mattresses laid out for sleeping. Later, perhaps, but being topside to watch the stars seemed a better deal right then.

The air dampened on the deck with mist from sea spray as the ship gathered speed. A radar grid twirled overhead checking out long shadows on the horizon which enlarged as we approached—the same Israeli gunboats that bombed the building next to Professor Abu Jawad's place. Some British sitting nearby worried aloud they might try to board and search our ship, but someone explained that doing so would cause an international incident since the Italian military vessel provided safe haven to refugees—as we were now classified. They were sitting there trying to intimidate and be a reminder that "we are here" just like the pilots of the F-16s buzzing Beirut.

After a few hours the damp spray stung and the wind whipped around me. I walked around to keep warm. Some people slept. Some danced around blaring cassettes and appeared heavily stoned while a few couples were being intimate out of the wind in alcoves near staircases. When I went down I found many had decided to warm up in the tank room so most mattresses were occupied. I found an available one and slept for a few hours but woke up with the suffocating smell of motor oil and petrol combined with heat. Feeling stuffy and gritty, but with no flea bites evident, I fled back topside to the cold, clean sea air and sat propped up against a pipe to watch the sun rise.

By seven we could see the faint outline of Cyprus on the horizon and a couple of hours later we docked at Larnaca. Tables had been set up with large flags of various countries and we were instructed to find our respective embassy representative to arrange transportation home. By luck I found myself near the head of the queue and half an hour later was talking to a cheery young man from the U.S. embassy whose crisp starched shirt held its pressed box shape despite the sticky heat of the morning. He told me to stay at the Holiday Inn for a night and that a flight would honor my ticket tomorrow.

To pass the time I bought a swimsuit at the hotel gift shop. White powdery sand, turquoise blue water, palm trees and sunbathers decorated the resort. As I settled onto a lounge chair in this fabulous resort, book in hand, it seemed incredible that I was only 24-hours away from a raging racist war. I was also unprepared for the young, shapely, blonde women who were walking, swimming and sunbathing nude. Hunky men strutted around in speedos, but then so did those with beer bellies. My own purple maillot was positively nun-like on this beach. After my fitful overnight ship's ride, I soon fell asleep and the book slipped from my hand.

From Chicago's O'Hare airport the taxi ride home to our apartment in Rogers Park took half an hour. The news that night reported on the war, but didn't come close to describing what I had lived the past few weeks. Civilian casualties weren't mentioned, only Abu Nidal. It was not reported that the PLO had condemned him as a renegade long ago and thus he had no base in Lebanon. Why did no one point out that the PLO had maintained the cease-fire since last summer and it was the Israelis who broke it to launch their old plan to occupy South Lebanon and control water from the Litani River? Why bother reporting at all if the facts were not included?

Chapter 11

Wilmette became my alternate home throughout the summer. Jeanette greeted me at the front door of the shuttered, two-story house with window boxes bulging with scarlet geraniums. The Abu Jawad family was everything mine was not.

Whereas my family's credo was that we were to depend on no one and rely on yourself—and make sure every activity had a practical, profitable edge to it; theirs was one where family and community mattered most. So for me there had been no possibility of my hitchhiking or backpacking through the U.S. in the summer; rather it was a must that I find a summer job. Student protest or challenging the social order was not to be countenanced in my family for we maintained the status quo and valued unquestioning conservatism.

The Abu Jawads actually encouraged everyone to be intellectually curious, to try one's hand in the art worlds of music and dance, to travel and explore the world. Critical thinking and leftist politics were not considered subversive or unpatriotic. Long hair and ethnic fashions were acceptable, for they were a family of the world whose neighborhood embraced cultures, nations and societies from the far corners of the globe.

"Liza, so glad to see you, come in." Jeanette pulled me in with an unexpected hug.

"It is good to see you. Here are letters from the professor," I said, handing her the small bundle.

"Have a seat in the living room. I'll bring some coffee." She opened a letter on the way to the kitchen.

I settled down in the spacious living room to give her time with her mail. Peacock blue swirls edged the warm Persian carpet mapped with intricate designs that sprawled out in front of me on the dark hardwood floor. Handsome handwoven tapestries on the walls looked down on a round copper table in the middle of the room strewn with sociology books. This was the home to have. Jeanette and the professor were American and Palestinian, like Soliman and me, but looking at the titles of her books made me realize that Jeanette ranked as an eminent world class scholar while I was just a nurse. But then Soliman was no Professor Abu Jawad either. Our future would take its own shape.

"So they really can't get out?" she persisted. "Soliman is stuck with a *laissez passez* but Mohamed has an American passport."

"True, but he must get past the green line to get out and he is known as a Palestinian leader and an advisor to Chairman Arafat. He is only safe if he stays in West Beirut. He would leave if he could, but he and the others are stuck."

She visibly paled and exclaimed, "But the fighting will get worse, you know that. The chance they will get killed is greater each day," she insisted, lighting a cigarette and inhaling deeply.

Having witnessed the indiscriminate Israeli bombing of civilian sites, I was more worried than I let on, and so replied, "Yes, but he has access to the best intelligence there. They will move around and won't take chances. Your friend Walleed Sayed, after all is the PLO representative in Lebanon, and he and his wife Warda will help them. They are not alone."

The front door banged open and a cheery voice called, "Hi, Mom."

"Hi, dear. Come in and meet Liza. She was just in Beirut with your father," instructed Jeanette.

"Hi."

"How are things going? Sort of hot over there now, huh?" She had a baby in her arms and was holding the hand of a petit toddler at her side.

"Yeah, it's a bit hot."

"Dad's okay? I'm sure he's lovin' it. This is what he lives for, you know, liberating Palestine. Are you staying for a while? These kids must go down for a nap." She started up the staircase.

"That's Marion, visiting us for the summer. She's our free spirit," sighed Jeanette as if concealing and admitting a family issue at the same time. She blew a long column of smoke and for another hour we covered every topic imaginable from growing up in Indiana, to nursing, to teaching, to Palestine. During the evening news we switched back and forth among the three networks to hear their coverage of Lebanon. Yes, they reported, the Israelis continued to bomb. A full-scale invasion was underway, but what else could they do—Israeli security was at stake. Not one journalist dared question how Israeli security could be threatened by penniless refugees stuck in camps.

It occurred to me that the real threat to Israeli security was the strength and depth of Palestinian nationalism. The Palestinian people were not going to disappear no matter how many times the Israelis tried to eradicate them. As long as Palestinians existed anywhere, the ability of Israelis to deceive themselves and their world could not be complete. In spite of the persecution, the Palestinians were growing in strength and number and their legitimate claim to self-determination sounded louder than ever—and this was the real threat to Israel's goal of regional domination through territorial expansion. None of their Arab neighbors—Palestine, Lebanon, Syria, Jordan or Egypt—had escaped occupation by Israel. But still the Israelis felt insecure.

The utter lack of curiosity or skepticism on the part of the U.S. media to the unfolding events sickened me. How could human life be so cheap, how could human rights protection be awarded so selectively? As I vented my frustration, Jeanette rocked back and forth in her chair, tears leaving tracks through her makeup. Finally I gave her a hug and left, promising to stop by again soon.

Once the door to my flat opened, I tossed the mail onto the table. A letter from Israel caught my attention. Written in Arabic. Drat that Soliman. An airline and a flight number were written in English. Soliman's village was the return address on the envelope. It had to be from his brother, coming this summer to start his Ph.D. studies, too. Our Palestinian friends who ran a travel agency could read the letter and tell me when my brother-in-law would arrive. Having a strange man live with me, even if he was Soliman's brother, did not appeal to me. But what else could I do?

Watching the nightly news became a habit. The war continued. How long could this go on before someone in power thought it was too much or simply wrong? I went to Indiana for my youngest brother's wedding, and a distant cousin commented, "How trim you look. Where did you get that tan?"

"It was easy to lose weight caring for casualties from the Israeli invasion. We didn't have time to eat much. The tan? Got that in Cyprus, lounging for a day or two after escaping the war in Lebanon on an Italian military ship. Why, where did you get yours?"

It was all too ludicrous. I didn't begrudge my brother a happy wedding, but no one could connect with me or the recent agony I had lived through. I tried to talk to another brother, a doctor doing his residency at the local medical center, but he would have none of it. "Is there any way you could help collect medicines, simple supplies like gauze? Do you know any drug reps I could talk to? The medical situation is desperate in Beirut because of the war." Pictures of the hospital and patients flashed in my mind.

"Listen, if you want to hang out with terrorists, that's up to you. I am not doing anything to help those Arab murderers. Don't involve me with your leftist junk," he countered with unforgettable vehemence.

"So that's what you think? Don't you know that is not the truth? Don't you know the Palestinians are refugees because they were routed out of their country in 1948? Don't you understand that we created the refugees, and all they are doing is fighting for their human rights which we deny them? We don't have the guts to tell the Israelis that enough is enough and they have to share the land of Palestine with its indigenous Arab people."

"Don't waste your propaganda on me. I'm really not interested in your politics either, understand?" He turned away, confident his priorities were correct. I was left wondering how this doctor-brother who had attended a Jesuit prep school and Notre Dame would not use the brains God had bestowed on him to try to understand that a world thrived out there beyond Indiana?

My sister Helen tried to be conciliatory, but there was little left to say. No family member had any regard for Soliman, but they were nonplussed he was stuck in Beirut. They believed his motives towards me were ill-intended and neither Palestinian politics nor the U.S. policy on Palestine mattered to them.

In retrospect, my preoccupation with the war in Lebanon must have come off as excessively intense, thus alienating people. But my husband and friends were in danger of being killed for political reasons that flew in the face of all the sacred traditions of civil rights and self-determination that Americans hold dear. Israel's Zionism, a mutation of 19th-century colonialism, was being sustained by the Reagan administration, which blithely presented the Zionist myths as facts to the American people.

My expectation that anyone in my family would be interested in the war went counter to all we had been taught. Activism of any kind was not encouraged. Besides, a wedding is still a wedding, so I realize I should have called a truce in my head for the day. Yet enjoying good food, champagne and dancing seemed like abandoning the people I'd recently left cringing in underground shelters praying to escape that day's bombing foray.

The next day I was back in Chicago starting the summer quarter. Sally, Lina and I went to Two Hermans for a snack. Although I was reticent to talk about the war again, since it struck me as egocentric, they convinced me it was for my own mental health—besides, we were still friends. The frustration that gripped me, Lina pointed out, stemmed from witnessing events that were beyond personal influence. The Israelis had told Secretary of State Haig that any pretext to launch the invasion would be used and to forward this policy to President Reagan. His "no comment" response sent a green light to the Israelis.

"But the Israelis have weapons enough on their own to launch a war, don't they?" asked Lina. "Do they need a green light?"

"Sure, for cover. The world community's criticisms of Israeli action can be deflected by the U.S. and especially its U.N. veto."

When Sally asked what caused the worst injuries, I explained what cluster bombs were. Like mines, their sole purpose is antipersonnel—to kill or maim people, not destroy buildings. The ones used in Lebanon had golf-ball-size metal cores that held explosive material with sharp blades attached like wings. When exploded, these wings flared out cutting off anything in its path—gutting flesh or sinking into bone. Sadly those that land without exploding, because they are small, are often picked up by children who think they are toys. When touched, they explode, cutting off the child's hand on the spot, if they don't kill them outright. Countless cylinders filled with them were dumped over refugee camps and hospitals.

What concerned Sally the most, though, was not the war but the thought that Soliman's brother was soon to arrive. She thought it ridiculous I should be housing a clan of relatives when Soliman might not even make it back. I agreed but until otherwise informed, I had to believe Soliman was still alive.

Leaving my friends at Two Hermans for Wilmette, I found myself depressed. Being with Jeanette and Marion helped in this life-or-death waiting game which ate us all from within. At least Jeanette did not need to worry about her husband's faithfulness throughout the ordeal. I was afraid that as long as Miss Daxon was there, Soliman could charm his way into the comfort of her empathetic arms, to commiserate together in luxurious angst. (Years later someone who had lived through this ordeal verified that my concerns about Soliman's betrayal were well-founded.)

That night, drinking Turkish coffee together, Marion and I planned Jeanette's birthday party on the sly, hoping it would cheer her up for she had fallen into a risky despair. At least we managed to make her laugh at my predicament of the impending in-laws about to descend.

Back home I found the mail contained Rick Chase's story on the Israeli military buildup and the U.S. contribution to it. He profusely thanked me for the photos and negatives I'd sent him which he'd used. I decided perhaps he wasn't such a jerk after all.

The spare bedroom was ready for Nabil, Soliman's brother, who arrived the next day. At the airport a mustached man with brown eyes waved at me, pointing to my sign with his name. He asked about Soliman while we waited at the baggage claim. The whole family in the village was under surveillance now that word had leaked out Soliman was in Lebanon. "Some of the little kids in the family overheard grownups and told their friends. Their friends' parents talk and word gets around. The Israelis infiltrate everything. They listen. It's easy for them. Don't worry."

He explained how the Israelis were now trying to prevent any anti-war marches, claiming the war was supposed to bring peace to Galilee. "But what do they expect?" Nabil asked. "They are killing our relatives who are stuck in Lebanon."

Despite my reservations, Nabil proved to be different than his brother. He was chatty and loved to talk politics. Since his wife was to join him in a few weeks, he rented the apartment above us. It was a surprise to hear more family news from him, "Mustapha, another brother, is coming to stay with us. He wants to go to college here. Soliman has arranged everything."

"What do you mean—another brother? Arranged everything?" I scoffed in anger. "Whom does he think supports us? Now his brother's tuition too?"

"What do you mean, doesn't Soliman work and have a job? He

said not to worry about money," Nabil clarified.

"Soliman has a few work study hours at the computer center which offsets some minor charges in the graduate school. My full-time job pays the bills, his tuition and anything else. When is this brother supposed to arrive?" My fury unlocked at this point visualizing Soliman languishing in Miss Daxon's empathetic embrace, but my gritted teeth held back what I was thinking.

"In time for the school year—the end of August," Nabil answered. "Well, nothing can change. He's already bought his ticket and our parents have told everyone. He's coming, like it or not."

"Are you going to work?"

"I have a scholarship and will arrange some work through work-study. You know with a student visa, we are not allowed to hold jobs. If we do and are discovered, we can be deported. It is not worth the risk since it is so hard to get here in the first place," he shook his head. "I have saved money, don't worry about me."

Worry about you? What about me? No one worried about me. Soliman conducted his life as if he were still living under the rules of a traditional village life. The trouble was, he married—announced or not—me, an American. My embrace of the political struggle of the Palestinian people did not mean the automatic embrace of every cultural and social rule that governed life in his village.

These conflicts were predictable since Soliman and I spent little time talking to each other. And then from my background, I had accepted the life script given me: to do more, never receive care or relief from work. We could not bridge cultural gaps because neither of us saw the need to cross the bridges. Soliman had no interest in them and I dared not provoke him by having an interest in them. But my anger simmered.

On the way to Jeanette's birthday party, I decided the time wasn't right to ask her my questions on how to deal with relatives. Besides, Michael Hout was coming and there was no need to discuss this in front of him.

"Hi, come on in, Liza," called Marion through the screen door.

Tonight she was dressed in a bright green sari. All the jewelry she wore jingled as she sashayed through the house. A woman, obviously her sister, entered the hallway, but in her long skirt and tunic sweater, she looked quite plain next to her sister's costume du jour.

After introductions, Lori, the sister, said, "Come on, let's go to the kitchen. Mom's in her office and has no idea about the party. She's actually angry; she thinks no one has remembered her birthday," laughed Lori. "Have you met Michael before?"

"No, but I've read his work. He's quite eloquent in his books about Palestine and orientalism."

"Don't tell him that. Like most big shot New York professors, he can be terribly arrogant, but around Mom he's a pussy cat. He's afraid of her. But, you'll like him, you'll see." Lori put a bowl in front of me with a knife and a bag of vegetables. "You make the salad."

"Okay." She had the same directive tone her mother had, but she closely resembled her father, too.

"I'll get it," called Marion from upstairs when the doorbell rang. She brought in Michael Hout cradling a dozen red roses.

"Is she here yet?" He asked, peering around. Marion waved him into the kitchen and took the flowers.

"Not yet. You sit over there out of the way," bossed Marion.

"Michael, this is Liza. She was with Dad in Beirut. She's Soliman's girl too," introduced Lori.

"So you were in Beirut? When did you get back? How is Professor Abu Jawad? Soliman's girl?" He fired off the questions then sat back on the barstool, hands clasped behind his head.

"Yes. Two weeks ago. As far as we know, everyone is alive, but since we can't contact them, it's anybody's guess."

The rhythm of Michael's voice plus his accent marked him as graduate of those elite schools favored by the Arab upper classes and his wavy dark hair and tortoise-shell glasses made him stand out in the crowd. Without thinking, I blurted, "You're much more handsome in person than on TV."

"Really?" he crooned, crossing his arms across his chest.

"Yes. I've been watching on these news shows and I must say, you are the only one to date that bothers to question the whole basis of the war and dispute the Israeli party line that everyone else seems to follow blindly." My eyes stayed on the cut vegetables.

"Well, that's my job. They all know my position and that's what I give them when they're inclined to give it air time, that is," he said. "So what's for supper?"

"The usual—humus, salad, lentil soup, rice, kebab, bread and birthday cake," said Marion, repositioning the scarf end of the sari across her shoulder with a sweep, all bells ringing.

"Sound's good. When does Jeanette come home?" he asked.

"In about half an hour. And help yourself to a drink, you know where it is." added Lori.

"Anyone else? Liza, have one with me," he urged smoothly.

"How can I resist? A small one, no ice please." Whew. If Refat was dangerous, Michael was treacherous. No one ever warned me about the seductive quality of Palestinian men.

By the time Jeanette walked through the front door, we had all hidden ourselves on the side in the dining room.

"Happy Birthday," we called in unison. The two grandchildren giggled at the commotion.

"Oh dear," she stopped. "All of you!" and then burst into tears.

We did our collective best to cheer her up. She had convinced herself that her husband was dead or dying—or worse yet, enjoying himself. All our efforts to cajole her into enjoying the evening seemed to backfire. She loved us for trying to lift her spirits, but maybe it was better to leave her alone. Perhaps that was how she coped with uncertainty.

"Sit with me, Liza. Have a coffee." Michael poured Turkish coffee into demitasse cups for Jeanette, me and himself.

"Now really, Michael, what is your sense of where this is all leading? You know it's a total disaster. It's all over now," said Jeanette, nervously smoking another cigarette with her coffee.

"It's not all over. That's ridiculous. As long as there are Palestinians, it is not over. What is over is the Palestinian presence as a state within a state. That is coming to an end even as we speak. And it should. The Israeli goal to destroy Palestinian nationalism is not going to be achieved. No matter how far the Palestinians are dispersed at the end of the fighting—which may yet continue for another month or so—and even though the expected dispersal will create new refugees, it will not crush our movement."

"But the destruction is so broad. How can you say that?" asked Jeanette.

"Sure, the Israelis are unleashing enormous military power, but in the process they will lose the moral basis which they have until now invoked for their colonial expansionist schemes. It will be a high priced bill they send to the U.S. government to pay, but it will not have bought them or the U.S. government what they wanted the most—the end of Palestinian national aspirations." Michael raised his cup to toast victory.

"What direction will the Palestinians have to take now?" My curiosity overcame my intention of keeping out of the fray.

"It's obvious we will have to focus on the only place Palestinians are still living on Palestinian lands. This should have been done from the start. That's the future."

"But be realistic, Michael. What future is that? We don't even know how this war is going to end. My husband may be dead even as we speak," Jeanette retorted ferociously.

"If I know him, he is quite safe, hunkered down with cronies sipping Black Label. Don't worry about him," Michael insisted.

"See, there, he is enjoying himself. You admit it." She angrily got up and walked out of the room.

"It's okay, Michael. Let her be." I swallowed the last bit of coffee. "It was so nice to meet you"

"Where are you going?" he asked. "It's early."

"Home. I have to be at the hospital early tomorrow."

"Hm. Well, till next time."

"Marion, Lori, thanks for everything." I hugged Jeanette who was pacing in the hallway. "Be strong."

"Oh, you know I'll just worry. It's just so awful. Good night dear." Jeanette shrugged and watched me leave.

By August, the war had escalated. The destruction by Israel of sovereign Lebanon together with its Christian Right parties neared completion. Even Michael Hout could not have predicted the immense scale of violence that consumed Lebanon and the Palestinians living there.

With no news of Soliman my letter to my South African friends Rita and Bo Rembutu remained unfinished. Their own struggle continued. Bo had been imprisoned for a few weeks, beaten for his alleged support of a student-run anti-apartheid protest rally at his university. He was never charged with any crime—sounded like the same treatment Palestinians suffered.

Writing to Rita about my extended in-law family would make her laugh. She had warned me about the danger of marrying an oldest son, for they become the next head of the family and so become the great provider for everything. "You will be secondary to the blood relatives' demands," she cautioned. "You, after all, are not kin, just a wife by marriage." I posted the letter on my way to Wilmette where a new crisis had developed.

"Hi, Marion, where is she?" No longer knocking on the door, I strode into the kitchen as if at home.

"On the porch. Maybe you can talk to her." Marion shook her head as she ground coffee beans to make fresh coffee.

"What triggered this whole thing?"

"Michael. He sent us a report from his sources about Ansar. She is convinced Dad is being held there. You talk to her. Maybe he is and maybe he isn't. But the thought is killing her." She placed three mugs of coffee on the tray.

Jeanette, sitting on the screened porch with her head curled over her knees, didn't look up but whispered a hello.

"Tell me what all this is about."

"You know. Ansar. Where else could he be? That's why we haven't heard from him or Soliman, too, for that matter." She stared out to the back yard.

"We have no reason to believe they are there or anywhere else in particular. Why are you so sure now?"

"Here is the report. See for yourself." She tossed it to me and then reached to light another cigarette. "It says right there—from the second day of the invasion they have rounded up all Palestinian males aged 15 to 60. First they demolished the refugee camps, then they bulldozed all the houses, dispersed the population and imprisoned the men. It's the Israeli pattern. And 9,000 people from Rashidiyeh were run out of the camp on the second day of the invasion. Where did those people go? Where have they been all summer?"

I read through the document which explained that the main purpose of international humanitarian organizations like the ICRC, the International Committee of the Red Cross, was to inspect prison camps to insure proper treatment and prevent torture and human rights violations. This had been agreed upon by the international community after World War II to prevent Nazi-like atrocities in concentration camps.

Unfortunately, the ICRC was denied access to Ansar, Israel's concentration camp in southern Lebanon holding an estimated 5,000 Palestinian prisoners. Lebanese prisoners were scattered in additional camps in atrocious conditions. The ICRC had repeatedly complained about Israel's delaying tactics and refusal to coöperate with their oversight at the various prison camps, but so far to no avail. When I was finished, I understood better why Jeanette was so upset, but really had nothing of comfort to say to her.

"You see why I am depressed? Where are all the human rights watch groups in America? My husband is an American citizen but because he was born Palestinian, he is expendable. What does that make my children? Are they expendable too? What is Michael doing? Can't he write something for the *New York Times*? Can't he call someone at the U.N.?"

"Michael is writing," I answered, "but one against a phalanx of expert lobbyists can't do much. Every resolution calling for the end to these Israeli attacks has been vetoed by the U.S.. There is absolute backing by the Reagan administration for the destruction of the Palestinian national movement."

Jeanette sipped some coffee, lit another cigarette and said, "I'll never see him again."

"Come now, you don't know that. He was in downtown Beirut—the Israelis aren't there."

Later I learned my statement might have been true for that moment—and I hope it gave Jeanette comfort—but a week later the Israelis did try to enter West Beirut by ground, but the fierce defense by the Palestinian and Lebanese Unified Forces actually inflicted 19 casualties on the Israelis. The Palestinians and Lebanese, defenseless against air and sea attack with no air force or navy, on the ground turned out to be formidable adversaries. Consequently, the Israelis abandoned ground fighting in Beirut and returned to the safer, for them, sea and air attacks. The Israelis, unable to enter West Beirut until after the PLO left, would eventually wreak an unimaginable revenge on their hapless neighbors.

I stayed with her for another hour before I had to leave to catch a flight to San Francisco—which was an umpteenth trip I had made to speak about the war. This had started when one of my uncles, a political science professor who taught at a college in Kentucky, had asked me to speak at his college. This enlightened and open-minded man's recognition of my activism and his courage at sponsoring me in presenting the Palestinian point of view remains one of my most cherished life-affirming moments.

To my surprise this was the first of other Americans who wanted to understand the competing claims to the land of Palestine. My uncle's sister-in-law called me one day. I had never met her, yet she lived only a half an hour away from me in a northwest Chicago suburb. A public health expert by career, she was an active person in her community and asked me to give a slide show of my work in Beirut and talk with her friends and neighbors about the war. So began my career on the speaker tour.

When the summer quarter ended Lina and Sally wanted to celebrate, but I demurred.

What's wrong?" Lina asked bluntly.

"It's just hard to party when all I can think about is the situation in Beirut. You two go on."

"We can listen one more time. It won't kill us to learn something. We just can't do much to help," Lina said as they dragged me along with them.

"I guess what is infuriating me is that a report on the news today said the Palestinians are holding Beirut hostage. It is a lie, but it's brilliant. The Israelis say Palestinian presence is what is causing the bombing of Lebanese neighborhoods."

"It's classic blame the victim," countered Lina, assuming her most professional therapist posture. "The Israelis launch the attacks and blame the damage to the Lebanese on the Palestinian refugees, who are fleeing the Israeli invasion of their homelands. The fact the Israelis invaded and are doing the bombing is not important when you blame the victim. It's no different from saying a girl was raped because she walked down the street alone, not because some bastard attacked her. The right to walk down a street, be you man or woman, is distorted to deflect criticism of the attacker."

I should have known my friends would understand my frustration. I continued, "It's all so misleading. After all, when the refugees were bombed out of their camps, what else could they do? Those who were not imprisoned went to the safety of West Beirut. The whole south is occupied by the Israeli army. There is a siege on the city, the water has been cut off, medical supplies are barred from entry and there's no electricity."

"This is all to put pressure on the PLO so they will leave," Sally commented quietly. "At least that's what I think. The Israelis are making it so bad in West Beirut the only way to stop their bombing is for the PLO to leave. So, you're right, Lina, blaming the victim is a great defense."

Despite their happy mood at wanting to celebrate the end of the quarter, I just couldn't get into the spirit, so when they decided to move the party to the Water Tower and shop, I decided they could do without my dragging spirit. My walk to the el through familiar scenery gave me a mindless time to get lost.

Chapter 12

On August 30 Sally's forecast came true as did Michael Hout's prediction of new refugees and additional dispersion. Chairman Arafat left Beirut for Tunis on the ship *Atlantis* with his fighters, PLO officers, the Palestinian medical teams of the Palestine Red Crescent Society and all other able bodied men—the women and children left behind. Reagan's envoy Philip Habib arranged U.S. assurances about protection of the civilian Palestinian population now left defenseless in a battered city and countryside.

Over the course of the summer, the Israeli invasion dispersed almost 400,000 Palestinian refugees from their camps to nothingness in the open terrain of Lebanon. Roughly 7,000 Palestinian men agonized in the squalor of the Ansar concentration camp alone, bringing the Red Cross's total to 15,000 imprisoned by the Israeli army. The estimate of Palestinian and Lebanese people killed was 19,085 with 6,775 killed in Beirut itself—84 percent of the casualties being civilian. The unknown dead, bulldozed during their camp's demolition or buried under the rubble of the collapsed city remained anyone's guess.

Approximately 300 Israeli soldiers died—all for peace in Galilee. When Arafat left, the defenseless civilian population was quickly surrounded by the Israeli army and their Lebanese allies who still had a taste for Palestinian blood. The American troops sent to protect the civilian population departed two weeks early, its mission un-fulfilled—Habib's U.S. assurances empty.

The light on my answering machine was flashing. I pushed the rewind and waited. "Hello, Miss Liza. This is Anwar at the travel agency. Soliman is coming home. He called today and will be coming Thursday on KLM. Please pick him up at the gate. Thank you."

Well then, he survived. Instead of happiness, I felt the collapse of my current freedom. I knew it would soon be a distant memory of a summertime fling to be recalled with nostalgia. Learning to drive the stick-shift VW would be interpreted as an aggressive move. It scared me to think of it. Did he have to know?

On Thursday, September 16, his brothers rushed to hug and kiss Soliman leaving me in the background. "How did you get here?" he asked, returning kisses to his brothers warmly, twice on each cheek plus two hugs. Third in line, he patted me on the back on the way to the baggage carousel. "Whose car did you bring?"

"The VW."

"Who drove?"

"Me. Your brothers don't have licenses yet."

"Oh, so you learned to drive a stick so you could use the car. Too good for the el now?" He laughed at his grand joke, but I felt the sting of his need to show authority in front of his brothers. It drained away any enthusiasm I'd had for his return.

Late on Friday, the phone rang. "Hello, Liza? This is Rick Chase," he began. Professor Abu Jawad had been right about him. We had become colleagues, linked through mutual participation in Palestinian activism and sharing information about the cause periodically, but little about ourselves.

"Oh, hi, how have you been. What's up?"

"Have you heard the news?" he asked.

"No, what?"

"Nader—you remember him from Beirut—just called with a horrendous story, going on right now, even as we speak, in Beirut," he paused to take a breath. "There's a massacre going on in Sabra and

Shatila refugee camp. No one can stop it."

"Why? Who's doing it?"

"The refugees who managed to escape went to Gaza Hospital and all report the same account identifying Israel and the Lebanese Phalangists. It seems on Thursday Israeli soldiers took up guard positions around the camps. Since technically they did not enter the camp itself, they're claiming immunity," he continued.

"What do you mean?"

"Since Thursday the Christian Phalangists and Israel's Haddad and his troops have entered Sabra and Shatila Camps by the truckload. The Israelis stand guard on the periphery letting them in so they can claim they saw nothing nor did anything inside the camp boundary—establishing that plausible deniability act they're famous for. Israeli officials are orchestrating this civilian massacre, but call it a 'mopping up' activity to scour out remaining terrorists," he explained.

"You're sure?"

"Yes. Nader said all the victims from the camps being treated by the medical workers are all women and children and are all suffering gunshot wounds."

"Of course they would have to be women and children, since the men were expelled. What next?"

"Remember, it's Friday night there. Nader told me no one can get into the area, the massacre is still going on. He and a few other reporters determined at least forty Israeli officers knew this very afternoon, Beirut time, that the massacre was still going on. The Palestinian women who managed to escape the camps pleaded with the Israeli officers to stop the massacre. The soldiers said they couldn't leave their guard posts and sent the women back to the camp." He fell silent.

"Rick, are you there?"

"Yeah, I am still here. Nader's Norwegian reporter friend tried to get into a camp but was blocked by a bulldozer with its scoop full of dead bodies."

"Can you go there? Will your paper send you to get the story? It is morally imperative to get the facts before the propaganda spin starts. Or can you work with Nader to get the story out. Be his link to the press here."

"No way to get there. Nader and I will work together. He will call later. Anyway, gotta keep the line open, just wanted you to know."

"Call any time."

Later that week, the opening lines of the first of his series of articles read, "On September 16th, with Israeli soldiers posting guard, the Israeli conspirators, Major Haddad's troops and the Christian Phalangist militia began a three-day massacre of the Palestinian civilians in Sabra and Shatila refugee camps. The slaughter, unabated, produced 2,000 dead."

Michael Hout had been right again. What did the Israelis have to show for the pricey military exercise? The machinations to invoke Israeli moral authority collapsed completely with the massacres of Palestinian civilians in unprotected refugee camps while the Palestinian movement survived, tattered and traumatized but still viable.

This shocking news made Soliman's arrival anticlimactic—and only aggravated his guilt about surviving the war at all. The aura of Miss Daxon—or rather my not being Miss Daxon—crowded out what little interpersonal space there was between us. My life cramped tighter—emotionally, intellectually and spatially with his younger brother Mustapha living with us.

Soon Soliman was the hero of the day. He spoke at local events set up by the Palestinian community eager to hear his eyewitness account. My efforts during the summer went unrecognized. My experience in Beirut's Akka Hospital emergency department and my summer activism were unheralded in his world where only one hero and one expert was allowed per household.

Soliman announced he was going to Boston for a conference the next week because everyone who had been in Beirut or had anything to do with it—medical relief workers, reporters and those sympathetic to the Palestinians—would be there for a collective catharsis. Everyone, that is, except myself.

Professor Abu Jawad arrived back safely a week after Soliman, delayed only due to a spontaneous visit he paid to his sister living in Jordan. He could not understand Soliman's position because the purpose was to energize everyone worn out by the long summer struggle for the next phase. "We are exhausted and the PLO sits in Tunis, separated from its constituents in and around Palestine. The key to our future lies in the West Bank and Gaza where we must reassert ourselves as a political force. You should be there for this."

Left out of the adventure, my isolation deepened. Soliman returned from his star-making conference invigorated and focused, but not toward his studies, which now seemed a ball and chain to him. The Fund claimed him, their showcase volunteer, full time. Every waking moment not spent at the Fund or at school, he spent in his brother's flat upstairs where he'd coo and cuddle with the newly arrived baby girl and gossip for hours with her mother, his sister-in-law. Around me they all spoke Arabic not feeling obliged to accommodate my presence. My refuge was reading or grading papers.

The cessation of outright war in Lebanon plus Soliman's presence brought an abrupt end to my action-packed summer. Besides I became totally engrossed at work. The question of Palestine remained a back-page issue but it had been dismissed from the media's center stage by fickle experts duped into thinking things had been settled. In the shadow of our household hero and with the movement momentarily adrift, my activist role petered out.

The next years gelled into a virtual maze of competing and parallel existences for me. Multiple layers of my life ran at different speeds, in a self-defensive mode to those around me. Instead of weaving an integrated life tapestry of harmonious but challenging threads and colors, my life became a compression of disparate events piled on top of each other—like a dense patternless fabric.

Jeanette facilitated my enrollment in the sociology department to begin doctoral study as my job required. Soliman insisted on buying a house and pressured me into borrowing $5,000 for the down payment from old family friends whom he shamelessly charmed and flattered. Having promised to pay it back in one year, I had another $500 in my monthly expenses.

Hard work satisfied my demon-pride and then I did not want to give up the Palestinian community and I still wrongly believed I needed Soliman for legitimacy. Besides, I kept thinking that around the next corner Soliman would become kinder, even appreciative. With a little more time and effort from me, I "offered it up."

In the meantime, our bills were paid and my studies progressed, thanks to what turned out to be a perfect second job for me at a psychiatric hospital on the night shift. Teaching by day, taking classes by afternoon, nursing on the night shift, I slept on the run. The protective shell of six uninterrupted hours of time available on each night shift while patients slept, allowed me to study and write sociology papers at the nurses' station for the next few years. No such protection existed for me at my house—occupied most of the time by the growing extended family of Soliman's brothers, wives, and new babies. Noise and clutter moved in along with them.

It remains a mystery to me what prompted Soliman, but one morning he announced he was ready to get married. To satisfy him, we had a small party. Sally and Lina were not invited because it seemed idiotic having already confessed to them this strange anomaly of marital status and I didn't want to taint them with the hypocritical festivities. The party served to elevate Soliman's status in the local Palestinian community.

Later I understood this was a necessary move if his ambition to be a formal leader was to be fulfilled. Married men were stable, secure, respectable—labels he coveted. Being publicly married gave me status in the community that long ago ceased to be important to me, but because my investment in Soliman was so deep, it was justified to recoup the small dividend my patience returned. Recast as a bona fide daughter-in-law of a family that knew no limits to the demands it placed on me, I was now granted the privilege of entertaining Soliman's parents who arrived for a four-month stay.

"Make some tea for them, hurry up," commanded Soliman who poked his head into the kitchen. "They are tired. And put the sweets on a tray and bring them in."

So began the first of many services rendered by me to his parents while his whole clan reveled in their presence or sat around as usual. "Here is some tea," I said, setting the tray on the coffee table. Soliman leaped to his feet to serve his parents—his mother first, then father. They nodded and smiled at me. At least they knew who made the tea.

This four-month siege on my life revolved around the wishes of Soliman's parents, who were actually very sweet people. The biggest problem was what to do with them in the daytime when everyone was at work. The sister-in-law and her baby daughter might have been the answer, but she did not want to spend time with them, regarding them as peasants, village dwellers, beneath her own urban, upscale family from a big city farther south in Palestine.

Someone devised a schedule to provide coverage during the work week. Some mornings I might sleep only for a few hours after an all-night shift since Soliman assured them they were free to wake me up anytime they needed anything. Being home-bound in a suburban community of Chicago stressed his parents who were used to the open air rambling of a village and the corresponding companionship of friends and neighbors available all day. Their isolation was reinforced by our own inability to communicate.

Soliman never varied his busy schedule and my sister-in-law used the napping schedule of the child to be unavailable. Mustapha, the younger brother, lounged as the perfect guest being totally undependable and indulged by his parents, who fawned over him, the pet child of their 14 children.

With no frame of reference I worked as hard as I could to be considered a good person and someone who could make it in their culture. While the macro geopolitical question of Palestine was clear to me, mundane Palestinian living was not—which made it easier for Soliman to exact from me terms, conditions, goods and money which he could never have gotten from a Palestinian wife who knew her rights and his limits in their culture and his family.

"I found another car," Soliman briefed me before going to sleep one night.

"Great, what kind?" My insistence that we get a cheap second-hand car for city use had been heard. Sometimes my night shift overlap meant the car wasn't home early enough for Soliman, causing no end of tirade.

"It's a brown VW bug. It needs some work but it can run," he explained.

That weekend a rust-tinged brown tin can pulled up in the drive way.

"So this is it?"

"Yeah, its engine is rough. The guy said it ran without oil for a few weeks. But now it has everything. Let's go for a spin." He started the car, which trembled and spurted into power.

"You'll get the knack. Don't worry."

"You really think this will hold up?" It chugged along, the gears shifting with effort, the motor grinding away. "Doesn't feel very reliable. You've paid the money?"

"Yeah, it's ours. It will be fine with a little more work," He assured me. "Here, you drive it."

We switched positions at the side of the road. With a slight jerk it eased into gear. I accelerated, holding tightly to the steering wheel to hold the car on track, resisting a severe pull to the right. "What's the matter with this car? Has it been knocked out of alignment? You expect me to drive a car that won't even go straight on its own?"

"I told you it needs work," spat Soliman. "We can drop it off today over at the Firestone place. They do all types of work there."

"We're half way there. Shall we drop it off now? We can take the el back home."

"No, go home. My brother can look at it and he and I will take it with the other car. You are not going anywhere are you? Don't you have to study or do laundry?" he asked.

"There's plenty to do, don't worry," I snapped. His jibes about my studying had increased as his interest in his own Ph.D. dwindled. In order to avoid another clash over my interfering with his business, I had found it easier just to write one more check for his tuition and hope he wouldn't squander his academic opportunity. This time again, to avoid his blistering wrath I gave in, "Sure, take the cars."

Although the car improved a little, it always pulled to the right. New tires, the work at Firestone plus the purchase price amounted to $2,000 of my hard-earned money, but I found liberation came with the second car even if it rode like an unwilling donkey.

Two weeks later, Soliman almost had an accident in the bug. "Help me," he called through the front screened door.

"What is it?"

"My leg, it just went out. Severe pain like an arrow and I couldn't push the clutch pedal at all so I drove from Howard Street in third gear." He winced.

"Where does it hurt?"

"My lower back," he pointed. He spoke to his parents, who were hysterical at seeing him lurched over in the chair in obvious pain. Everyone came at the big news of his illness for it was cultural to swarm en masse over a suffering individual to show how much they commiserated—and such attention is expected of relatives and friends. After two weeks of doctors' visits, tests and discussions, Soliman was diagnosed with a herniated disc, so a laminectomy, rehab and bed rest for him filled the next few weeks.

Strangely, he adopted a passive demeanor and was surprisingly scared by the whole experience. While he was hospitalized, nurses who knew me hovered around extending many kindnesses to us. Sally and Lina worried that I was being pushed to the breaking point since there was no reduction in my work schedule—cooking requirements plus caring for his parents—while attending to Soliman.

With my family's training, it was virtually impossible for me to ask for help or admit I couldn't handle it all alone. So I found myself trapped by Palestinian culture forces that no one interpreted for me and over-extended with the academic projects of my university job—which provided the health insurance and salary that supported our whole motley clan.

My friends began urging me to leave Soliman—something I was not ready to do. I wanted to succeed and overcome these challenges to show the doubting spectators of my life I wasn't a failure. My investment in Soliman at this point was too great, my belief in the dream too solid, so my suffering seemed noble. At least I felt alive.

Soliman recovered and went back to his normal schedule. His parents' lives merged into our general household routine until one day the festering irritations burst out. Coming into the house from work, I found my sister-in-law draped on the couch in my living room with her child and my in-laws in attendance surrounded by half-drunk cups of tea scattered on the coffee table. Cookie crumbs on the carpet formed a trail from the table to the child mushing them in her mouth. "Where is the bug car?" I asked. "I have a meeting at the health center in half an hour."

"Oh, it's gone. Our dear little brother-in-law Mustapha has it," my sister-in-law answered in saccharine tones.

"Why does he have it? Who said he could take it?"

"It's not your car," she laughed.

"It is my car," I asserted.

"You are wrong, Liza. It's not your car. It's his car." She smiled sarcastically and winked at our mother-in-law. "Didn't you know about it?"

"Know about what? It's not his car."

"Soliman gave him the car because his mother said it was not right he not have a car. All the brothers should have a car. That's all there is to it. So our dear baby brother-in-law picked up the car about an hour ago." She nodded to our mother-in-law. "See how happy she is. She has managed to arrange cars for her sons and can proudly gossip about that back home."

"You can't be serious. I paid for that car and worked extra weekend nights just to come up with the money. Soliman has no right to give it away. It's mine. I will get it back."

"You can't. There is no way this car will be given back to you. Forget it." Her advice was a prophecy.

When Soliman came home on time minutes later, I accosted him at the front door, "What do you mean giving my car to your brother?"

"Get away from me," he glowered, pushing me aside calling me a rude name. "Don't you ever question me or what I do. Is this any way to greet your husband?"

"Why you idiot," I rejoindered. "I worked for that car and I need it. Doesn't anything I do matter or count for you? Why do you do this to me? What more do you want from me? For heaven's sake, I have been killing myself since your parents got here?"

"If you don't like it here, there's the door. You are free to leave or stay. Makes no difference to me. And don't mention the car again." His hostile, contorted face sickened me.

"Then I'm taking your car now for a meeting."

He swore in Arabic. "Touch my car and you're dead. You can take the bus."

Rage carried me out the door. His mother crying at the spectacle disgusted me. She, like her son Soliman, had become used to milking their American cash cow. Heaven sent, a bus came within minutes, but a catastrophic aneurysm had torn in my soul that day which would extend slowly over time—painful, energy draining and ultimately fatal. The last rip was a few years off, but to live with this emotional aneurysm and contain its chronic pain, I juggled my existences: my academic job, my hospital job, graduate school, domestic household duties, Sally and Lina, the Palestinian ethnic community, my in-laws, Jeanette and Professor Abu Jawad.

I still needed them all, even the bad ones, even Soliman the worst one, a little while longer.

Chapter 13

So many lives changed after the war in Lebanon that summer of 1982. The political devastation had numbed our psyches, but our spirits were unable to relax lest we miss an opportunity to refocus and repair the damaged struggle to liberate Palestine. No other activity held as much meaning for us, nor did anything else seem more valuable. A survivor's guilt set in, making us desperate to prove we were even better activists in support of the Palestinian people wherever they lived. It was our duty.

Rick Chase called frequently with stories from Nader in Beirut, who refused to leave even for a few days rest. The struggle to survive by the women and children left in Lebanon grew more desperate. Nader wrote "The massacres at Sabra and Shatila Camps have left ghosts all over the city. The people are ridden with nightmares, lethargy or cry all day. Some sit all day in silence. So many children are orphaned or their only living relative is a father idling in forced exile in Tunis. Will they ever see their fathers again? Who will care for these children in the meantime? It could take years."

Soliman could not focus on anything but Palestine. To go to a movie tired him for he couldn't sit still. He never studied and finally took Incompletes in his courses, unconcerned that his tuition had to be paid (by me) to keep his student status active.

The initial euphoria from the conference that so elated Soliman and others soon gave way to bickering and personal attacks and power plays. Blame for the defeat in Lebanon spread liberally, tearing apart the PLO and inflaming the tortured relationship of the PLO to the rest of the Arab governments. Interference by some Arab governments compounded the ferocity of the internal Palestinian conflict about the future and how to get there in the wake of the Israeli invasion of Lebanon.

Abu Musa, the dissident member of Arafat's political party Fateh, and a few followers opposed Arafat's handling of the war and the postwar situation. While his criticisms had validity, it became clear his goal was to get rid of Arafat, not reform the policies of the Fateh political party. This stance angered the leaders of the other political parties who together form the PLO and who believed Arafat, as duly elected chairman of the PLO, was the legitimate leader. Any change would have to come from a democratic process, not by Abu Musa's threats and his rogue military strikes on Palestinian refugee camps with Syrian military backup, basically starting a civil war or attempting a palace coup.

As an American, it mattered little to me what Arafat's position was. He happened to head the Fateh political party and since that party had more seats in the Palestine National Council, their parliament, he led the PLO. Simple. The Palestinian people designated the PLO to represent them, but if the Palestinian people are cut from the equation, there is no PLO. It seemed to me an internal conflict within the PLO could easily destroy it so Abu Musa's gang could do what the Israelis failed to do in Lebanon. The struggle for the soul of the PLO and the future national aspirations, all were at stake.

My own life was becoming an extension of the turmoil rampant at the PLO. Soliman seemed daily to grow more hostile, angry and combative about everything. His parents' interference in my life seemed on a small scale no different than the Syrians trying to stir things up in the PLO. Whatever conflicts I had with Soliman, they were ours to deal with, not his parents', just as the PLO's internal conflicts were theirs to sort out, not the Syrians' through their agent

Abu Musa. The questions were the same: Who was in charge? Who could set the agenda? Unfortunately, the PLO emerged as master of its own fate much sooner than I did of my own.

The local Palestinian community mirrored the PLO as it floundered in its own political morass. Vicious expressions of the conflicts by people believed to be docile, good-natured friends became common. One night we were invited to a dinner party on the south side of Chicago by our friends, the Salehs.

"*Marhaba, Marhaba,* welcome, *Ahlan Wa Sahlan.*" Naseem Saleh always greeted us with flourishes, gestures and a sing-song *Ahlan Wa Sahlan.* His big smile always made me feel comfortable even though he was reticent about speaking English, preferring Arabic. Although he kept himself somewhat insulated from the American English-speaking world, his kids spoke excellent English and would sit telling me names of things in Arabic so, only eight and eleven years old, they were excellent Arabic teachers for me.

"*Marhaba,*" Soliman replied. Clear plastic cushion covers on the royal blue sofa squeaked as he sat down. Across the room Ahmad Farrah and Professor Abu Jawad squeaked with every reach for a cashew nut from the bowl on the polyurethane varnished driftwood coffee table.

The women were in the kitchen. I went in saying, "*Marhaba Farida,*" giving them all a kiss on each cheek.

"My, you're getting good at all these cultural niceties, my dear," commented Jeanette lighting a cigarette.

"How have you been, Liza?" Muna Farrah stirred the cauldron of bamia, okra and meat cooked in tomato sauce.

"Fine, and you?"

"Oh, so overworked. Ahmad's parents are in town. Tonight, thank Allah, they are visiting some other family. This is like a break for me." She poked Farida Saleh in the ribs who laughed.

"So you came here and you help with the cooking, some break. But at least we have Jeanette and Liza here, some fresh faces for us," replied Farida Saleh.

"Give me something to do," implored Jeanette. "Farida, have you gotten any farther on your master's degree?"

"Here, you can chop some parsley." She dumped three bunches onto a cutting board and handed her a knife. "Two classes left, then my thesis. I can finish this next academic year, but it is hard with the children and Naseem."

"Oh, yes," Jeanette agreed, "I wrote my dissertation between naps and feedings. And now I have grandchildren."

"How many?" asked Muna Farrah.

"Two. They are great fun." Jeanette chopped the parsley with precision and obvious experience. "Farida, are you making *knafeh* for dessert? Yours is the best, I believe."

"Yes, Naseem wants it and Professor Abu Jawad loves it, too. That's incentive enough," she laughed. "Have you ever had it, Liza?"

"Yes, It's made from filo dough filled with baked cheese, browned then smothered in attar syrup, right?"

"Bravo, exactly. I will teach you to make it some day," Farida said.

"Great."

"Think twice, Liza," Jeanette cautioned. "The more you know the more you will be expected to do." She obviously saw through Soliman's manipulative charm, but we didn't discuss him directly.

Steamy lentil soup filled the soup tureen. The rice and raisin stuffed leg of lamb covered a huge round platter. The plates of felafel, kibbi, and pickled turnips crowded around the bowls of humus, *baba ghannouj* and tabbouleh while the bread spilled out of two baskets. Small bowls of yogurt with cucumbers sat at each end of the table near spinach pies, and potatoes were wedged in any left-over space. Soon the lemon-tinged aroma of the stuffed grape leaves drifted like a siren's call to the men who sniffed first then wandered in. Their conversation ebbed as they gazed at the banquet table. With enough food for an army, Farida could use the leftovers for the next week.

The men sat at the table next to their wives, but their glowing compliments about the cuisine were not enough to forestall disaster. Our host started in, "After all Arafat did for us, how can he be treated like he is now, by dissident members of Fateh, his own political party," shrugged Naseem Saleh. "Pass the bread, please."

"Come now, Naseem, you can't mean that. He is so corrupt and in it for himself, he gets what he deserves. What do you mean all he did? Lebanon was a debacle for us." Ahmad Farrah tossed his fork onto his plate. He searched around the table. "What do you think, Professor Abu Jawad? You are one of his men."

"Habibi, dear friend, calm down. These lovely ladies have gone to a lot of trouble to fix this wonderful meal," soothed Professor Abu Jawad. "Arafat is not without fault, but neither is he the sole reason for our internal conflicts. You are right—he controls too much power and controls all the money, but he has been a master of diplomacy, getting the message of our struggle out to the world community. This is no small feat in the face of the U.S./Israeli axis."

"Let me speak to my brother, Ahmad," demanded Naseem Saleh. "Abu Musa and his crowd have every right to raise opposition to Arafat's policies, but he should do so within the structure of the PLO. That is what it is there for. No one believes all the political factions, whatever name you call them, will agree all the time—just like the Republicans and Democrats fight here in the States. But what they don't do is get additional military help from other governments to wage a civil war. It is all internal and nonviolent. So why did Abu Musa turn to Syria? He wanted Syria to finance his own private military machine with which to oust Arafat. And take over the control of the PLO. But he is a stupid lackey of the Syrians. They are the real enemy of the PLO. The Syrians will dump Abu Musa when they are through with him."

"Naseem, you are wrong about Abu Musa and the Syrians. They are stepping in to fill a vacuum of leadership, since Arafat is clearly not up to the job. What did his diplomacy bring us? Nothing? Our land? No, only more bombs." Ahmad Farrah sneered and cleared his throat. "Abu Musa calls for a return to armed struggle and we should consider this. Why should we give up our weapons when Israel doesn't? Or the U.S. for that matter? How else do we fight for our land?" Ahmad looked around at the table of troubled faces.

"So you are with Abu Musa, that traitor, that harlot?" roared Naseem Saleh. "Armed conflict you say? Whom is he killing? He was willing to slaughter additional Palestinian lives in Tripoli, to fight Arafat in al-Baddawi Camp with Syrian fighters giving him assistance. Even Libyans were helping him. Why are we killing ourselves in the refugee camps? The Syrians didn't put us there. The Israelis did. Did you forget who is our real enemy?"

"Harlot? Who is the harlot?" retorted Ahmad Farrah. "Arafat surrounds himself with limited, simpleminded loyalists who do nothing but serve him. All Abu Musa did was confront it. Why shouldn't he try and change the PLO?"

No one at the table moved. Such language in polite company was unheard of. A pall fell over the group. None of the women spoke—at least not yet.

"That is precisely the problem, you donkey," Naseem snapped. Abu Musa wants to change the whole PLO to suit himself and his Syrian, Libyan patrons. But he has no right to do that. He is a member of Fateh, the political party, and should have confronted changes with Arafat at their party level. The Popular Front for the Liberation of Palestine and the Popular Democratic Front for the Liberation of Palestine both agree that Abu Musa has valid points. But they also say his tactics are wrong. Civil wars in the camps? Don't you see that is wrong?" Naseem stopped long enough to gulp some water. "Furthermore, the two Popular Fronts coexist in a balance with Arafat. No one knows about Abu Musa. They don't trust him as a leader. They prefer Arafat, who no doubt will adapt because of this crisis."

"Soliman, you've said nothing. Don't you have an opinion?" Ahmad Farrar dabbed beads of sweat on his brow and fidgeted in his chair.

"You both have points but remember it was Israel who drove us out of Palestine and now Lebanon," he said.

"And Jordan? Who drove us out of Jordan?" challenged Naseem Saleh.

"The Jordanians," Soliman answered.

"But why?" pressed Naseem Saleh.

Soliman looked to Professor Abu Jawad who sighed and said, "You can all argue for the rest of the night. I came for a pleasant evening with friends. Look at what is happening here. This will kill us faster than any Israeli bomb. Discontent, suspicion, subterfuge will destroy our national movement," he glared at the men. "Now, it is quite true that Arafat has his faults. That's number one. However valid Abu Musa's complaints were, his methods were sorely lacking in sensitivity or patriotism. Further, with his broad swipe at the PLO, Abu Musa lost the chance to influence Arafat in a way that Arafat could save face changing the party, thereby changing the PLO. That's number two."

"But," interrupted Ahmad Farrah.

"No, let me finish." Professor Abu Jawad waved him off. His angry voice thickened. "It is so easy to insult one another. Now, number three as to Naseem's point: Who drove the Palestinians out of Jordan? King Hussein. Nothing threatens the hegemony of the Arab regimes more than the idea of a secular democratic state of Palestine. The PLO is literally a functioning state apparatus in exile. It scared King Hussein back in 1970 and it scares Syria, Libya and the rest of the Arab world now. If popular local elections were held, their populations would likely get rid of all the current leaders be they kings, presidents or pharaohs. And the idea that all religions can live together with full human rights threatens them even more since religion can't be used to coerce."

"But Lebanon," began Naseem Saleh.

"Wait. Lebanon had its own civil war break out precisely because it was not a secular democratic state. The PLO presents an alternative to the Arab world. The Lebanese Moslems and Christians who both supported Arafat see the benefit of a secular democratic state and wanted one in Lebanon." Professor Abu Jawad looked at Jeanette who shrugged.

"Excuse me, Professor Abu Jawad. Then would you see the role of Syria and Libya backing Abu Musa's dissident movement against Arafat as simply a method of those Arab regimes trying to get rid of the PLO too?" the question popped out of me and I dared not look at Soliman.

"Exactly. They are using Abu Musa to liquidate the PLO as a factor in the Arab world. They are not concerned with the Palestinian people and the denial of their rights but are merely protecting their own regimes against change," he smiled an approving smile at me.

Jeanette added as an aside to me, "As for the U.S., the Reagan plan is to reclassify Jordan as a state for Palestinians (note the twisted use of the terms) not a Palestinian State, since that plan erases any vestige of Palestinians as the indigenous population of Palestine. It invalidates any claim of human rights and self-determination and is another method by which the PLO can be eradicated. No need for a PLO if Jordan agrees to house the Palestinian people. I doubt the Jordanian people are very happy about this reclassification either."

"With all due respect Jeanette, you are an Arafat person, Professor Abu Jawad. It is true," said Ahmad Farrah.

"I am a Palestinian. That's number one. Number two, I support the legitimate representative of the Palestinian people, the PLO, currently lead by Yassir Arafat elected by the executive council which is made up of various parties. Number three, if in following the due process of the rules and regulations of the PLO a new chairman is elected, he will receive my support. But I will not subscribe to interference in the PLO's internal affairs by external agents or agencies of other governments. I am a Palestinian nationalist. I am my own man." Professor Abu Jawad stared at everyone around the table. "By the way, what sort of man are you, Ahmad?"

"Arafat has been in too long and should go. We will see," he huffed.

"Please eat. Let us not forget this was a party," urged Farida Saleh.

"Excuse me, but we are no longer hungry," said Ahmad Farrah pulling Muna to her feet.

"Come on, now, why are you leaving? Why can't we agree to disagree?" asked Soliman. "You'll miss the *knafeh*."

No one laughed at Soliman's attempt to lighten the mood.

"Another time. Thank you, Farida," said Ahmad Farrah moving toward the door. "Muna."

"I am sorry, Farida," whispered Muna as she hugged Farida good-bye. "I disagree with him but I don't dare say it here. You understand."

"Yes, I'll call you tomorrow." Farida turned toward the table, her eyes filled with tears. "Must you all be experts on everything? Doesn't friendship count? Should we start shooting each other here in La Grange?"

"Come, now, sit down," Naseem Saleh said.

The rest of us stayed because we didn't want to upset Farida Saleh anymore. Soliman tried valiant attempts at jokes, but they fell flat. The palpable rifts in Palestinian ranks were manifest in our own community. The chilling lack of direction disoriented us. The party broke up after the *knafeh,* and I had to endure the ride home in cold silence—Soliman's punishment for my raising a question.

The phone rang as we entered the door and Soliman grabbed it. His scowl relaxed and he hung up the phone. "Our young brother Mustapha is in the hospital. He totaled the car."

"Are you going there now?"

"No, he is not hurt much. I'll go in the morning. At least it was not his fault. The other guy had insurance so his medical bills will get paid."

A month later completely healed from minor injuries, Mustapha, the family pet, pulled into our driveway with a Chevy Citation.

"Hey, come look at my new car," he called.

"Where did you get this?"

"From the insurance company. My car was totaled. It was the other guy's fault. With the money I bought this new used car. Runs great, low mileage. New tires. Great, isn't' it?" His pride ran in front of him.

My bug, my hard-earned transportation, had been transformed into his new perfectly safe Citation. Did he even see the irony of it? He, just like Soliman, didn't have to. They didn't care.

The years progressed with constant management of my non-mixable spheres. Soliman's demands on me usually meant work. Hosting 50 people for cookouts in the back yard was not uncommon. His parents came to visit again for another killing four-month stay. My sister-in-law had two more incorrigible baby girls.

Soliman's new full-time salaried job with the Fund meant travel which suited him. His world revolved around cultivating support for educational and health care institutions in the West Bank and Gaza, but his graduate studies were abandoned. My course-by-course progress toward a Ph.D. brought only ridicule from him. He taunted me with dismissive jokes or outright accusations of intellectual snobbery. But with my self-esteem problems, I could hardly think of myself as a threat to him. It also helped me cope to believe Soliman was more deeply involved in Palestinian politics than he let on.

Often a woman would call and ask for him. When he wasn't there she would hang up. She never left a name. She never left a number for him to call back. I never thought about it, but years later I finally met his blonde Swedish lover in Cairo.

My greatest joy came from our friendship with Jeanette and Professor Abu Jawad. Their kindness and mentoring knew no limit for me. Their graduate courses in urban sociology and political science outshone all the rest. The chronic fatigue of multiple jobs and midnight-shift work discouraged much activism on my part, but something in me had passed the point of no return.

The familiarity of my negative routine provided me with structure and motion to get through each day. The ratio of the pain in staying versus the pain in leaving remained even for a long time. But by 1987 the ratio began shifting. I saw my existence as a dichotomy—the world of Palestine vs. the world of everything else. I couldn't live without Palestine because I didn't know how. Believing that it was a zero sum game, I endured Soliman, whom I did not love or respect, for Palestine, which I did.

PART VI – CHICAGO/PALESTINE 1987-1988

Chapter 14

"Hello. Hello." The overseas phone line crackled.

"Hello, Hala, this is Liza calling from Chicago. Happy New Year!" It was not quite a yell into the phone. "How is Athens?"

"Ah, Liza, Habibti, dear sweetie. Happy New Year to you. Fine. Athens is fine. How kind of you to call. I loved your last letter."

The lilt in her accent never failed to make me smile. An unexpected outcome of the otherwise miserable 1982 war in Lebanon was our friendship. Hala remained for some time in Beirut, a leading figure for the Palestine Red Crescent Society. When Dr. Fathi Arafat, the president and all his male directors, managers, physicians and nurses were forced to leave with the rest of the male population, Hala, as director for public relations, became the most senior member of the PRCS executive committee on site. Her leadership rallied the remaining physicians, nurses and staff of the PRCS system—for the most part all women.

Thus had the women's era emerged in the aftermath of the invasion. Women provided direction and support to the hospitals and clinics—what was left of them—and the refugee population at large. The men only slowly began to make their way back during the next five years. The otherwise joyful return sputtered in an uneasy tension as the men expected the women to relinquish their new roles and hand the power back to them willingly.

The women changed because they had to, but the men had not. Their reality, suspended in Tunisian time framed by the past, reconnected to a future of ill fitting, unwanted roles. Who could know who suffered the most—the men forced into camps, sitting idle and powerless, or the women left behind who buried the smelly rotting bodies in the camps, foraged for food to feed their children, cleaned floors in clinics and camp latrines and kept the community viable? A useless debate—everyone suffered.

Hala never complained in her letters to me of the meetings she convened, the floors she swept or the toilets she cleaned. Her loyalty to PRCS President Dr. Fathi remained absolute yet she was fiercely independent and did not hesitate to disagree with him. Her life represented the antithesis of the stereotyped subservient, Moslem Arab woman. She was a role model for all modern progressive women, principled to the core. I needed her help this New Year's Day, 1987.

"It's so good to hear your voice. Are you busy?" My heart raced with anxiety.

"Not at all. What's wrong, Liza? It's in your voice."

"I hate to tell you this, but I didn't know whom else to call."

"What is the matter?"

"Oh, everything is all right, don't worry, it is just that I wondered if you knew where Soliman was? He left for Jordan, he wouldn't say exactly, about two weeks ago and there has been no word from him since."

"He hasn't called you at all?"

"No, usually he never calls, but last night was New Year's Eve. I stayed home in case he would call and he didn't. You might have seen him or heard about him since he is doing some project for Dr. Fathi and the PRCS."

"Well, first, he is all right. I saw him three nights ago here in Athens. Now today he is in Cairo. That is all. Darling, Liza, do not worry about him. He will be home soon." Her words sounded kind to me although her message sliced at my heart like a saber. No, it couldn't be my heart that hurt—it must be my pride.

"Well, that's good news. Please, Hala, do not tell anyone I called looking for him. Especially Soliman because he will be so angry. I thought he would call because of the holiday."

"No, it was right that you called me, your friend. You are dear to me. He is wrong not to call you. What is his problem? Leaving you wondering like this? Now, don't worry. I will not say anything." Her assurance was gold to me.

"Thank you so much, Hala. Sorry to bother you. I will write soon and send the material on nursing curriculum you wanted."

"Fine. Looking forward to your letter and the material. Liza, do not feel ashamed to confide in me. I am your big sister. We must help each other. It is not an easy world and Soliman is not an easy man. I can see how he acts and he is not the best Palestinian on the personal level. But don't worry, Habibti. Eh?"

"Thank you so, so much, Hala. Also, regards to your sister and mother. Take care. Good-bye."

"You're welcome. Good-bye for now. 'Bye." She hung up.

What an insensitive jerk. I stayed home on New Year's Eve thinking he'd call. Where was he? Athens? No, Cairo probably. Alone? Surely not. Having fun? Absolutely. How much more to take? Not much. My courses will be finished soon. A year of field work to do. Not much longer. Just stay busy and forget about him. Who cares where he goes as long as he doesn't bother me too much. Hope his girlfriend will keep him busy. Why does he still hurt me? Why does it still hurt? Maybe that is the only feeling left.

The last letter from Rita and Bo Rembutu in South Africa lay on the coffee table. Rita was pregnant and Bo worried about the tension near the village where they lived. The state security forces at his university had been increased, inciting more resentment, fueling an already volatile situation. They worried about the pregnancy since miscarriages were common in areas of poverty and war. Tear gas bombs could precipitate early labor with fatal consequences— whether from the chemical mist or the terror itself no one was sure. Whether exploded in the West Bank, Gaza or South Africa, bombs produced the same results. Bo worried because as he said, "We are making some progress, keeping up the pressure on the apartheid regime. The violence always gets worse just before the breakthrough. But our leader Nelson Mandela is certain and steady. He is a leader for all time, for all people."

They asked about Soliman, but he had been peripheral in our friendship and they were really more my friends than his. Soliman had not written or talked to them since we had left Washington, DC years before. What an interesting thought. Was this burst of insight the first sign of fraying on the rope of dependency that Soliman had used to lasso me for years of dutiful, unquestioning service?

The latest bulletin from the Israeli League for Human and Civil Rights sat on the table. Bo should read it to give him hope. If some Israeli human rights activists were willing to document the abuse endured by the Palestinians in direct confrontation with their own government, then perhaps some equally enlightened white South Africans would be able to do the same. Perhaps their opposition would help Bo's human rights struggle. I mailed it the next day.

Soon came a message blinking on the answering machine. Soliman ended the message with a hesitant, contrite "I love you." That was the first time he had ever said it to me. Somehow, hearing it on an answering machine, from a call no doubt prompted by the direct but discreet rebuke supplied by Hala meant nothing. Too little, too late. Far past emotion. Far past response. My indifference and disdain only frayed the rotting rope faster.

Silence was my motto now. I drove him home from the airport with no question or comment—and he didn't mind. He'd brought me a few presents as he always did—the usual *jalabiya,* the long dress, a snake-skin purse or a necklace—bribes meant to humor me, to make me think there was a relationship. Maybe this was the way he showed love, not by words, but by presents. Respect was more important to me, but that was the gift he would never give.

Other wives existed in a world of respect from Palestinian husbands. These Arab men were kind and helpful to their wives and played with the children. Being Arab or Palestinian wasn't the problem since I knew too many men whose lives directly contradicted the stereotyped sexist, belligerent Arab male. Cross- cultural marriages could be rich and profound. They required work to succeed like any marriage, but you had to want to do the work. In theory you liked the person you married. A false premise lay at the base of our marriage and I was party to it, as guilty as Soliman.

Farida Saleh told me once she would walk out on her husband if he dared swear in front of her. The thought that he would swear at her was unthinkable for her. No need to tell her that most of the Arabic I picked up from Soliman was curse and swear words, mostly aimed at me.

Jeanette told Professor Abu Jawad that she wanted to interview for a new faculty position. The four of us were having a glass of wine before dinner one night.

"Go right ahead, wherever you want," he said.

"You mean you would move for her?" I asked.

"Of course, why not? She is entitled to pursue her career. Politics can be done from anywhere and I am not too shabby either as a scholar. Jeanette's work is important and she deserves the best." He threw a wink and intimate smile to Jeanette and she nodded with a half smile in return. "It's an issue of respect, Liza. Respect is the finest gift we can give each other."

Soliman remained quiet with sullen concentration. Thick-skinned and insulated, his shell protected him from any criticism or introspection. Besides, he would do what he wanted since he considered external opinion to be an intrusion into his personal business. His world was no one else's business. My hope had been that we'd be like the Abu Jawads, but our different paths were rapidly approaching a crossroads—and a crisis.

With little direction from the Palestinian leadership abroad, the stateside Palestinians tried to fill the void with local diplomacy. Encounter groups became the rage as Palestinians sought out American Jews interested in Palestinian rights. Soliman had been going to one in Chicago for a year—a group consisting of wealthy, well-connected Jewish socialites, businessmen and a few human rights groups participants. Some professional conflict resolution technicians would attend to manipulate the discussion and keep it peaceful.

Soliman never discussed his encounter group with me, but Farida Saleh did. Attending as a representative of the Palestine Women's Council of Chicago, hers could never truly confront the core issue—that the Jews were an occupying power inflicting enormous misery on the Palestinian people even while this dialogue was going on in the encounter group. No one wanted to confront the fact that Israel was responsible for the creation of millions of refugees and the acquisition of their homeland. The professionals restricted the topics for fear of upsetting the Jewish participants.

"So what's the point?" I asked.

"To diffuse the issues or, better yet, confuse everyone," she answered. "It's a way for the Israelis through their American network of supporters to discover the soft spots and figure out how many concessions Palestinians might make for limited peace or limited settlement." Since statehood and human rights were not evident goals, Farida finally got disgusted at the strictures on the conversation and quit the group fuming because while these encounter groups met, the stories of exhausted lives tyrannized from Israeli occupation played on and on, the same story over and over.

The sun radiated heat even if the air breathed cool. The brisk morning air condensed hot breath into puffs of mist. School children dressed in wool sweaters shed them in the warmed-up afternoon and knotted them around their waists for the walk home. By late afternoon the sun dropped low in the winter sky. After a day's work of manual labor, the tired pensive faces of the men who form Israel's cheap labor, a secondary work force, watched the landscape of their homeland—ruled by their employer/occupier—rush by from the windows of their cramped stuffy minivans. Like regimented herds, they were transported from the occupied Gaza Strip to Israel proper where the menial and unskilled labor needs of the Israeli economy were met by Palestinians. Pauperized by the colonial settlement of their land, brutalized by the military occupation, tormented by various regulations and rules—but no rule of law—these men eke out an existence to support their families—just to do what men do: work.

I gleaned this scenario from Rick Chase's most recent draft essay about the Palestinian labor force. It interested me but since it was pushing midnight, I decided to read the rest in the morning. It was strange being home at midnight instead of at the hospital, so it took a bit of effort to fall asleep. The night, stricken with dreams plagued with uncertainty, eventually turned to day. Fatigue followed too as my eyes resisted the light of morning.

"Hey, did you see what happened in Gaza yesterday?" Soliman was already downstairs drinking morning coffee when a TV news program broadcast a report from Gaza. The footage showed swarming mourners holding up wooden coffins, wailing women, Israeli soldiers outfitted in riot gear.

"According to our sources, a minivan filled with workers returning home to Gaza Strip from their jobs inside Israel was rammed by an Israeli army truck. Witnesses say the army vehicle approached the minivan, sped up and hit the minivan straight on. Four Palestinian workers are dead with nine injured. The Israeli authorities initially gave no response. Today they issued a statement that the incident was an accident. This did not answer the questions of the Palestinian families or their community as 3,000 angry mourners attended the funerals held early this morning. According to our latest reports, the funeral turned violent as Israeli soldiers tried to disperse the crowd of mourners. Palestinians threw stones at the soldiers who opened fire on the crowd, killing two and wounding 30 more. We will keep you updated on this story. And now, let's take a look at the nation's weather map, today December 13, 1987."

And so began what was soon labeled the *Intifada.*

"This is only the beginning," Soliman called back to me.

"Why do you say that?"

"Just read your boyfriend's essay. It will tell you why. It's good." Before I could protest that Rick was merely a friend, he had slammed the front door saying, "You take the el."

With Rick Chase's article stuffed into my brief case, I was at the office an hour later, my door closed, when someone knocked. "Hi, what are you doing so secretively? Your door is never shut," inquired Lina.

"Reading a story draft from Rick Chase in light of the news today. Want some coffee?" The percolator hissed as if on cue.

"What news?" asked Lina pouring a mug of coffee.

"Some Palestinians were killed in Gaza yesterday on their way home from work. Whether the deaths were intentional or accidental, some 3,000 people turned out for the funerals and more violence erupted. Soldiers opened fire on the crowd, killing a couple more."

"Really, you'd think in this day and age people would have figured out that prolonged abuse leads to anger. At some point anger gets expressed and those 3,000 mourners are angry. It reminds me of the civil rights movement. One day, and you never know when, but it's just not okay anymore to sit at the back of the bus. All it takes is one harsh incident too many to shatter the balance of oppressed and oppressor." Lina leaned back in the chair blowing steam off the mug.

"You are quite insightful for someone who claims not to like politics."

"What is the phrase, the personal is political? Like it or not we cannot escape it. What else did Rick write?"

"He writes about the settlements. Hundreds of Jewish settlements have been built in Arab land now housing Israelis or Jewish immigrants from anywhere in the world. They are armed and have government authority to open fire on any Palestinian they perceive as a threat."

"So that essentially means shoot first, ask questions later?" asked Lina.

"There are incidents of fatal shootings out of fear, no Palestinian believes there could be an accident anymore. There is total lack of faith at this point because settlers want to get rid of the Palestinian population," I said.

"How does the government confiscate land for settlers if someone already owns it?" Lina asked with a frown on her face.

"Rick describes how the Israeli government takes Arab land invoking military occupation law in the West Bank and Gaza. Military law can justify taking fields from farmers for military security. If military law doesn't quite fit the situation, the government invokes an old British law dating to the time of the British Mandate. Any house built without a permit can be demolished. A hundred-year-old house in a village more than 500 years old surely has no permit. If there is no permit from the Mandate era either, too bad. The house gets blown up, the family displaced, the land now belongs to the government."

"How can there be more than one law?"

"Nothing between Israel and Palestine is fixed—not the borders, the national status, nor a legal system. That suits the Israelis fine. Rick writes since they invoke multiple laws of several legal systems with new laws constantly added, the Palestinians never feel relaxed. They never know when a normal activity suddenly becomes a crime punishable by prison, house demolition or land confiscation."

"Rick Chase has done a lot of work. This is quite a story don't you think?" asked Lina.

"It is a dense work, a great document, but what major newspaper would print it? It's too critical. Maybe *The Reader*."

"They might, but that has a very limited readership. Outside of urban leftist Chicagoans, who would even see it?" Lina pointed out.

Later that afternoon, the melodramatic end of Rick's article, that I read while the el train stopped midway between two stations for an unknown reason, foreshadowed a future that should have surprised no one. The Palestinian people cannot absorb much more oppression regardless of the type or source. They are the proverbial camels waiting for the last straw to land on their backs, yet even though it will fall eventually, it is unlikely to break their backs.

The deaths of the workers returning home in a minivan and the violence wreaked on those who came to mourn them was the catalyst that, as Michael Hout would later write, would launch one of the greatest anti-colonial insurrections of the modern period. Within days, this insurrection's name, *Intifada*, was heard around the world. Uprising. Soliman had been right.

It was just the beginning.

Chapter 15

In the spring of 1988 Dr. Fathi Arafat called me after the start of the *Intifada* to ask if I would be willing to make a health and social assessment of conditions in the West Bank for him. Soliman arranged the travel with great irritation—since he was not included—but he could hardly refuse Dr. Fathi's orders. So two weeks later I anxiously flew into Tel Aviv, apprehensive about my first encounter with Israelis on their colonial turf.

Scanning the people holding signs with names, I finally found my name on a white cardboard held by a stately woman coiffed with an elegant chignon, wearing graded pearls. Madam Randah I had been told would be awaiting me.

"Hello, Madam Randah?"

"*Marhaba,* Madam Liza. Did you have any trouble getting through?" She gave me a slight motherly hug.

"Not at all. It is so lovely to meet you."

"Come, let us be on our way. My son is waiting with the car. You must be tired. We will also eat as it is lunch soon. Are you hungry?" She hustled me to the car park.

"*Marhaba*, Madam Liza. I am Hani." Her son's manner surprised me, his accent wispy light. Tall, olive skinned, black hair and a handsome square face. "All right, everybody in, let's go." We sped off to their home.

"We are going to our home where you will stay. We'll have lunch, then you can take your rest. With the curfew we cannot take a little tour as I had hoped," said Madam Randah.

Their home was near Jerusalem—an hour-and-a-half away in Ramallah, once a small village on the outskirts of Jerusalem which had grown to be a town. We rode in silence watching the pretty countryside go by. Trees, hills, some sheep. This was home to an ancient indigenous people, now dispossessed.

The land and the Palestinian people knew each other, nurtured each other with the intimacy of lovers in a timeless relationship. Ripped from their homelands, the Native American knew what this amputation felt like, as did American Blacks who kept trying to explain to white folks their wrenching collective legacy of rupture from African land and ancestral lives. My job was to capture for my PRCS report the current events of the Palestinians as they tried to halt the encroachment on their culture, their land, their lives in order to survive.

Madam Randah pointed to a stone and brick building at the intersection where we stopped. "That is my school, rather, the school where I teach. It was started years ago by some missionaries but they are long gone. A local committee runs it now. The language of instruction is English. We still have a few English teachers from Britain but most of the staff now is Palestinian."

"So that is where Hani learned his British English."

"Yes," he said, "but I do love American slang. Perhaps you can teach me some of the latest. You are from Chicago, right?"

"Yes."

"Still gangsters there? And Eliot Ness?"

"No. We try to be more respectable now, with completely modern criminals. You need to stop watching old movies."

"Hand me your passport please," instructed Hani, his tone changed, the easiness gone. "We are approaching a checkpoint. "

He stopped the car. A young tanned Israeli soldier leaned over the window and grunted something. Hani handed him my passport and their papers.

"American?" said the soldier peering at me.

He handed the papers back to Hani and waved us through.

"You know, Liza, I would love just one day, just once in my life to drive somewhere without being stopped, without having papers examined, without worrying some soldier is having a bad day and might hurt me, just once. To me, freedom, self-determination, human rights are not words. They are actions such as driving to the store, going to school, going to church, or attending the mosque without fear or interruption. When that happens, Palestine will exist and I will be happy for the first day in my life."

"Come now, Hani, you are being dramatic for our guest," commented his mother.

"But you agree with him?"

"Actually, yes. Freedom is not a document. Nor a signing ceremony. It's having small enjoyable things, like a party in the evening and not worrying about curfews. Freedom to forget your purse at home and not worry you will be jailed at a checkpoint because you can't identify yourself. Freedom is enjoying the despair of having too much to choose from, not the resignation of having no choice at all." Madam Randah stared out the window.

"Mother, did you read that in a book? It's not bad," teased Hani. "We take ourselves so seriously all the time. It is as oppressive as the Israelis."

"Hani, stop joking. Madam Liza has just arrived. We don't want to scare her or bore her."

"Madam Randah, on the contrary, you must help me to make an accurate report on the *Intifada* and what you are doing with it."

"Oh, my dear, tomorrow you will get a full view of everything. Don't worry. We know you are here at the request of Dr. Fathi. We understand," she said. "Here we are. Welcome, *ahlan wa sahlan*."

Thankfully, Madam Randah did not invite friends for lunch, so our own getting-acquainted proceeded without extra commotion. Dr. Kamal, her husband, joined us just before we sat down. His manner reminded me of Professor Abu Jawad, but his hair was not yet as gray. Their house seemed familiar too, decorated with Palestine tapestries, brass and copper tables, plus Oriental carpets. The house had been built 100 years ago on Dr. Kamal's family land which they'd owned for at least 400 years.

"How do you do, Madam Liza? In my experience, if you can stay awake until early evening on your first day, you will adjust quickly from jet lag. Isn't that so, my dear?" He smiled at Madam Randah as she placed a platter of *malowbi* on the table. The steamy aroma of onions, cumin and garlic was familiar.

"Do you know this dish?" asked Hani.

"Yes, but with eggplant on top of the rice and chicken instead of cauliflower."

"Not many Americans are familiar with our Palestinian cuisine. Your husband must be very proud of you," observed Dr. Kamal.

"Anything new at the university, Father?" asked Hani.

"Not today. The students are spending more time on organizing for *Intifada* than their studies. The Israelis will close all schools soon, from elementary to university in retaliation."

"What will happen to all the school-age children?"

"We will teach them at home, in the neighborhoods, anywhere. Madam Liza, education does not depend on a building. Teachers can instruct anywhere. We will manage," replied Madam Randah.

"Yes, mother, but be realistic. If all education is shut down for years, we lose time—and we won't have formal certificates or degrees. That affects our job chances. Not everyone runs a home-based school as well as you. In the poor areas, nothing happens. The kids just run wild. All they get is street education from radical fundamentalists, violence and prison. It is a disaster for us when the Israelis close the schools." Hani looked to his father.

"Actually, Hani is right. Without schools, children do not learn discipline, respect for authority, the social skills of play and negotiation. They are not exposed to Palestinian literature, poetry or music, nor that of any other culture. A hostile, restless youth is produced, possessing no marketable skills with no future other than more military occupation and the Israeli plan to dispose of us." Dr. Kamal picked up the basket of bread. "Would you like some more bread?"

"Thank you, no. I've eaten more than enough. It was a great meal," I replied.

After lunch the conversation continued in their cool and shaded front room. They all seemed eager to explain what was happening.

"You know, Madam Liza, some of us believe Israel wants to produce this hostile youth population to use as a self-fulfilling prophecy," remarked Hani. "I am two courses from finishing my Master's degree in engineering. If the university closes, how long will I have to wait for those two courses?"

"I don't understand."

"Well, it makes me angry to wait for two courses just because the Israelis want to demonstrate their power over us. When lots of poor and disenfranchised people organize themselves, their individual anger merges into a societal one. That predisposes them to messages of revenge, hate and violence—so they can strike back at the Israelis. The Palestinians are then labeled as racists with no one paying attention to the fact that they are merely reacting to the severity of their occupation."

"Hm."

"The Israelis and their world supporters throw up their hands and rant about how the Arabs hate them justifying their need to establish their own security through repressive brutal occupation." Hani stopped to sip some water. "In my case, I am angry. I might throw a stone at a soldier who is armed with an Uzi, grenades and who knows what else. But he can shoot me dead or jail me without charge for months at a time. So the Israelis need an angry, hostile Palestine to justify strutting around like a macho nation of Rambos."

"Indeed, the whole identity and psyche of the Israelis are threatened by peace with the Arab neighbors and with Palestinians. If they have no external enemy to fight, they will have to look at themselves. What would they see? Descendants of European settler colonialists, who brutally robbed a people of their human rights and homeland. It's not a pretty picture," added Madam Randah who had just entered with a tray of coffee and cookies.

"Surprisingly, the Israelis have actually promoted the Islamic fundamentalism they so noisily claim to abhor. It is another constructed foe because poverty and despair are the two conditions that can seed any fundamentalist reactionary ideology," Dr. Kamal commented as he handed me a demitasse cup of very strong coffee.

"How does the *Intifada* affect you, or does it?" I asked.

"Let's face it, the *Intifada* is not just an incident but a way of life. It is a refusal by our people to continue to be less human for the convenience of others. *Intifada* is our claim to the right to resist occupation. You'll see all around you this new spirit of resolve and self-reliance tomorrow. Our words today cannot convey its profound importance to us," suggested Madam Randah.

"I think you have a saying, 'I'm mad as a hornet and am not going to take it anymore.' That's *Intifada*," said Hani with a laugh.

"Clever. It does capture the message."

As she picked up the empty coffee cups, Madam Randah said, "Madam Liza, don't let us keep you if you would like to rest. I know it's been a long day for you."

She was right. Even though I tried to stay awake, my system was closing down and a short time later, sleep swept over me. It was only seven, but my body acted as if it were midnight. Then about midnight, my jet-lagged restlessness woke me. The moonlight slit a path through the dark house toward the salon.

"Madam Liza, out here." My shadow detected, Hani waved for me to come stand by the window.

"Look at the stars. They are spectacular tonight," he said without turning to me.

"You like stars?"

"I want to be an astronaut for NASA. But it is impossible." He shrugged still staring out at space.

"Why?"

"Don't you understand? I am Palestinian, majoring in engineering, but now I may not finish for years. The universities are being closed tomorrow."

"How did you find out?"

"There are ways," he said.

"Are you part of the Unified National Command of the Uprising?" He was the right age for the popular leadership committee, a generation younger than the one currently running the PLO. Although coördinating with the PLO, the Unified National Command held gold-standard legitimacy with the people as it orchestrated the day-to-day demonstrations and strikes of resistance, the soul of *Intifada*.

"You ask a question like that," he laughed. "It must never be known who are the leaders. We are all the leaders. Every man, woman and child is a leader. We are everywhere. Every house is the headquarters. But I will tell you this. I want to be an astronaut and one day will be accepted in the astronaut-training program. That's all I want, the opportunity to try. That is what we are fighting for. Opportunities to try, just like everyone else."

"*Inshallah*, God willing."

"We'll have a busy day tomorrow. I worry about my mother because she is stubborn and does not hesitate to confront the soldiers. You'll see," he said. "Good night."

"Good night." Crawling back into bed, I forced my jet-lagged body to lie still so sleep could once more come.

The sun rose quickly. We finished a light breakfast before half past seven.

"Where are you going today?" asked Dr. Kamal.

"Just a general tour. We'll start at the Kalandia camp to see the co-op and the women's industries and then pass by some schools. Of course, it will depend on the situation, now that the universities have been closed indefinitely," said Madam Randah.

"Mother, remember there is a strike and curfew today. Shops will be open only two hours. We must be careful to grocery shop only during the open hours," cautioned Hani.

"Curfew, by the Israelis?"

"No, by the Unified Command. This is our curfew. This is *Intifada*. Since the universities have just been closed, we don't want the angry students out demonstrating without some plan. We want our people to stay in today, to sort of cool off. No need for more casualties. And today, you see, we also have a strike."

"A strike?"

"Yes, a strike. Israel depends on us for cheap goods, for cheap labor and as a market for their manufactured goods. If we don't open our shops, we don't sell the Israeli goods we are forced to carry. So their produce rots, their juice goes bad, their milk sours because we refuse to open our shops and sell. Simple and effective. It hits them where it hurts, at their economy." Hani smiled with confidence. "And it is nonviolent. No loss of life unless the Israelis shoot us—which they do for any reason. We are trying the methods of Gandhi and Martin Luther King—the freedom fighters."

"So some of the restrictions you have now are self-imposed?"

"Sure. We know the situation will get worse. We must preserve our own limited resources of food, water, oil, gas and the rest. We consume much less of everything when we impose a curfew on our people." Hani stood up and walked to the window. "It is not easy. The Israelis have stepped up the number of checkpoints. If any paper is out of order, or on any pretext, they will arrest you. And they're more outrageous. If you respond to their insults, they will accuse you of aggression. Again, arrest."

"Let us go now. We want to be at the market when it opens," said Madam Randah. "Dr. Kamal, what will you do?"

"Since my office has been closed, I'll read or work on my research. Maybe cook you a surprise," he said.

"Shookran, thank you. We'll see you soon," she answered.

We got into the worn Subaru, but Dr. Kamal's remark that he might cook a surprise for his wife stuck like a broken record. I simply could no longer regard Soliman's tireless rudeness as cultural, but rather a function of his own warped ideas of how to treat a wife. Too many Palestinian men contradicted his pattern. My eyes, the window to a soul darkened by shutters of denial, slowly began to loosen enough to let bright cracks of reality bring dawn to me.

The day turned out to be long, hot and dusty. There seemed to be interminable queues of cars at checkpoints where we sat, windows open, hot dust swirling around us. "We will be very deliberate in our drive. Mother, you have the *koufiya* ready?" Hani asked.

"Yes, here under the seat. Just tell me when you want it."

After we were waved through a checkpoint by an Israeli soldier, Hani asked his mother to place the *koufiya* visibly on the dashboard and then answered my unspoken question. "Since we have imposed a curfew, it is dangerous for our car to be out. The black-and-white-checked *koufiya,* our historic Palestinian head scarf, signals to Palestinians on watch to enforce our curfew that the car is Palestinian with permission to be out. We stuff it back under the seat when we approach an Israeli checkpoint, of course."

"Do we have permission to be out?"

"Yes, of course. Your movements had to be cleared by the Unified Command. Otherwise, we would never dare to break the curfew." Hani glanced in the rear-view mirror.

"I'll go this way to stop and see a family. Do you mind, Mother, if we take a detour? It will only be half an hour." He smiled an "I am in charge" smile to her.

"If it is only half an hour. We can walk around the village. It will be good for Madam Liza to see a village," she replied.

The car lurched off the paved road onto a bumpy dirt path. Hani wound his way up the small hill to the village. A primary health care sign hung next to the UNRWA logo on a small building. "That is a U.N. public health station," confirmed Madam Randah.

Hani stopped the car outside a stone-and-cement brick house and we got out to the delight of a group of children who immediately gathered around. Madam Randah greeted them but shooed them away as we walked down the main path. Her black low-heeled pumps somehow seemed incongruous on these grimy walking paths of the camp.

"The smell in the air?"

"That's from the latrines and open sewers. The Israelis refuse to allow any housing improvements even in these centuries-old villages. Denying permits for plumbing is one of their harassment tactics. A bit silly, don't you think? How on earth would a proper toilet and bathroom in a Palestinian village threaten Israel's security?" She waved to a woman peering out of her window.

"Why are these women sitting on the steps of their houses?"

"I don't know. Let's ask them," she answered. She greeted them politely and asked what was going on. Soon all four of the women were shouting and pointing to the lock on the door. One of them sat down weeping.

Madam Randah finally turned to me and exclaimed, "Madam Liza, this is a story for your report. According to this lady, her ten-year-old son was out past the Israeli nighttime curfew searching for one of their new kittens in the field. His cat had kittens a few weeks ago and the boy was enthralled with caring for them. The mother didn't know he was out, thinking he was at a neighbor's home. The Israelis found the young lad but did not believe his story. He resisted, calling them names, throwing dust in their faces. The soldiers beat him and took him to prison where he remains. The next day the soldiers appeared and told the woman to get all her children outside the house. While they stood there, the soldiers took a lock and wire and welded the lock shut, explaining that since she could not keep her son in the house, she didn't deserve to live in it at all. If she tried to break the lock and enter her house, she would never see her son again."

"Where is her husband?"

"He is in Kuwait working. He sends money back home to support the family, as many men do. He doesn't know anything about this." Madam Randah spoke again to the woman. "It only happened a few days ago. I'll have to get in touch with the human rights lawyers," she said. "They have an office in Ramallah, but they can barely keep up with the caseload."

"What will happen to the rest of the family? All of them locked out? For a ten-year-old child's search for a kitten?"

"She and the children are staying with relatives next door. We must get the boy out somehow and have the house reopened with a wire cutter not a bulldozer." She sighed, "I'll tell Hani. Perhaps he can arrange some quick intervention." She spoke to the women who nodded in understanding at her plan. As we left they all said thank you over and over again to Madam Randah.

"Hani is important, isn't he?"

"Yes. He is a very good son. He wants to be an astronaut. *Inshallah*, some day."

We turned to walk back toward the car. Hani waved to us. He listened intently to the story and nodded. "Don't worry. Now, to Kalandia Camp."

Although it was only three kilometers away, it took another 45 minutes of stop and go through checkpoints. "Checkpoints are multiplying as the *Intifada* intensifies and solidifies. We are able to initiate collective action almost immediately 24 hours a day," boasted Hani.

"What is your most effective resistance tool?"

"Not following the orders of our Israeli occupiers. We civilians fight the Israeli army any way we can," he said. "Sometimes we march in demonstrations to demand human rights. Or we throw stones at armed Israeli soldiers when they taunt us or prevent us from exercising our basic human rights—like standing with friends on a street corner to tell a joke or gossip."

"The soldiers stop you for that?"

"Yeah. They are authorized to open fire at will with live ammunition. A fair fight?" he snorted, "We exercise our right to go to church or the mosque but expect to be tear gassed while praying. With *Intifada* we refuse to live in fear anymore."

"But those actions hardly seem serious enough to provoke the wrath of the Israelis to shut down schools—which seems a severe punishment in my estimation."

"You're right. The most effective weapons of the *Intifada* are our strikes. We now refuse to sell Israeli goods or produce and we buy little else because our shops are closed most of the day so the income and sales taxes Israel imposed on us has dropped. Also, we strike from our jobs. Almost 200,000 wage laborers stay at home from work in Israel. Without them Israeli agricultural and industrial production has fallen way off."

Madam Randah added, "The strikes have proven that Israel's colonial structured economy can't function without a scared, hopeless colonial labor force. So they close the schools and enforce curfews to prevent any further organized resistance especially by the youth. We are not impressed by their violent measures anymore. We simply refuse to be victims."

"You see, Madam Liza, the *Intifada* was not just a spontaneous eruption—although it seemed like that at the beginning. Many events had set the conditions for it," said Hani.

"Like what? The minivan incident in Gaza?"

"No, I think it was actually a collection of failures and misplaced trust—the war in Lebanon, the internal fighting of Abu Musa and Syria's attempt to control the PLO, the willingness of Jordan to cut a deal so Palestine would not exist, the arrogance of the Egyptians who felt they could somehow engineer a peace process for us, but without us and even forget us at the signing ceremony at Camp David." Hani turned around for an instant and stared at me. "And then all those plans, the Reagan Plan, the shuttle diplomacy, all meant to erase us from existence. You know what we learned?"

"No, what?" I knew I was being set up to ask that question, but wanted this private political science lesson from a future astronaut to continue.

"We learned as Palestinians that no one was going to give us our homeland back. We were wrong to expect other Arab countries struggling to achieve their own national aspirations would also make our cause their priority. No one was going to sacrifice or fight on our behalf and then give our homeland back to us on a silver platter. Only we, the Palestinians still living on Palestinian land, could get it back. Only we could rescue ourselves. The lifeboats are our own actions, our demonstrations, our strikes. All the PLO diplomacy in the past two decades didn't do it. So you see the time was right for action from the grassroots level—the refugee camps in West Bank and Gaza and the villages."

"That was some speech. Professor Abu Jawad said awhile back that grassroots organizations and the youth held Palestine's future."

Of course, what Hani neglected to point out was that their strikes from work—although noble and politically necessary—sent families into abysmal poverty, leaving them utterly vulnerable. For the *Intifada* to succeed, to bring social change, the Palestinian communities worldwide would have to start to support them financially for many more months to come.

"We're here. This is Kalandia Camp," announced Hani, turning the car sharply to the left and stopping. The camp's narrow entrance was framed with sand-filled oil barrels stacked on top of each other, three barrels high. Barbed wire cascaded over the top and down the sides. An Israeli soldier approached the car. Hani spoke to him. The soldier waved us through.

"Imagine having to ask permission to enter a refugee camp of your own people," he said.

"Don't you think they are more worried now since the *Intifada*? If you close the schools, there's nothing to do. Now everyone will put all their energy into thinking up ways to resist. Why doesn't it dawn on them their security would be enhanced by good relations with the Palestinians and the Arabs?" I asked.

Hani steered the lurching car along the narrow potholed path into the refugee camp while Madam Randah answered, "It is useful for them to play the role of victim. Then you never have to take responsibility for your own actions or decide what you truly believe. I don't understand them, but could live with them as a neighbor. If only they would award us the same respect they keep demanding from us. We are quite willing to recognize the Israeli people and the existence of their country if only they would do us the same courtesy. They must recognize my people, the Palestinians, and our right to a country on what is left of our own land of Palestine. It is clear we must both share. Only then will there be peace."

"This camp was formed in 1967 by people from villages destroyed in the surrounding area. It is typical," added Hani. "There are the usual open sewers, little potable water, abject poverty and dense crowding."

"The women organized themselves long ago into a clothing co-op to produce and sell items in the camp too expensive to buy on the outside. With *Intifada* they have become one of the chief sources for clothes in West Bank. This is their workshop," pointed out Madam Randah.

Hani turned the car down another path and parked.

"*Marhaba*," called Madam Randah to the woman standing on the stairway.

"*Marhaba*," she replied. The two women embraced and kissed each other's cheeks. They waved at me to follow.

"Mother, I am going to follow up that lost kitten case from the village. I'll be here though by the time you are finished," Hani said.

"Be careful, Hani," admonished his mother. Turning to me, she continued, "This is the main workshop," nodding to the eight women sitting at sewing machines. The long fluorescent light tubes drained their faces of color but their brightness prevented eyestrain during the long hours of sewing. Most smiled, one waved a casual salute.

Two vintage treadle Singer sewing machines decorated with quaint gold filigree thumped and pumped in contrast to the whir of the antique electrified machines. Piles of fabric, sorted by cloth and weight formed rainbow towers leaning up against the wall. Several stuffed baskets overflowed with garment patterns. The small windows, high on the wall, captured small breezes while two floor-stand fans circulated the tepid air throughout the workroom.

"Tell me about these women."

"They are mothers who live in this camp. Two have husbands working in the Gulf. Three have husbands currently in Israeli prisons, detained without charge, who have been there at least a year. Two others have husbands who work in day labor in Israel but now stay home because of the *Intifada* strikes. The youngest is a widow. Rubber bullets shot during a demonstration paralyzed her husband from the neck down. He died a month later from complications and infection. She is due to have their first baby next month."

"The other women have children?"

"Yes, but I don't remember how old or how many they all have. These women support not only their immediate families, but also their extended families of grandparents, aunts, uncles and related children," she said. "Come, let us proceed to the embroidery center."

Madam Randah's stylish pumps led us into another room, similarly equipped with fluorescent tubes and humming fans. Six women sat around a folding card table heaped with embroidery threads. Thimbles, scissors, needles, wooden embroidery hoops of all sizes filled a large flat basket usually used to carry bread.

"*Marhaba*," Madam Randah greeted the women.

"*Marhaba*," replied the chorus.

"Liza, these women are embroidering dresses, shawls, purses and decorative hangings using the ancient traditional colors and designs of the Palestinian people. The designs embroidered on either white or black, cotton or wool signify your hometown. Small villages would use that of the dominant city closest to it and these patterns have remained essentially unchanged for centuries. Since traditional designs tend to be geometric, lately some innovators have tried to weave floral designs in with the old ones." Madam Randah picked up a finished piece.

"That is beautiful."

"Yes, this is one of the more modern designs, but I prefer the traditional authentic ones," she said.

"Granted, but don't you think it is still authentically Palestinian if a Palestinian designs a modern pattern?"

"You know, I never thought of it that way. We must not get so stuck on the past we forget to live in the present. Smart girl," she laughed.

We examined some finished pillows. The black shawls, embroidered with tomato red borders were edged with long, black fringes dangling with elegance. They could have been from Madam Khadijah's shop in Fakhani Camp. "Do these women make much money from this work?"

"Yes, if they sell several large pieces they can make a year's income. We sell them in specialty shops in Jordan, Egypt and a few places in Europe. Unfortunately, no one in the U.S. is willing to carry these. For some reason they question how something this beautiful can be made by a Palestinian." she explained.

"Your cynicism is showing."

"My fatigue is showing. How many more years do we have to endure this life? We are tired of it and are ready to share Palestine with the Jews. Let's just get on with it. Truly, Liza, I cannot understand what is so threatening about us. The PLO renounced everything it can. We have accepted our fate that part of Palestine is now Israel. We want to live in peace. I want my son to be an astronaut, not a refugee, not a soldier, not a prisoner, not dead."

"It is difficult for Americans to think positively about Arabs and Palestinians. Arab is synonymous with terrorist. Palestinians are called grasshoppers and cockroaches by the leaders of Israel. Americans hear that and think it must be true since no one official from our government contradicts them."

"Well, at least we are now known to exist. Golda Meir went around for years telling the world that Palestinians didn't even exist, that the land was empty and she had no clue about hundreds of thousands of refugees." Madam Randah laughed. "Imagine, this housewife from Milwaukee, Wisconsin, telling the world that I, Madam Randah, and my family do not exist. Leave politics aside.

Don't you think it is the most outrageous statement you ever heard? How could the world choose to believe her? Did no one see the refugee camps filled with suffering people driven from their homes in Palestine? The refugees came from somewhere. It is absurd."

There was no rational answer to this ludicrous question. Never answer an irrational question with a rational answer, Lina reminded me whenever my frustration rose at the gross illogic of the question of Palestine. How did it become a question in the first place? I thought the 20th century had brought us to a new era where human rights and self-determination were our new American gospel.

"Let's move on to another section," directed Madam Randah who thanked the women. "Now here, we have knitting."

This room was much larger, but it had the same lights, fans and windows. Instead of fabric here were heaps of yarn sorted on the tables. Three industrial size electric knitting machines were operated by six women who switched off the various tasks. Completed sweaters, cardigans or pullovers were folded and labeled in the corner.

"This shop supplies many villages and camps with sweaters, scarves, hats and gloves in all sizes and colors. Our winters are cold and damp. Remember we don't have central heating in our homes so it is as cold inside as it is outside," reminded Madam Randah.

"Where did the machines come from?"

"One was donated and two were bought with grant money from a development project. We could use one more, but I have resisted buying one outright hoping for another donation." Madam Randah picked up a yellow pullover. "Why don't you take this for Dr. Soliman. Perhaps he will get us our fourth knitting machine."

"Perhaps. You are clever."

"We should go. Hani is worried about getting to the shops for groceries. If we go later, there is usually nothing left," she said.

We said good-bye for a third time. The sunlight stung my eyes as we stepped back outside. "There's Hani," said his mother. "See those children around him?"

"Yes."

"They are his science club. He meets once a week with them to give some extra help in science and math. They study the stars, of course, Hani's passion." She walked toward the car.

"Hi, ready to go?" he asked.

"Yes, we must hurry," said Madam Randah.

"Hani, what makes you so interested in stars and in space?"

"Because the sky is free and belongs to no one and to all of us," he answered with a grim look on his face.

We drove down the narrow path passing all these stateless refugees in their own homeland. The camp geography, the smell, the sounds were similar yet different from the camps in Lebanon. Historic catastrophe profoundly haunted these camps. By standing on their rooftops, residents could see past a grove of centuries-old olive trees to the remains of their village—only a few hundred yards away, but now separated by a lifetime of barbed wire fencing.

The drive to the market was interrupted with many more checkpoints. Israeli soldiers snapped at Hani when he presented our papers. The number of checkpoints had grown since the announcement that schools and universities were to be closed indefinitely. Denying youth a place to meet did not mean they wouldn't meet together, but it required a net of Israeli soldiers densely spread to keep even a modicum of peace and order. This was such a classic colonial stance to order soldiers of war to keep peace among the natives by using violence and repression.

Two hours later we arrived at Madam Randah's house and carried in the plastic sacks of groceries. Living every day with the restrictions, whether from the Israelis or self-imposed, meant finding creative alternatives for a lot of the daily chores of life.

I finally asked, "Hani, do you ever get bored with the occupation and the constant fuss with the Israelis? Is the occupation the all-consuming topic of conversation?"

"Actually, yes. Nothing is more boring than the incessant discussion of this horrible act or that unfair situation. My studies save me, taking me away, in my head that is. With the stars you can go so far away from this tragic place, it's sort of a transcendental vacation." He took a deep breath. "But, Liza, beyond the routine violence, unfairness and misery, this is a fight over our existence as a people. If we don't struggle and resist being erased from the world of societies, what then? The ancient and beautiful culture of Palestine's indigenous people will not even be a memory. It won't be a category in an encyclopedia, it won't be a flag in a hall of nations."

"I don't quite understand your last statement."

"The Israelis don't want just to take our land or control our cheap labor, they want to erase us completely as a people. They want to rewrite history and write us out of it. That's what originated their lie about 'a land without people for a people without a land'. What about the centuries we've been here in Palestine? So, yes, it's tedious, but it's a necessary routine if our society is to escape oblivion. All it takes is one small child shot in the chest for throwing stones or, as you saw today, jail for a child searching for a pet, to remind us how precarious our life actually is. Can you understand?"

"Of course. Only I've never talked to a Palestinian who grew up in Palestine and stayed here."

"Well, I, too, someday want to leave—for NASA—but that may never happen," he replied.

"That must be hard to live with."

"It is my fate being born Palestinian. Something great will come of it."

The next day ended my stay with Madam Randah and her family. Hani insisted on driving me to Jerusalem alone. He assured his mother and father he would be all right since on the way to Jerusalem he would have me in the car and on the way back his cousin Dina was coming for a visit. It was commonly believed that a young man was less likely to be picked up or roughed up by the Israelis if a woman or girl was with him. After a warm good-bye, we took off toward Jerusalem.

The American Colony Hotel could have been a movie set—old, historic, pink stucco, grand Palladian windows, an interior tiled courtyard with tables under umbrellas, large sweeping palm trees and ferns. Omar Sharif could have flung open the door, strode onto the patio, robes flowing, romance just an Arab stallion away.

"Here we are." Hani lifted my bag out of the car. "You'll be picked up tomorrow morning by Dr. Ali who will take you on the tour of *Intifada* health-care operations. Oh, a warning."

"What's that?"

"This hotel is known for two things—reporters and spies. It's sometimes hard to tell the difference. There are all nationalities of them trying to get the latest scoop on whatever. Many angles are played here. Talk to no one—at least don't say what you're doing."

"Thanks, Hani. Good luck."

"Thanks, *Inshallah*, we will meet again. Be careful." He got in and waved jauntily out the window as he sped down the hill toward downtown Jerusalem.

Checking in was easy. My room on the third floor had a view of the local houses and trees, not the panoramic view of Jerusalem usually seen on holy cards or calendars. I drank a lemonade and ate a salad in the courtyard. Unlucky me—two elderly women from Georgia joined my table. They were not reporters or spies.

"We're Christians, you see. We have come to see the Holy Land," the chubby one with pink jowls said.

"Yes, to see the holy places. And you know the Jews here have done such a nice job fixing up the place," the other continued. She sported a motionless bouffant hairdo, freeze-dried with hair spray.

"You are right, those Arabs are, well, so dirty. If you see a poor person here, you know right away they're Arab." The chubby one dived into a huge chocolate sundae, shivering at the cold concoction.

"They beg from you at the market. So impolite." The breeze could not dislodge one hair from her helmet.

"I hope we see some Muslims, although I am not sure what they look like. Who are the Muslims? My daughter told me to get a picture of a Muslim. Have you ever seen one?" asked the chubby one.

"If you'll excuse me. Enjoy your dessert." I stood up and left.

Flopping into the easy chair near the window of my room brought no respite as my chest filled with anguish. How can this be? How clueless can Christians be who go to Palestine, the Holy Land, yet remain so ignorant about the Palestinian people and then be so bigoted about Arabs in general? Why don't they know there are Christians, descendants from the time of Christ, living here–the Christian Palestinians? These women would listen and believe what their ministers said. Why were they totally uniformed? And complete racists to boot. No wonder I felt isolated from my own people.

Tours of the Holy Land can make enormous money for churches or travel agencies. How many include a stop at a refugee camp to witness to God's poorest, most maligned, most suffering children in Israel? Children of God's own Holy Land are instead erased from the collective, authoritative knowledge of what goes on here, replaced with myths spun by an historically recent colonial group composed originally of Western European Jews, later American Jews, now called Israelis.

Christians and Moslems have learned to live as neighbors and friends in the Holy Land. Why wouldn't a minister of Christ question the repression of both groups by the Israelis who now control the tourist places in Christ's homeland? It was all too selective. Selective ideologies to assuage the fear of strangers, one group to another. Selective human rights. Whose side is God on? I sought refuge in my private spiritual cave, curled up in the chair, alone.

Chapter 16

"Good morning, *Marhaba*, Madam Liza," greeted Dr. Ali.

"*Marhaba*, how are you?"

"Let's go. We have many places to go today. There is no *Intifada* curfew so we can move around better than yesterday, although there could be a clash with the Israelis over the closure of the university. There may be a student demonstration today or they may go to the universities to demand they be reopened." He opened the car door for me. "Please." Short, stocky with a large mustache, he seemed to be irritated at having to escort me.

Our first stop was the Medical Relief Association office, small and crowded with health literature in English and Arabic, a few cartons of U.N. or WHO materials spilled onto a table. Dr. Ali spoke with a young woman for a few moments and then explained to me, "This is a classroom where we train community health personnel whose work is very critical during curfews when no one can move. So we decentralize both our operations and knowledge and spread it around for all to use. Circumstances prevent doctors and nurses getting to patients at hospitals or at home, so we rely on community workers for primary health care interventions."

He went on to describe the same decentralization and training of local workers that Rita directed in South Africa. If people cannot come to an office or clinic, the health care worker must go to the people. Education built self-reliance and strength. The visit was soon ended and he said, "Let's go." Whipping the car down the hill, he went on, "We are going to the walled Old City of Jerusalem where Christian Palestinian families live."

"Someone is sick?"

"We are collecting blood for typing since the Israelis do not allow us to build a blood bank. For normal surgery at the hospital a patient must bring relatives or friends at the same time for us to collect the amount of blood we need for the surgery on the spot."

"You are typing the communities so you can build a data base?"

"Right. Instead of waiting until the last moment and being unsure of getting what the patient needs, we can directly contact people and ask them to come give blood. It is a voluntary program, but most see it as a patriotic duty," he explained.

Dr. Ali parked the car near the YMCA building across from the Palestine Pottery Company and then we walked down the street to the Damascus Gate, an arched entrance to the Old City located in Arab East Jerusalem. Descending several flights of steps to an open plaza, we were surrounded by Israeli soldiers decked out like models for a Jane's Weapons Publications. They were perched only on high spots where they keep an eye on all movement. A few pairs of soldiers were in the plaza watching Palestinians shop for vegetables. Old women were sitting on the ground, their wares spread out on cloths beside them. Palestinians went about the routine of living while oblivious tour groups followed their guides' pennants on a search to find the holy buildings of their God.

We waded through the clog of those buying zucchinis and grape leaves by the main archway. Dr. Ali led me up a staircase that curved up and around to a second level platform. There we knocked on a heavy arched wooden door, old as Palestine. It opened slowly, only after Dr. Ali yelled through it, "It's Dr. Ali."

"*Marhaba,*" a young woman smiled and gestured to us to enter.

"*Marhaba,*" he replied and then quickly explained my presence. He talked briefly and then drew blood. I looked around the two-room flat; an old stove, a sink and a three-quarter size refrigerator crowded in one corner of the first room. A heavy brocade drape, pulled back and secured with a worn tasseled rope exposed the bedroom beyond where I could see four beds squeezed in between two large armoires. A bathroom was tucked inside an interior corner. Despite the glamorized notion of living in the Old City, this flat was dark, damp and crowded—perfect place to incubate pneumonia or TB.

"Yes, we watch for all kinds of infectious diseases around here," was his answer to my question as we made our way to the next door on his list. This routine kept up for the next two hours. By that time, Dr. Ali had finally warmed up to me. Despite his professionalism he regarded me as another gawking foreigner, not worth the investment. I recalled Maria El Asmar and her description of one-visit guests—those you meet but don't invest in. Dr. Ali probably considered me not much more than a data collector. He didn't know I would have moved in a minute to work in Palestine, but Soliman never seemed so inclined—which I found a huge disappointment. At least by the time we were through that afternoon Dr. Ali was letting me carry the case with the blood samples.

"That's it. Now some stops at a few hospitals."

"Good."

"I decided the best thing for you to do was to see a normal day for me. Medical procedures you know; it is our situation that makes providing health care so different. Our limited resources and out-of-date equipment strain our efforts to provide quality care, especially in hospitals. You'll see." He guided me back out from under Damascus Gate. I never did see the holy places, the shrines and the churches which the Christian tours advertise. Nor did I bother to go to the Haram Al Sharif—the third holiest place for Moslems. God wouldn't be there. For me, God exists in damp tiny flats or on the mats where old women watch grandchildren and sell their harvest, in the women's co-op at the refugee camp, in a science club for school-aged children locked out of their learning establishments or in a four-story walk-up in Chicago. God is out and about, present and visible if you bother to see.

Intifada demonstrations could erupt at anytime and anywhere, some well-planned, many spontaneous. Absorbed in discussion about the purpose of our next home visit, we slowly became aware of crowd noise.

"Stay still and near me. Do as I say," ordered Dr. Ali.

University-age youth had gathered in the street ahead, some chanting but most throwing stones into the green clusters of Israeli soldiers maneuvering toward them. Those soldiers nearest the crowd showered them with bullet sprays—their faces no older than the students they shot. A few faces shirked in distaste as they fired; many more gazed methodically ahead wearing "just doing my job" masks.

Screams burst out as the mayhem escalated. People ran every direction—some toward the injured students—reenacting for me the familiar photo of our own Kent State massacre only here Israeli soldiers were gunning down unarmed students protesting their rights to go to school.

"Come on Liza, we must get to the students. First we'll get across the street to the car. Then we'll drive back down and load as many wounded as we can. Ready?"

"Ready."

We dodged the zones of assault where Israeli soldiers were beating the students with billy clubs. Rabid vengeance reddened the faces of the soldiers as they beat a student cold. These attacks were man-to-man, not mediated by the speed of a jet or blip on a computer insulating them from their victims like the Israeli pilots in Lebanon. Passing close enough to hear their terrified cries of pain, we couldn't help the students being beaten. They were already arrested, now to face the well-documented torture, endemic in Israeli prisons, which often killed those beaten the most badly on the street.

Dr. Ali signaled to students bent over a bleeding man that he was bringing his car. They nodded, keeping pressure on the hemorrhaging holes. It seemed forever, but it was only a few minutes later that we got the car and drove back down to the demonstration.

Tear gas saturated the air with noxious fumes. The stink of rage and terror mixed with odors of splayed tissue, burns, sweat and fear. Someone squeezed three bleeding men and a writhing woman into the subcompact Fiat. Dr. Ali drove to the nearest Palestinian hospital, Makassed. He never stopped talking calmly to his shattered passengers in the soothing rhythm of the language my husband told me it was not necessary to learn.

The soldiers kept firing into the crowd, even after the students began to disperse. How do they rationalize shooting civilians at point-blank range or clubbing them unconscious? Who convinced them Palestinians were animals, grasshoppers, cockroaches? Perhaps at an inquiry, conducted to assuage the revulsion of foreign onlookers or foreign financiers with delicate sensitivities, the soldiers would answer, "I was just following orders." The sorrowful irony is lost on them that their own history rejects such an empty excuse for inhuman behavior perpetrated by soldiers on unarmed civilians.

Bigotry and racism rationalized under claims of national security interest serve only the interests of a tiny nexus of powerful elite. This was the same excuse made for the attack by the Chicago police against the student protestors at the 1968 Democratic Convention. For some reason, here in Palestine, there were no chants of "The whole world's watching."

Despite the traumatic experience of being an observer of that horrible melée, the next day proved to be more catastrophic for me. Mr. Anwar arrived at the American Colony Hotel to have dinner with me. An overworked attorney, he spent his days typically in legal battles with the Israelis so the purpose of our meeting was to discuss the legal ramifications of the *Intifada* on the people. We had never met, so his opening remark took me off guard.

"Aren't you Soliman Munir's wife?" he asked sliding into the chair.

"Yes, why?"

"He was in my office this morning, but said nothing about you, although it occurred to me that I had an appointment with you later.

I said nothing about you because it felt strange and surely he'd have said something about me seeing you." Mr. Anwar leaned over the table. "I don't mean to upset you."

"He is here? That's news to me. As far a I know he is in Chicago." What do you say to a total stranger? Do you say that your own marriage is so rotten that the two of you don't even share travel plans to the same city? Who was he visiting and for what purpose? Why was I here if he was too? A different mission? Classified? For culture? For politics? Why wouldn't he have made contact with me? He knew my itinerary. The weight of deception and decay finally sank our marital boat. I quit Soliman at that moment. There would be no rescue from anywhere but myself. No one else was going to do it for me. My own *Intifada* was born.

Chapter 17

The drive through Gaza was slow and hot. I was on my way to brief Dr. Fathi in Cairo. The checkpoint at Rafah on the Egyptian border had been backed up for hours. Grimy with the day's heat and dust, I finally passed through to Egypt, land of eternal history and gentle people.

Screams startled me awake my first night in Cairo. Outside my hotel window in Heliopolis there was only gray stillness and shadows flickering from street lamps—the face of nighttime as it should be. I lay down again realizing I'd been mistaken. Only two days since Palestine and the *Intifada*, but the images did not fade and the sounds blistered my dreams.

The next morning I was greeted warmly by Dr. Fathi Arafat who hugged me with affection. "My dear, this is an excellent report. We only wish you would stay with us here. We need your help." He continued, "You are like a dear daughter to me. How can I kidnap you to stay with us here?"

There was no smile, wink or nod. Instead he paced back and forth and then stopped directly in front of me. With a slight bow, he clasped his hands behind him, standing motionless.

"Dr. Soliman might not like that," commented Dr. Refat leaning forward in his chair. "But after all, we need her more than he does."

Uncertain if they were teasing me or giving me a message, I

now needed no encouragement to begin my personal revolution. Witnessing the student demonstration had galvanized my determination to find an active role in the PRCS. There was more for me to do than pontificate on human rights issues. My clinical and academic skills would be available to Palestinians, if I came to live with them. Soliman was no longer a necessary connector for me.

"Madam Liza, I must go to my house now for lunch, but you will be tonight later at a reception for a friend of ours from Norway. She is a nurse like you and you both will enjoy meeting each other." Dr. Fathi stood up, took two steps toward the door, stopped and turned. "Until then."

Dr. Refat and Madam Hala remained in the conference room with me. Similar to the office in Beirut, but smaller, it had another massive carved wooden desk, made in the PRCS wood shop no doubt. Dr. Fathi was managing the Palestine Red Crescent Society, now headquartered in Cairo. He, Madam Hala and the others had rebuilt the society here after its devastation in Beirut. Their goal remained to meet the varied health needs of the scattered refugee populations of Palestine including Lebanon.

Madam Hala also left for her apartment and an afternoon nap, leaving Dr. Refat to present their proposal to me. He explained Dr. Fathi would talk about it more that night, but that my decision should be made quickly. For the first time in many years, I felt a lightness around me, as if a corset had been unlaced allowing me to breathe deeply. Their request was an authentication of who I was and what I could offer. It buoyed my spirits enormously.

Later at the reception, glasses of orange cola sat on the table amidst shallow plates of nuts, cheeses and sliced cucumber sprinkled with cumin and lemon juice. Dr. Fathi personally greeted every activist, journalist, health worker—and probably a few spies—who attended the reception in honor of Synne Holan, the Norwegian nurse, that night. He then took me aside for an earnest 15 minutes of conversation—an act which did not go unnoticed at this quasi-political function.

"Our nursing school and the hospital need so much work. They need leadership, teacher training and clinical training. You could do so much if you stayed here," insisted Dr. Fathi. "You know my house and my sister's home are open to you. You have a family that wants you here. You are one of us, one of my dear daughters," he reiterated.

We were sitting next to each other on a squishy velveteen sofa and I glanced up to find Dr. Refat smiling at us from across the room where he stood with two blonde Dutch women in stylish dress. The crowded reception was in full swing in this flat only a few streets from the hospital. "Don't you think I see how you suffer with Soliman? Take a vacation from him. Be with us. Decide later to return to him or not."

"So you see everything."

"Everything, my dear Liza, my daughter." Dr. Fathi tousled my hair then stood up. "We'll make all the arrangements. Madam Hala, will help you." A pair of Japanese reporters seized their moment, fluttering about him with honorific bows.

"It is settled then." Madam Hala had been sitting silently on the other side of me listening. Still I had no idea where Soliman was, but it mattered little to me now.

"Many men work abroad for years. He should not object if you do the same," huffed Madam Hala. "My darling Liza, divorce is not automatic but probably inevitable for you. He is a peasant."

"He will object to my coming to the PRCS without him," I predicted, which turned out to be true. But with my course work finished and my field work done, I only had to complete my dissertation—which could just as well be done in Cairo. A job to tailor-make a Palestinian-centered nursing curriculum and then train nursing teachers at the PRCS's Faloujah Nursing school in Cairo would be too great an opportunity to miss at this point in my career.

By the end of the summer of 1988 Soliman grudgingly surmised that a divorce would follow. He didn't mind that so much as the fact that his fellow Palestinians wanted me, with or without him, at the

PRCS in Cairo. Also, having this decision made without his imprimatur rendered a grievous insult to his pride and reputation. It never occurred to him that his abysmal treatment of me, his wife, was what hurt his reputation. If he had paid attention, he would have discovered that most Palestinian men do not abuse their wives and in fact care for them and respect them.

Soliman came home early the day I moved from Chicago. As I was locking the door of the house where I had never missed a mortgage payment, he pulled up and parked on the street. The divorce papers had been filed the week before. The stamped final copies would be mailed in a month. Mine would be forwarded to Cairo.

"So you are leaving?" Soliman said weakly.

"Yes." I climbed into the truck to drive to my sister's house to store books and boxes of stuff. Not wanting to be accused of taking his house away from him, I had signed it over to him, fully furnished, even stocked with groceries. "All the gold jewelry, rings, purses and anything else you gave me is in a box on the bed for you. My wrist watch stays because it is the only one I have."

He had demanded everything and I agreed. When he asked for my jewelry back I winced at the depth of disregard he had for me. In Palestine gifts given to wives are sacred, gold in particular representing a dowry or her personal wealth are for her own security. No Arab man would diminish himself by demanding them back, as if they were mere accouterments lent to the current occupant of the wife position.

"I love you," Soliman stated, standing by the truck door.

"You love the fruits of my labor, my dear." With a flick of the directional lever to signal a right turn, I revved up the U-Haul with a grueling slow groan as my foot depressed the accelerator. Slowly the truck blustered onto the street. The rear-view mirror showed Soliman standing in the yard. He would be okay.

For many weeks, his resistance to the divorce had taken many manipulative turns. He attempted to court me again, maybe prodded on by a self-help book or perhaps by his experience with one of his many women friends. The roses and champagne only provoked my pity and poignant sadness. Once craving such attention from him, I found these current renditions false—expedient measures to make in a crisis—anything to avoid the public exposure of personal rejection. When these strategies failed, he tried more dramatic demonstrations of woe. His most pathetic attempt drew my utter contempt. "I can't take this," Soliman wailed to me at one point, walking into the living room.

"Yes, you can. We both can. Don't con yourself about us being happy or in love. Spare me the charade." I was finding it barely tolerable to be living in the house with him and was glad it would be over soon. I was trying to concentrate on the newspaper I had been reading when I realized he had pulled a silver hand gun out of his pocket and was waving it around.

"Put that away. You don't need it."

"I am going to kill myself." Soliman put the stubby barrel to his temple and pulled the trigger. Nothing happened. He tried to fix it and pulled the trigger again. Again, nothing. I leapt toward him, knocking him to the ground. The gun slipped away from him and I grabbed it.

"Give it to me," he screamed.

"No, now you get out or I will."

"Oh, God. Oh, God." Soliman sat on the floor rocking back and forth, hitting his head with his hands.

His brother finally came to stay with him at my insistence. As I drove off in the U-Haul, I felt I could finally relax. I didn't have to worry about being sucked into caring for him again. Regardless of his manipulations, I had to keep remembering that nothing had changed. If I had succumbed to his game, on the basis of pity, I would have been doomed to a life of misery and self-hate. His self-serving "I love you" at the eleventh hour could hardly be trusted. But the hardest part was giving up the dream I conjured up long ago in sweet naïve times.

Soliman was engaged two months later. They had met three months before I filed for divorce, were dating during our renewed pseudo courtship and shopping for the house at the time of the failed pistol show. My friend worried about me after she told me, but there was no need.

The three-hour drive to my sister's house reminded me of my trek from Washington DC to Chicago in 1980. Soliman drove his overloaded car with me following in a small U-Haul truck. At the time I was so full of anticipation, so secure in my dream of what our life would be, so invested in a flawed relationship, so unaware of how I repeated a pattern I had desperately wanted to escape.

On this drive to Indianapolis I was at least comforted by the knowledge that I had learned a lot from all this about myself. I had grown up in a big family where I had learned early on that doing my chores would make my parents happy. But never for long, for housework only shows up when it is not done, being otherwise invisible.

My role in the family had been to take care of everyone else. Thus I had learned responsibility and accountability, how to cook, how to do laundry, how to iron, how to clean a house. But eight is too young an age to stop having friends over, to stop slumber parties, to stop ballet lessons, to wash and feed an infant and a toddler before you go to school each morning as part of household routine. When you work where you live, you can never have a day off. Convinced as a child that working harder would mean some time back to play, to do what I wanted, I kept on working, ever hoping playtime, free time would come. But it never did. And it barely kept my parents happy. There was always some housework I could be doing.

The summer I was 14, I stared out my bedroom window at the rest of the family, lounging around the patio. While my brothers played catch in the yard, my parents watched the youngest two girls. My hands still damp from dinner dish cleanup, I understood that none of them had respected me as a child nor did they now respect my adolescence. I was the uncool big sister, the maid of the house.

No teasing was cruel enough from my brothers. No after-school activity was judged by my parents as vital enough to waive my household chores. I vowed then to leave and never come back. There was a world out there that I was going to escape to, leaving behind the familiar, oppressive regimen.

Graduate school was my first step outside of Indiana. Never wanting to run away just to leave without a destination, I wanted to be in charge of my own life, yet it was difficult to break loose. It was seen as an act of rebellion when I told my parents I would not come home that summer in Washington DC to pick up my chores where I'd left off.

Yet as predictable as sunrise, I now recognized, guiding the truck east past the billowing exhaust from the steel mills of Gary towards the cornfield prairie ahead, I simply replicated the only pattern I knew with Soliman. I might have wanted to love him dearly, but it would never be enough because the flaw in the setup was the lack of respect which was so familiar to me. Just as at home, I was never respected as an equal partner, but rather as a manageable drone able to produce untold amounts of work. When after years of self-deception I finally realized that I did not need Soliman to legitimize my own choices and actions, I was free.

So this was one more step to freedom. A couple hours later I pulled into my sister's driveway. My question then was whether we could jettison the parent-child relationship we had developed when I had been so involved in raising her. I was grateful to find that passing years had changed both of us. I realized the burden was on me not to repeat the destructively familiar pattern. It was easy to develop a normal sisterly relationship. After unloading the truck together and filling her basement with my boxes, we got caught up on what was happening in our worlds before we checked in with our parents. Helen was eager to talk about the man she was seeing and her plans for the future.

Mom and Dad were relieved that I had finally dumped that foreigner after almost 10 years, but they were baffled about Cairo. I didn't try to explain what they could never understand. In rejecting Soliman, I did not turn my back on my support for Palestine and my appreciation of the Arab world, nor did I abandon my human rights beliefs and the many friends I'd made in that world. I had merely rejected a man who was personally destructive for me. They interpreted my moving to Egypt as a reflection of a lingering Soliman influence. With him gone now, why wouldn't I want to join the Junior League or the symphony auxiliary?

I flew back to Chicago the next day to stay a few days before leaving for Cairo, Egypt.

PART VII - CAIRO 1989-1995

Chapter 18

And thus I had come to this enchanting view where stars studded the sky across the Nile toward Giza. The Sphinx and Pyramids, visible from my balcony during the sound and light show conducted just after sunset, now coalesced with the dark desert, invisible at this late hour.

Pete Glaeser, semi-slouched in the chair, smiled at me but said nothing. His button-down cotton shirt brightened in the cool light of the rising full moon. The security field lights occasionally crackled and friendly shadows were already visiting the balcony. It was time to close this story and for this he waited. What of Palestine now, and what of me?

By New Year's Eve 1989 the Berlin Wall had fallen, the Soviet Union had ceased to exist and my divorce was filed. The 1990s, only hours away, would usher in a new era of freedom for the East Germans, the Eastern Bloc and the Soviet peoples. I was relating to them because my own personal freedom was only a few weeks off.

Unfortunately colonialism was not yet dead. Palestine did not enjoy the freedom lavished on the former Soviet Bloc. No television newscasters were reporting the dismantling of refugee camps in Lebanon, Syria, Jordan, Egypt, Tunisia, West Bank or Gaza with glittering live-action shots as they did for the dismantling of the Berlin Wall. No official announcement was made ending Israeli military occupation to establish an independent Palestine with East Jerusalem as the capital. No proclamation fulfilled the promise made by the British to Sharif Hussein more than half a century before.

So we watched the Blacks in South Africa win their human rights in 1991 and Bo and Rita Rembutu turned their efforts "to gut this infected rotten apartheid, to build a clean, respectable society based on human rights and rule of law, a just law." Such words could not yet be written about Palestine. Rather 1990 saw Palestine's *Intifada,* protesting the military occupation of their land, begin another grueling year. Hani still waited to finish his Master's in Engineering at Birzeit University, closed now for four years, two courses away. Refusing to trade on pity for his fate, he wouldn't send in his astronaut application until he had his degree.

I found it wrenching to say good-bye to Lina and Sally. We had helped each other survive divorces, the grind of doctoral study and the finding of our deepest selves. We had lived entwined in each other's lives for eight years and, fortunately, although that phase ended we have never lost touch. Our friendships of mutual respect have lasted. In fact, it turned out that we all embarked on new adventures that year. I was just the first to take off.

Finally I was finding that adventure I had sought. After the invasion of Lebanon and the expulsion of formal Palestinian institutions, the headquarters of the PRCS had been reconstituted in Cairo. President Gamal Abdul Nasser had set aside a clinic in the suburb of Heliopolis for Palestinian use with a presidential decree, and subsequent regimes had not raised serious opposition to this. Who was going to argue about a hospital anyway? Thus Dr. Fathi had established the PRCS headquarters in Cairo.

During the next few years my work focused on developing competency-based curricula for nurses, lab technicians, pharmacy techs and X-ray techs at the Faloujah Nursing Institute, the PRCS school in Cairo. Between school and hospital responsibilities, plus my membership in the scientific committee, my life overflowed with challenges—and freedom. But it was a heavy load to carry alone.

Frustration became a constant companion. The official start of the school year began with a convocation in the main lecture hall. The noisy greetings of returning students bounced off the wood-paneled walls, while the honks from the traffic blew in at the open windows. The students from Canada Refugee Camp just inside the Egyptian border were always there on schedule, but the sunny faces framed in head scarves of the returning students from the Occupied Territories—West Bank and Gaza—were not. No one ever explained the reason for their delay, only that they would sometimes show up weeks late due to typical harassment by the Israelis.

One day Mr. Younis, Dr. Fathi's personal secretary, called me to his office and then escorted me to the office parking lot where he stopped at a green Fiat hatchback parked under a palm tree. Without a word he handed me the car key and ordered me to start it. "From Dr. Fathi," was all he said with a wink. Later when Dr. Fathi came to school, we embraced and he again called me "daughter."

This car became famous with the students. The school, the hospital and the nursing student dorm were not within walking distance of each other. Since my world revolved among these three points, whenever I went anywhere it seemed that my car was crammed full of students needing rides, windows down, hot wind blowing dust on us. Since my goal was also to learn the streets of Cairo, I had an added incentive to get students to go with me, for my Arabic was still weak. If we got lost, the students could ask directions. Thus I managed to find all the good sweet shops in Cairo where I rewarded my guides with baklava, *bes boosa*, biscuits or gateau. In time I learned a lot about Cairo and its sweet shops and also heard the stories of these students—about brothers detained in Israeli jails, their jobless fathers, mothers dead in childbirth and houses demolished to make room for Jewish settlers from America.

The most famous moment for the green Fiat came when a student, Amel, asked me to drive her from the dorm to the house of her fiancé for their official engagement. Her family lived in Gaza and had requested a travel pass from the Israelis so they could attend the engagement of their only daughter. They were refused, no reason given. Amel's closest friends helped her adjust a new white *hejab* head scarf with lace trim and polish the scuffs off her worn shoes. Others decorated the car with white ribbons trailing tin cans. Her friends and I represented her family on this symbolic drive of Amel's moving from the household of her father to that of her future husband.

A Palestinian community, Ain Shams—a remote, poverty-ridden area on the outskirts of Cairo—was our destination. Dr. Jane lived here in the reëstablished hospital for disabilities and rehabilitation serving the poorest Palestinians and Egyptians. Many large families were cramped into two-room flats here, so cooking was often done over kerosene burners on the balconies. Dust from dirt roads pockmarked with ruts and holes billowed around laundry dripping from strung plastic ropes. The neighborhood was watching and cheered as we bounced and honked our way down the road trying to avoid goats and donkeys casually grazing at the roadside. Hours later, after being officially engaged with rings exchanged, the new fiancée left the celebration where orange cola and simple butter cookies had been served and songs of celebration sung, and folded herself back into my faithful green car for a ride back to the dorm. Her tears spoke a volume about how Amel wished she could have had her parents with her that night.

With myriad such experiences my life in Cairo was full working with the Palestine Red Crescent. As with all development work, my goal was always to work myself out of a job. If you teach well and establish programs that fit the local institutions and culture, then your role should diminish as the local people begin to take over. When that point for me was reached in the PRCS, good luck would have it that a job with an international health-care-development organization opened up in Cairo. This new opportunity to work with Egyptians challenged me professionally while allowing my services to remain available to my Palestinian colleagues as needed. So my life progressed in Egypt, *Um el Donya*, the Mother of the World.

The presence of Pete Glaeser, the pediatric ER doctor from Milwaukee, Wisconsin, did complicate the scene. Very few people outside my PRCS family knew my story, my own kin knew next to nothing, yet here I was spilling it all out to Pete. When I finally stopped the tale, Pete folded his hands behind his head and eased into his words. "My first reaction is embarrassment."

"Embarrassment? What are you embarrassed about?"

"That I could have been so oblivious to what was happening over here and that my suspicion wasn't tweaked by the reporting, the movies, the stories about the Middle East conflict, the Israelis, the Palestinians because it is so one-sided. The lopsided portrayal of the Middle East should have cued me to question the source and motive of the reports and stories. That's an embarrassment." He shrugged and poured a fresh glass of tonic water. "You must be happy to see the peace process underway now?"

"Happy? About capitulation? About a leader so exhausted that he buckled to the glamor of a photo-op at the White House with his aging enemy?"

"Whoa, you just lost me. Isn't this peace process supposed to be fixing the problem?" he asked.

"As a loyal supporter of the PLO, my position is in total disagreement with the direction Chairman Arafat took. He should have followed Professor Abu Jawad's prescription for the international peace conference and negotiations outlined in June 1988. The Oslo Accords gave them nothing at all."

"Nothing?"

"Nothing. Palestinians had to recognize Israel's existence and their right to self-determination. But the state of Israel refused to recognize the Palestinian people and their right to self-determination in return."

"Well, those points are not made clear in the press at all," he replied. "What else?"

"It was not a two-way deal. Arafat made concessions that did not bring a State of Palestine or freedom. The Military Occupation of Israel still controls the West Bank and Gaza. There has been no change, only shifting PR images that collapse on close inspection."

"What about all the refugees?" he asked.

"The Israelis do not want to acknowledge the millions of refugees living around them in neighboring Arab countries because if they do, the dirty secret of how Israel came into existence might get out. Discussion about refugees is postponed indefinitely–a classic delay tactic."

"Why shouldn't they return to their homes?"

"If the refugees return, the Arab population on the land would be greater than the Jewish population, and this is intolerable in a racially pure, Zionist-Jewish State. That is, after all, the whole goal of the State of Israel. It is a democracy only if you are Jewish. The Palestinian Israelis, Palestinians like Soliman and his family, who managed to stay within Israel, live as second-class citizens with only second-class human rights."

Pete calmly absorbed my heated words, but it seemed evident to both of us that my passion for Palestine might interfere in our friendship.

"So Arafat just gave the refugees up?"

"He postponed their fate until final discussion which will be late in negotiations–too late to extract much help for them. There is not even talk of reparations to the refugees to pay them for the loss of their homes, livelihoods and statehood. Those women in the Kalandia Camp co-op will be sewing and knitting side-by-side with their grandchildren at the rate these negotiations proceed."

"But how can that be? The Israelis are the masters of arranging reparations to holocaust victims. Why shouldn't the Israeli government, the World Zionist Organization or other Jewish groups pay reparations and damages to the refugees they created. It's only fair," he commented.

"Don't hold your breath. Chairman Arafat made a bad deal. If he speaks out against the Israelis now, they say he is ungrateful. The Israeli government wants him to get rid of violence but there has been no structural change in the society to warrant that. If anything, the Israeli rules and regulations of the West Bank and Gaza are even more restrictive and detrimental to economic development."

It began to dawn on me as I looked over the Cairo skyline that Pete's presence in my life could cause an abrupt change and that I soon might be facing a choice with unknowns. The question would be whether this would be a change in my interest.

He continued his line of questioning, not knowing my thoughts, "In what way do they restrict economic development?"

Although continued discussion of Palestine kept me safe and in charge of the conversation, sooner or later, we would sometime have to shift to the personal and there my control would slip. I appropriated a few more minutes to shore up my courage by highlighting a few more facts about Palestine today. "Economic restrictions work in many forms." I went on to describe how trucks jammed with beans, tomatoes, eggs, milk or citrus fruits were corralled at border crossings between the Gaza or West Bank and Israel while tense drivers paced and waited for hours, days or weeks, hostage to the whim of the Israeli officers. Reasons for delays are never given, but Palestinian drivers watch helplessly as their products rot in the hot sun instead of getting to market. Then the stores in Israel which have ordered them castigate the Palestinians as unreliable.

"The easy movement of cars on the street by my building," I pointed them out to Pete, "is not possible in West Bank or Gaza." Israeli settlements slice up the Arab land, cutting off centuries-old passageways between ancient Palestinian villages. Armed settlers traveling in cars with bullet-proof glass are authorized to shoot at will; guidelines are nonexistent. Old Palestinian women weighed down with plastic sacks of goods, mothers herding small children forced to walk miles out of their way to get to the market or each other's homes are said to pose an enormous threat to gun-toting settlers. Rocks thrown by frustrated youth are said to intimidate the formidable nuclear power of Israel and its soldiers sporting Bausch and Lombe goggles on titanium-gray helmets with machine guns slung over their shoulders. A geographical lockdown contains the physical movement of the Palestinian people but not their aspirations for freedom and human rights.

"This sort of oppression seems anachronistic. It is hard to imagine the U.S. government supporting it," Pete remarked quietly. Unruffled by my saga, he posed another question. "The Jewish people I know support human rights, equality and justice, so how could they also support the Israelis who violate Palestinian human rights?"

Sally had demonstrated to me the beauty of Jewish faith with its moral obligation to share in the care of each other and the world around them. Being Jewish is not the problem, I explained. Supporting the racist political goals of Zionism is the problem. You don't have to be Jewish to be Zionist.

Christian groups who support Israel do so, not because they love Jewish people—for some of these Christian groups believe the Jews continue to be guilty for killing Jesus—but because they believe Jesus will not come back again the second time unless the State of Israel exists. They interpret Israel as a physical state in this world, not a spiritual one, but they want to hurry up Jesus' return so they laud the Zionist leadership of Israel and relish in repression of the Palestinian Moslems, labeled the anti-Christ. That the Palestinian population worldwide includes hundreds of thousands of Christians escapes their notice somehow.

Nazareth, Bethlehem and Jerusalem—the heartland of Palestinian Christianity—is home to seminarians, nuns, priests and ministers who daily watch the loss of their congregations to the violence of Israel's occupation of their homeland. So you see an old preacher fumbling heavy keys to open church doors warily, keeping an eye on nearby Israeli soldiers lest they slam shut the door, declaring that attending Sunday service is a security risk that day. Christ-like living can land a youth in jail or close a middle-aged person's family business—no explanations required. The peace and camaraderie of Christ's teachings remain an irritant to Israelis who believe they can bulldoze houses, confiscate family land, close schools and prevent church or mosque attendance with impunity because they are "chosen".

"Wasn't Christ's message about a new social order where no one was chosen but we are all to be children of God?" asked Peter. "That's certainly how we were taught. And also that those who claim to know when Christ will return and think they can facilitate it fools themselves with the sin of arrogance. In the meantime, the Palestinian people, Christian and Moslem alike, suffer harshly under a colonial settler state regime supported by a superpower nation in the closing years of the 20th century."

"Couldn't the Palestinians simply declare themselves independent like the U.S. did from Britain?" he asked.

"The Israelis would crush a revolt like that militarily within hours. The Palestinians cannot fight the Israelis militarily—only politically and morally. This is not 1948. It's 1995. What with global news, the internet and instant communication, it should be more difficult for the Israelis to cover up mass expulsion and massacres today than it was 50 years ago. But I am not sure. "

"Why not?"

"Well, for one thing, why would we expect outrage from the world community when in the face of other human rights violations nothing is ever done, no one holds them accountable. What would be different? The scale of the violation? They could use the same words as in 1948—that the Palestinians are running away, rather than the truth—that they are running for cover from Israeli military attack. Palestinians would be blamed as the victims, as usual. They should be content to remain a passive, cheap labor force while they are being harassed and expelled from their land as we colonize their heritage, erasing it."

The breeze cooling my face reminded me that I needed to cool my passion. Poor Peter. He was getting a lifetime of inquiry, study and politics dumped like a waterfall in a few hours.

"What are you going to do about it?" he challenged. "Don't you have the moral obligation to tell people like me what you know? How else will we know? How else can you hope for world opinion to change if you don't tell your story?"

"It's hard to explain my beliefs to people who are steeped in stereotyped questions and pat answers. They will label me anti-Semitic or some sort of radical."

"Are you?" He stared at my PLO posters on the wall.

"Not at all. It is human rights first, because we are human first. No selective human rights. It is very simple. You don't believe me?"

"I believe you," he acknowledged. "And your passion for Palestinian rights is genuine and important to you. It must have been rough to be married to that jerk. It was probably worse than you have told me."

"Let's not dwell on him. It almost killed me but for Dr. Fathi, my dear uncle, who offered a safe haven in which to recover. My life is good and was unruffled until you arrived in Cairo. My adventure is my own and it fulfills me. What about you?"

"I am fascinated with you." Pete faced the Nile. "I have never been so impressed with anyone as I am with you."

"You are very sweet. And there is no one in your life? You are too good looking not to have been plucked by some lucky woman somewhere along the line?"

"Oh, I was plucked once, but it did not work out although I gave it my all," he admitted. But this was not tonight's story and his would be told later, on another balcony visit.

My attraction to him seemed illogical. My life needed no change. Yet since he arrived in Cairo, a simple lightness, a sense of fun, bubbled up from a deep recess in my spirit which had been shut away long ago, the year the first of my two sisters was born. Peter invoked the name of my favorite TV hero at the time I was a little girl, before my sisters were born, when he saw a low-flying twin-engine airplane cross over the Nile. "It's Sky King," he called out to no one. How did he know of Sky King? What other core commonalities did we share? It felt like finding a long-lost friend, or maybe better, it was like finding a long-lost self.

Pete stood up and leaned on the balcony. We lived halfway

around the world from each other. His world was now foreign to me. Vacations, cars, football games, "brats and beer" were not part of mine. If we were to close the gap between us, someone would have to move. I turned toward the Nile, my adored River Nile.

"Why does a personal life with an American affect your relationship with Palestine? You seem to view them as mutually exclusive," he said.

"It is not the personal life or romance. It is living in the U.S. again. How can I go back there when home is in the Arab world? Here we understand about the persistent inaccuracy and racism of the American and Western views of us. How do I live with people who still think Pakistan is Palestine, who believe Israel sprang to life out of nowhere just to take care of Holocaust victims? How can I live with people who challenge the lack of human rights in China and Tibet, but don't challenge the abysmal human rights record of Israel toward the Palestinian people?

"Do you think I should go back to a country which for 50 years has consistently voted 'no' in the U.N. on any resolution that would bring self-determination and freedom to Palestine? To a country that brokered a peace agreement where mutual recognition of civil and national rights to statehood were not required? Isn't the U.S. supposed to be the bastion and the leader of freedom and self-determination in the world? Do you understand what I'm saying?" I knew my anger was putting a damper on that special evening, but I couldn't stop. Maybe now he wouldn't press me just to go home. Maybe all the fun we'd been having together was a dreadful mistake.

After a quiet moment, he commented, "You are choosing the easy way out, sitting here cloistered in your tower of like-minded friends and colleagues. You wallow in the certainty of your own views but you are preaching to the converted. You are not in a position here to influence the foreign policy you complain about where it counts—back in the States. If your personal life suffers a bit, that is a trade-off you are willing to make. I just don't think you have to make that trade-off."

"You don't?"

"No. Palestine is a part of you, don't segment it. It and all the other hardships made you what you are today–the person I am attracted to. Never change or abandon your politics. Continue it."

His rational thinking sounded good, almost too good. Was he self-serving or was there really a new adventure before me, one that would draw on all my experiences to date? Standing next to him, absorbing the Nile breeze, made me feel solid and fresh.

Pete continued, "We have an opportunity before us. Take it or not. Just how or why we could come to feel about each other so deeply in such a short time cannot be explained. But we are not 20. We've hit the 40s. Haven't we learned anything in these 20-plus years?"

Suddenly, being 40 didn't seem so finished. The chance for happiness with Pete notwithstanding, I was filled with fear at the thought of going back to the empty consumer life of America, to another endless prairie. Being the wife of a doctor in Milwaukee seemed a short distance from there, and the thrill of independence after a bad marriage had not worn off. Still, Pete had reached the most recessed, most defended part of my soul with his sense of humor and breezy self confidence. The Arabs call it *dammo khafif*, light-blooded. He was that and extremely smart. I didn't want him to leave Cairo tomorrow.

Finally Pete turned from the balcony and studied me. Sitting down in the bent-cane chair, he leaned back, relaxed, and a slight smile broke across his face. He knew he had won. I leaned down and kissed him lightly. What is the song? *A kiss to build a dream on.* "Shall I make you a coffee?"

"Yes, Turkish coffee, *mazbut*, that is a little sugar?" he answered.

"Now, don't go away," I said, stepping into the salon.

"You must write a book about Palestine," he called after me.

"One day, *Inshallah!*"

Bibliography

Abu-Lughod, Janet. "The Demographic Transformation of Palestine," in *The Transformation of Palestine*, ed., Ibrahim Abu-Lughod, Northwestern University Press, Evanston, IL, pp. 139-164, 1987.

Abu-Lughod, Ibrahim. *The Transformation of Palestine*. Northwestern University Press, Evanston, 2nd edition, 1987.

– Feature Story. *The Chicago Lawyer*, August, 1981.

– *The Palestinian Uprising and the International Peace Conference*. Northwestern University lecture, June, 1988.

Al Haq. *Punishing A Nation*. Ramallah, 1988.

Antonius, George. *The Arab Awakening*. Librairie Du Liban, Beirut, 1969.

Bassiouni, M. Cherif. *The Palestinian Intifada – A Record of Israeli Repression*. Data Base Project on Palestinian Human Rights, Chicago, 1989.

Chomsky, Noam. *The Fateful Triangle; The United States, Israel, and the Palestinians*. South End Press, Boston, 1983.

Davis, John H. *The Evasive Peace: A Study of the Zionist-Arab Problem*. John Murray, London, 1968.

El Asmar, Fouzi. *To Be An Arab in Israel*. Washington, DC, Institute for Palestine Studies, 1978.

Hundley, Tom. "The Bitter Battle over a Young Arab's Fate. *Detroit Free Press*. July 24, 1981.

The Israeli League for Human and Civil Rights. *Report on the Violations of Human Rights in the Territories During the Uprising,* 1988. Tel Aviv, 1988.

Jabara, Abdeen. *"No Facts Accepted."* Ziad Abu Eain Defense Committee, Chicago, August, 1981.

Johnson, Alexandra U. "Israeli Torture of Palestinian Political Prisoners in Jerusalem and the West Bank: Three State Department Reports." *Palestine Human Rights Bulletin.* Number 17, April 1979.

Journal of Palestine Studies. Vol. 13, 1983/1984.

Mallison, Sally, and W. Thomas Mallison, "Israeli Settlements in Occupied Territory versus International Humanitarian Law." *Arab Perspectives,* May 1980.

Menuhin, Moshe. "A Tribute to Count Folke Bernadotte." *The Arab World.* March–April 1969.

Mouat, Lucia. "Israel Wants Him Extradited for Trial; Defenders Appeal, Argue Bombing Charge False." *Christian Science Monitor.* July 16, 1981.

Naughtie, James. "Palestinian Jailed in Chicago, Fighting Extradition to Israel." *Washington Post,* July 24, 1981.

Palestine Human Rights Newsletter. Vol. 1, No. 7, September, 1981 and Vol. 1, No. 8, October, 1981, Chicago.

Palumbo, Michael. *The Palestinian Catastrophe.* Quartet Books, London. 1989.

Rempel, William C. "U.S. in the Middle as Arabs, Israel Fight over Palestine. *Los Angeles Times,* August 19, 1981.

Said, Edward W. *Orientalism.* Pantheon Books, NY, 1978.
  – *The Question of Palestine.* Vintage Books, NY, 1992.
  – *The Politics of Dispossession.* Vintage Books, NY, 1995.
  – *Peace and its Discontents.* Vintage Books, NY, 1996.

Sayeh, Fayez A. *Camp David and Palestine: A Preliminary Analysis.* Arab Information Center, NY, Volume 8.

Schmitz, Anthony. "He Wastes Away in a Downtown Cell While the U.S. Authorities Consider the Case against Him." *Chicago Reader,* June 18, 1981.

Appendices and Maps

INTRODUCTION

One of my favorite books, *The Arab Awakening* by George Antonius (Librairie du Liban, Beirut, 1969), contains what seemed to me when I stumbled on them a lost treasure—the McMahon Correspondence and the Sykes-Picot Agreement. It was amazing finally to see copies of the actual exchange between Sir Henry McMahon and Sharif Husain regarding the future independence of the Arabs. I had heard the story anecdotally from various Palestinian friends who were not recounting episodes about an era long past; they were telling me family stories only a grandparent or great-grandparent away.

It was strangely moving to read the assurances by McMahon that held so much promise for the Arabs and then, in black-and-white, to read how not even a year later others—the French, British and Russian ministers of foreign affairs—rendered the McMahon Correspondence null and void through their Sykes-Picot Agreement. Here are recorded the official intents and betrayals by Western nations of the Arab's land that included the Holy Land.

Because the documents are rather long, I have excerpted here relevant portions. *The Arab Awakening,* still in print, contains the full correspondence and the complete Sykes-Picot Agreement. To demonstrate how the UN has failed to implement its own resolutions that would institute peace in Palestine, included here are the UN Resolutions 242 and 338.

The three accompanying maps are included as an aid for understanding the time and space of the conflicts in the Middle East.

Appendix A

The McMahon Correspondence
Sir Henry McMahon's Second Note to the Sharif Husain

Cairo, October 24, 1915

Complimentary titles.

I have, with gratification and pleasure, received your note of the 29th Shawwal, 1333, and its tokens of sincere friendship have fill me with satisfaction and contentment.

I regret to find that you inferred from my last note that my attitude towards the question of frontiers and boundaries was one of hesitancy and lukewarmth. Such was in no wise the intention of my note. All I meant was that I considered that the time had not yet come in which that question could be discussed in a conclusive manner.

But, having realised from your last note that you considered the question important, vital and urgent, I hastened to communicate to the Government of Great Britain the purport of your note. It gives me the greatest pleasure to convey to you, on their behalf, the following declarations which, I have no doubt, you will receive with satisfaction and acceptance.

The districts of Mersin and Alexandretta, and portions of Syria lying to the west of the districts of Damascus, Homs, Hama and Aleppo, cannot be said to be purely Arab, and must on that account be excepted from the proposed delimitation.

Subject to that modification, and without prejudice to the treaties concluded between us and certain Arab Chiefs, we accept that delimitation.

As for the regions lying within the proposed frontiers, in which Great Britain is free to act without detriment to the interests of her ally France, I am authorised to give you the following pledges on behalf of the Government of Great Britain, and to reply as follows to your note:

(1). That, subject to the modifications stated above, Great Britain is prepared to recognise and uphold the independence of the Arabs in all the regions lying within the frontiers proposed by the Sharif of Mecca:

(2). That Great Britain will guarantee the Holy Places against all external aggression, and will recognise the obligation of preserving them from aggression;

(3). That, when circumstances permit, Great Britain will help the Arabs with her advice and assist them in the establishment of governments to suit those diverse regions;

(4). That it is understood that the Arabs have already decided to seek the counsels and advice of Great Britain exclusively and that such European advisers and officials as may be needed to establish a sound system of administration shall be British;

(5). That, as regards the two vilayets of Baghdad and of Basra, the Arabs recognise that the fact of Great Britain's established position and interests there will call for the setting up of special administrative arrangements to protect those regions from foreign aggression, to promote the welfare of their inhabitants, and to safeguard our mutual economic interests.

I am confident that this declaration will convince you, beyond all doubt, of Great Britain's sympathy with the aspirations of her friends the Arabs; and that it will result in a lasting and solid alliance with them, of which one of the immediate consequences will be the expulsion of the Turks from the Arab countries and the liberation of the Arab peoples from the Turkish yoke which has weighed on them all these long years.

I have confined myself in this note to vital questions of primary importance. If there are any other matters in your notes, which have been overlooked, we can revert to them at some suitable time in the future.

I have heard with great satisfaction and pleasure that the Sacred Kiswa and the charitable gifts which had gone with it, had arrived safely and that, thanks to your wise directions and arrangements, they were landed without trouble or damage in spite of the risks and difficulties created by the present deplorable war. We pray Almighty God that He may bring a lasting peace and freedom to mankind.

I am sending this note with your faithful messenger, Shaikh Muhammad ibn 'Aref ibn 'Urafifan, who will lay before you certain interesting matters which, as they are of secondary importance, I have abstained from mentioning in this note.

Compliments.

Appendix B

Sykes-Picot Agreement

May 1916 (excerpted)

1. France and Great Britain are prepared to recognize and uphold an independent Arab State or a Confederation of Arab States in the areas shown as (A) and (B) on the annexed map under the suzerainty of an Arab Chief. France in area (A) and Great Britain in area (B) shall have a right of priority in enterprises and local loans. France in area (A) and Great Britain in area (B) shall alone supply foreign advisers or officials on the request of the Arab State or the Confederation of Arab states.

2. France in the Blue area and Great Britain in the Red area shall be at liberty to establish such direct or indirect administration or control as they may desire or as they may deem fit to establish after agreement with the Arab State or Confederation of Arab States.

3. In the Brown area there shall be established an international administration of which the form will be decided upon after consultation with Russia, and after subsequent agreement with the other Allies and the representatives of the Sharif of Mecca.

4 There shall be accorded to Great Britain

    (a) The ports of Haifa and Acre;

    (b) Guarantee of a specific supply of water from the Tigris and the Euphrates in area (A) and (B).

Appendix C

United Nations Security Council Resolution 242

22 November 1967

The Security Council

Expressing its continuing concern with the grave situation in the Middle East,

Emphasizing the inadmissibility of the acquisition of territory by war and the need to work for a just and lasting peace in which every State in the area can live in security,

Emphasizing further that all Member States in their acceptance of the Charter of the United Nations have undertaken a commitment to act in accordance with Article 2 of the Charter,

1. *Affirms* that the fulfilment of Charter principles requires the establishment of a just and lasting peace in the Middle East which should include the application of both of the following principles:

(i) Withdrawal of Israel armed forces from territories occupied in the recent conflict;

(ii) Termination of all claims or states of belligerency and respect for and acknowledgment of the sovereignty, territorial integrity, and political independence of every State in the area and their right to live in peace within secure and recognized boundaries free from threats or acts of force;

2. *Affirms further* the necessity

(a) For guaranteeing freedom of navigation through international waterways in the area;

(b) For achieving a just settlement of the refugee problem;

(c) For guaranteeing the territorial inviolability and political independence of every State in the area, through measures including the establishment of demilitarized zones;

3. *Requests* the Secretary General to designate a Special Representative to proceed to the Middle East to establish and maintain contacts with the States concerned in order to promote agreement and assist efforts to achieve a peaceful and accepted settlement in accordance with the provisions and principles in this resolution;

4. *Requests* the Secretary General to report to the Security Council on the progress of the efforts of the Special Representative as soon as possible.

Appendix D

United Nations Security Council Resolution 338

15 October 1973

The Security Council

1. *Calls* upon all parties to the present fighting to cease all firing and terminate all military activity immediately, no later than 12 hours after the moment of the adoption of this decision, in the positions they now occupy;

2. *Calls* upon the parties concerned to start immediately after the cease-fire the implementation of Security Council Resolution 242 (1967) in all of its parts;

3. *Decides* that, immediately and concurrently with the cease-fire, negotiations shall start between the parties concerned under appropriate auspices aimed at establishing a just and durable peace in the Middle East.

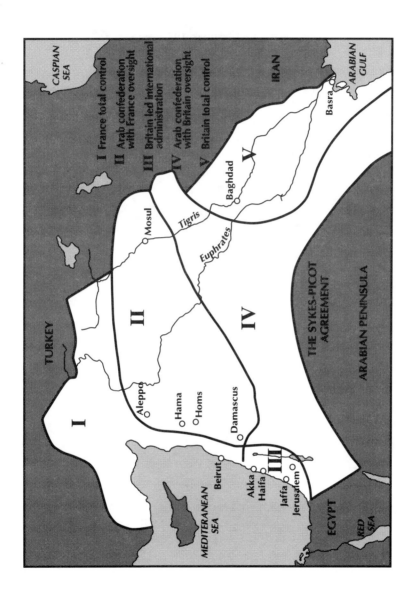

I France total control
II Arab confederation with France oversight
III Britain led international administration
IV Arab confederation with Britain oversight
V Britain total control

THE SYKES-PICOT AGREEMENT

CASPIAN SEA

IRAN

ARABIAN GULF

Basra

Baghdad

V

Mosul

Tigris

Euphrates

TURKEY

II

IV

ARABIAN PENINSULA

Aleppo

Hama

Homs

Damascus

I

Beirut

Akka

Haifa

III

Jaffa

Jerusalem

MEDITERANEAN SEA

EGYPT

RED SEA

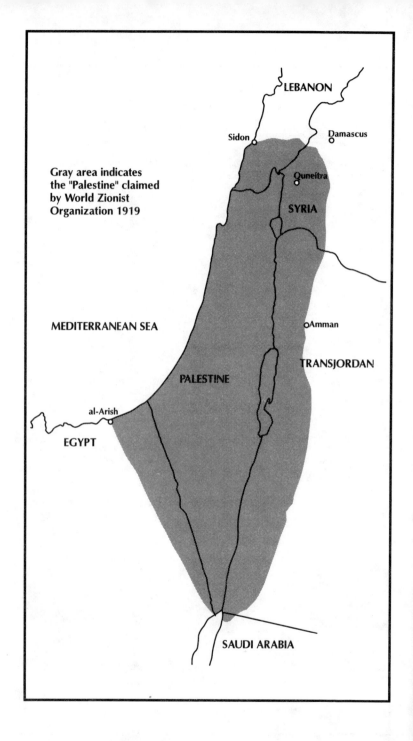

Gray area indicates
the "Palestine" claimed
by World Zionist
Organization 1919

LEBANON

Sidon

Damascus

Quneitra

SYRIA

MEDITERRANEAN SEA

oAmman

TRANSJORDAN

PALESTINE

al-Arish

EGYPT

SAUDI ARABIA

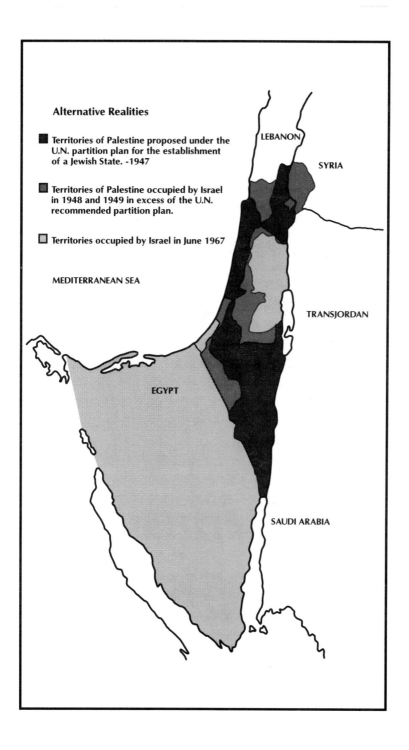

Alternative Realities

■ Territories of Palestine proposed under the U.N. partition plan for the establishment of a Jewish State. -1947

▨ Territories of Palestine occupied by Israel in 1948 and 1949 in excess of the U.N. recommended partition plan.

▢ Territories occupied by Israel in June 1967

MEDITERRANEAN SEA

LEBANON

SYRIA

TRANSJORDAN

EGYPT

SAUDI ARABIA

About the Author

Liza Elliott, a graduate nurse with a PhD in sociology, has worked extensively as a consultant with the Red Crescent Society ever since encountering war in Beirut in 1982. Currently she is active in many organizations trying to promote international peace and is also an adjunct professor at the University of Alabama, Birmingham, where she lectures on refugee health care. She lives in Birmingham with her husband Peter Glaeser.

Additional copies of this book may be obtained from your bookstore
or by contacting
Hope Publishing House
P.O. Box 60008
Pasadena, CA 91116
(626) 792-6123 / (800) 326-2671
Fax (626) 792-2121
E-mail: hopepub@loop.com
Visit our Web site: http://www.hope-pub.com